# Praise for
## *Opening Digital Markets*

"The glory of the Internet is that it provides global presence, and it's the great equalizer. This book details a very important corporate role for Internet commerce. It is necessary reading for all executives interested in propelling their organizations into the new global iMarket."

LAURIE A. TUCKER
Senior Vice President, Logistics
Electronic Commerce & Catalog
Federal Express

"Internet-driven electronic commerce is essential for organizations entering a virtual distribution marketplace and wishing to survive in it. This book is the road map for business leaders. Mougayar's descriptions and advice are crisp and enlightening."

ROBERT EDELMAN
Vice President
Marshall Industries

"From strategy to technology, *Opening Digital Markets* shows the business executive how to think and discover new opportunities in the new world of cybercommerce. With sharp insights, Mougayar takes us beyond Intranets, deep into Internet commerce territory, with an exhilarating array of ideas and breakthrough business models to learn from."

JENNIFER BAILEY
Vice President, Website
Netscape Communications Corporation

"Unquestionably, electronic commerce on the Internet will, before the end of the century, profoundly redefine many basics of business. This book is invaluable in helping business managers get ready for the opportunity and challenge. It's cogent, hype-free, focused, and practical."

PETER G. W. KEEN
Founder and Chairman
The International Center for Information Technologies

# OPENING DIGITAL MARKETS

## OTHER BOOKS FROM COMMERCENET PRESS

*The Search for Digital Excellence* by Amir Hartman, Malu Roldan, James Ware, and Judith Gebauer

*Understanding Digital Signatures: Establishing Trust over the Internet and Other Networks* by Gail L. Grant

## OTHER BOOKS BY WALID MOUGAYAR

*The Business Internet and Intranet: A Manager's Guide to Key Terms and Concepts* by Peter G. W. Keen, Walid Mougayar, and Tracy Torregrossa

*In order to receive additional information on these or any other McGraw-Hill titles, in the United States please call 1-800-722-4726. In other countries, contact your local McGraw-Hill representative. Or visit us at www.computing.mcgraw-hill.com.*

# OPENING DIGITAL MARKETS

## BATTLE PLANS AND BUSINESS STRATEGIES FOR INTERNET COMMERCE

WALID MOUGAYAR

SECOND EDITION

**McGraw-Hill**

New York   San Francisco   Washington, D.C.   Auckland   Bogotá
Caracas   Lisbon   London   Madrid   Mexico City   Milan
Montreal   New Delhi   San Juan   Singapore
Sydney   Tokyo   Toronto

Library of Congress Cataloging-in-Publication Data

Mougayar, Walid.
    Opening digital markets : battle plans and business strategies for
Internet commerce / Walid Mougayar.—2nd ed.
        p.    cm.
    Includes index.
    ISBN 0-07-043542-1
    1. Electronic commerce—Planning.   2. Strategic planning.
    3. Internet marketing—Planning.   4. Business enterprises—Computer
    networks—Planning.
    HF5548.32.M68    1998
    658.8′4—dc21                                                     97-41318
                                                                        CIP

# McGraw-Hill

A Division of The McGraw·Hill Companies

        6 7 8 9 0    DOC/DOC    9 0 2 1 0 9

ISBN 0-07-043542-1

*The sponsoring editor for this book was Scott Grillo, the editing
supervisor was Jane Palmieri, and the production supervisor was
Sherri Souffrance. It was set in Fairfield by Renee Lipton of
McGraw-Hill's Professional Book Group composition unit.*

*Printed and bound by R. R. Donnelley & Sons Company.*

McGraw-Hill books are available at special quantity discounts to use as
premiums and sales promotions, or for use in corporate training programs. For more information, please write to the Director of Special
Sales, McGraw-Hill, 11 West 19th Street, New York, NY 10011. Or contact your local bookstore.

*To my loving parents—Raymonde and Antoine—*
*whom I admire and thank for all their guidance.*


*And to Maureen, for your love and understanding.*

# CONTENTS

Preface    *xv*
Acknowledgments    *xvii*


**INTRODUCTION**                                                                 1


**CHAPTER ONE.  INTRODUCTION TO INTERNET
COMMERCE**                                                                       7
The Big Picture    *9*
New Meanings for a New World    *11*
    Buying and Selling    *11*
    (Digital) Value Creation    *12*
    New Intermediaries' Arrival    *13*
    Opening Digital Markets    *14*
The Internet Effect    *15*
The Evolution of Electronic Commerce    *16*
    Business-to-Business versus Business-to-Consumer Electronic
      Commerce    *17*
    Comparison of Traditional Electronic Commerce with
      Internet-Driven Electronic Commerce    *18*
The Future of EDI: Open, Lighter, and Cheaper    *21*
The Role of Intranets    *24*
Do-It-Yourself Market Size Assessment    *26*


**CHAPTER TWO.  BUSINESS CATALYSTS**                                             29
Distribution Costs and Value Chain Inefficiencies    *29*
Costs of Business Transactions    *32*
Search for Growth Markets    *33*
Competitive Pressures    *34*
Demands of the Electronic Consumer    *35*
Globalization Issues and Location Optimization for Commerce    *36*
Government Role and Competitive Positioning of Nations    *37*
United States versus Europe versus Japan: Lessons for the Future    *39*

## CHAPTER THREE.  TECHNOLOGY DRIVERS AND TRENDS                                         43

Convergence of Technologies and Capabilities    43
    Convergence of Infrastructure Components    43
    Convergence of Information Appliances    44
    Convergence of Vendors and Industry Services Capabilities    44

Cost of Technology    45
Content Liquidity    45
The Internetworked Enterprise    48
A Human Dimension to Technology    48
Rapidity of Software Development    49

## CHAPTER FOUR.  CHALLENGES AND SOLUTIONS TO INTERNET COMMERCE                        51

Characteristics of Internet Commerce Challenges    51
Categorizing Challenges    52
Technological Challenges    54
    Strength of Security    54
    Availability/Interoperability of Payment Instruments    55
    Interoperability of Technologies and Applications    58
    Comparative Buying Capabilities    59
    Richness and Depth of Content    60
    Lack of Reliable Network Infrastructure Services    60
    Lack of Standards    60
    Deployment of Public Key Infrastructure (PKI)    61
    Technical Integration with Existing Applications    64
    Bandwidth Costs    64

Legal and Regulatory Framework    65
    Lack of Consistent Rules and Policies    65
    Customs and Tax Uncertainties    67
    The Role of Governments and Nations    68
    Other Regulatory Issues    70

Behavioral and Educational Challenges    70
    Trust and Privacy    70
    TRUSTe    71
    Complexity of PKI    73
    Fraud    73
    Hype    73
    Awareness about Availability of Services    74
    E-money Laundering    74
Organizational and Business Barriers    75

Other Miscellaneous Challenges    76
    Channel Conflict    76
    Critical Mass    77
    Fulfillment Process    78


**CHAPTER FIVE.  EMBARKING ON INTERNET
COMMERCE**    **81**
Approaching the Strategy    82
Your View of the Internet    83
    It's a Network    83
    It's a Medium    84
    It's a Market    84
    It's a Transaction Platform    84
    It's an Applications Development Platform    84
The Buyer/Seller Model    85
The New Value Chain    87
    Scenario 1: It Gets Smaller    87
    Scenario 2: It Gets Redefined    89
    Scenario 3: It Becomes Virtual    89
The Three Spheres of Connectivity    90
The Main Web Site Is Dead: Strategies for Expanding Multiple
  Electronic Channels    91
    Direct Web    92
    Indirect Web    92
    Agent Web    93
The Internet Commerce Value Chain    94
    Network Infrastructure    95
    Commerce Infrastructure    95
    Commerce Applications    96
    New Intermediaries    99
    Commercial Agents and Information Appliances    99
The Role of CommerceNet    102
    The Vision    104
    The E-co Architecture: Response to Digital Anarchy    107
    COINs: Internet Commerce Applications at Work    110


**CHAPTER SIX.  STRATEGY ACTIONS**    **113**
Setting Internet's Expectations    113
Answering Strategic Questions    114
10 Steps to Cybermaturity    116
    Step 1: Conduct Necessary Education    116
    Step 2: Review Current Distribution and Supply Chain Models    119

Step 3: Understand What Your Customers and Partners Expect
from the Internet    *122*
Step 4: Reevaluate the Nature of Your Products and Services    *123*
Step 5: Give a New Role to Your Human Resources
Department    *128*
Step 6: Extend Your Current Systems to the Outside    *131*
Step 7: Track New Competitors and Market Shares in the
New Digital Marketspace    *132*
Step 8: Develop a Web-Centric Marketing Strategy    *133*
Step 9: Participate in the Creation and Development of Virtual
Marketplaces and Intermediaries, *Now*    *134*
Step 10: Instill Electronic Markets Management Style    *137*

## CHAPTER SEVEN.  UNCOVERING NEW OPPORTUNITIES                                                    139

The New Intermediaries    *140*
Theory and Behavior of Virtual Marketplaces    *140*
Principle 1: Organization of Information Leads to New
Market Power    *140*
Principle 2: The Uncertainty of a Transaction Journey Leads
to Market Efficiency    *144*
Principle 3: The Order-of-Magnitude Factor Is the Paradigm
Shifter    *145*
Principle 4: Markets Will Do Business with Other Markets    *145*

A Sample List of Intermediaries    *146*
Checklist for New Intermediaries    *149*
A Case of a "Multibroker"    *150*

New Intermediaries Examples    *152*
Electronic Auctions    *152*
On-Line Software Delivery    *152*
On-Line Support and Service    *153*
Outsourced Professional Services    *153*
Multimedia Content Delivery    *154*
Financial Transaction Brokers    *154*
Marketplace Concentrators    *155*
Products and Services Brokers    *155*
VAN-less EDI    *156*
Virtual Trading Communities    *157*
Digital Rights Intermediaries    *158*
Customer Information Intermediaries    *159*

Beyond Intermediaries: Real Virtual Marketplaces    *159*
Intermediaries on Top of Other Intermediaries    *160*
Virtual Everything, Inc.: Four Examples    *161*

# CHAPTER EIGHT. THE WIRED CONSUMER 165

Why First-Generation Consumer Malls Failed *166*
Evolution of the Wired Consumer *167*
  Early and Curious Adopters *167*
  Advantage-Driven Users *167*
  Requirement-Driven Users *168*
  Pervasive Users *169*
Key Needs for Consumer Internet Commerce *169*
  Need 1: Customer Self-Service *170*
  Need 2: Efficient Information Access *171*
  Need 3: User-Centric Queries Allowing Bidding *175*
  Need 4: Information Appliances *177*
  Need 5: Virtual Reality Experience *178*
  Need 6: On-Line Customer Service and Transaction History *179*
  Need 7: Universal Payment Instruments, Digital Wallets, and
    Smart Cards *181*
  Need 8: Microtransactions *184*
  Need 9: Casting Technologies *185*
Ideal Virtual Shopping Store on the Internet *187*
Anatomy of an Ideal Super Virtual Retail Store *188*

# CHAPTER NINE. IT STRATEGIES FOR ELECTRONIC COMMERCE 191

Technical Strategy Starting Points *191*
Strategies for CIOs and Corporate Web Executives *193*
  Issue 1: The Internet Redefines the Term *Legacy* *193*
  Issue 2: The Internet Is a Strategic IT Platform *193*
  Issue 3: Take Care of the Internetworking Platform Quickly *194*
  Issue 4: IT Needs Webmaster, Webmaster Needs IT, Management
    Needs Both *194*
  Issue 5: You Want It Done in Three Months? *195*
  Issue 6: Build versus Integrate *195*
  Issue 7: Outsourcing versus BOT *196*
  Issue 8: Get to Know the New Electronic Commerce Standards *197*
Architectural Approaches to Internet Commerce *198*
Systems Architecture Framework *199*
Costs of Implementation *202*
Security Architecture *204*
Web Delivery Architecture *205*
Internet Computing Goes Live *205*
Distributed Design Requirements and Plug-and-Go Software *207*
  Netscape's ONE Model *208*
  Oracle's Network Computing Architecture™ *209*
  Java Electronic Commerce Framework *209*

The Future of the Browser    *209*
Internet/Intranet Integration Issues    *210*
Don't Integrate, Automate!    *214*
Evolution of Business-to-Business Applications    *215*


## CHAPTER TEN.  IN PURSUIT OF VALUE-ADDED DISTRIBUTION: MARSHALL INDUSTRIES' EXPERIENCE    217

Company Background    *217*
The Birth of a Vision    *218*
Readying the Organization by Sensing the Changing Environment    *219*
Introducing "Virtual Distribution"    *221*
Evolution of the Web to Enhance the Business    *222*
Web Site Features That Produce Results    *223*
Redefining Supply Chain Management    *225*
From Digital Value to Digital Service to Digital Business    *226*
A Look Ahead    *227*
10 Lessons Learned    *228*
Conclusion    *229*


## CHAPTER ELEVEN.  MANAGING SUCCESSFUL INTERNET COMMERCE    233

Top 10 Reasons for Not Embracing Internet Commerce    *234*
Positioning the Case for Action    *234*
    Guiding Principles    *237*
Business Value of Electronic Commerce    *238*
Benchmarking Your Evolution    *239*
Scenario Planning    *240*
Apply Chaos and Complexity Theory    *242*
From Digital Value to Digital Markets    *243*
The Rise of Digital Markets    *244*


## EPILOGUE    247

## APPENDIX A.  DIGITAL PAYMENT OPTIONS    249

Generic Flavors of Internet Payment Instruments    *249*
    Digital Cash    *249*
    Smart Cards    *250*
    Encrypted Credit Cards    *251*
    Electronic Checks    *251*
    Internet Financial EDI    *251*
Criteria for Choosing Internet Instruments    *252*

**APPENDIX B.  INTERNATIONAL ELECTRONIC COMMERCE ORGANIZATIONS**                    255

**APPENDIX C.  WEB INDEX OF COMPANIES CITED**      265

**APPENDIX D.  GLOSSARY OF ACRONYMS**              271

**APPENDIX E.  THE FUTURE OF DIGITAL MARKETS**     273


Bibliography    277
Index    281

# PREFACE

O*pening Digital Markets*, second edition, one year later. What happened in 1997? Some things happened, some didn't. But is this relevant? The fact that we were still headed in the right direction is crucial. Electronic commerce business opportunities on the Internet are going to be with us for a long time to come, so inasmuch as the road is long, it is important to remember only the relevant events of the journey, and not get nostalgic about distractions along the way. This book takes the high road to electronic commerce on the Internet by focusing only on the relevant and strategic parts of the journey.

Without the shadow of a doubt, the Internet and electronic commerce have captured our imagination by giving us new dreams of success and power. All over the world, every week, an astonishing number of Internet start-ups get established, without objection from initial venture capital. Several of them swear they are the next Marc Andreesen–Jim Clark duo. They think everything is up for grabs. They think everything can be redefined. They think all the rules are to be changed. They know that millions of consumers and businesses are waiting in line to participate in the expansion of intergalactic and gigantic virtual marketplaces. They definitely want a piece of it.

These are exciting times for those small companies, but equally exciting for large companies. Yes, the Internet allows small new companies to grow and develop, but it also allows big companies to get bigger. Even large organizations are now owing their success directly to the Internet. If the Internet wasn't here, all the start-ups would be in real trouble; moreover, some large companies would suffer drastically. Ask Cisco or Marshall Industries about it.

Amid this optimism, the words *success* and *failure* are being redefined. In 1996 Amazon had sales of $16 million and losses of $6 million, and that was success. During the honeymoon, it's the honeymoon.

Regardless of what happens next, there is a shortage of business knowledge about extracting value and sound strategies from the Internet and its most important application: the process of conducting business electronically. Most early electronic commerce books were incomplete and did not present a holistic view of the lessons learned in a manner that could be practically applied by business managers. Is there a cookbook for Internet-based electronic commerce? This is the closest to a cookbook for profiting from electronic commerce on the Internet, in a time when the ingredients, utensils, and tastes are still changing.

On the dark side, electronic commerce on the Internet is still a chaotic marketplace. It has even been referred to as a digital anarchy. Others have claimed the Internet has reached its apex, which is the point at which managers start to make improper decisions. And in spite of the instant fascination it offers, electronic commerce is still open to many misinterpretations.

As someone who has been totally immersed in Internet commerce for the last three years, I have successfully helped startups and large multinationals exploit the opportunity of the turn of this century: electronic commerce on the Net. Throughout my consulting engagements, presentations, research, and travel in North America and Europe, I kept asking myself: What have we learned, what does it mean, what is the business model, is this important from a business perspective, what is the strategy behind the actions, and what if we extrapolated and imagined even further? The lessons are all here for your taking.

This isn't a book about a far-reaching future, but rather about one within reach. This is a book with compelling reasons for acting now to determine your future. If you have seen your electronic commerce future, you must part with the past.

The only prediction I will make is: the Internet is still full of surprises, mostly unexpected ones!

*Walid Mougayar*
*walid@cyberm.com*
*October 1997*

# ACKNOWLEDGMENTS

The origin of this book has been like a seed in my mind. But once the seed was planted, others came to energize its growth by watering it, fertilizing it, protecting it, and helping it withstand nature's unpredictable behaviors. (Comparing Internet's vicissitudes to nature's unpredictable behaviors holds true.) I gratefully acknowledge the role of several people and organizations in contributing to the growth of this work. My association with them has been, and continues to be, the best seeds for my growth.

I owe a great deal to my clients, for validating key concepts and even pushing them further for me. They allowed me to write the theory and principles, modeled after their practice. Without them, this book would have been incomplete.

Special thanks to a number of key industry and profession al contacts I became associated with. My ongoing consultation and relationship with them has always been enlightening. I owe a debt of gratitude to two key people who served as my motivational mentors: Ravi Kalakota, electronic commerce author and professor, who helped very early in the process by providing feedback to the first edition, and Jay M. Tenenbaum, founder and chairman of CommerceNet, for insights into his profound vision, second to none in the world of Internet commerce.

Overall, and at the risk of leaving a few unnamed, the following people stimulated my thinking, introduced me to a new concept, helped me understand their company's strategy better, or provided me with valuable feedback while I was writing this book. In alphabetical order: Shahla Aly of IBM Canada Ltd., Mary Cronin of Boston College, Keith Ellis of webMethods, Steve Gesner of TD-Bank, Mark Gross of Cowles Media Company, David Ticoll of the Alliance for Converging Technologies, and Harriet Velazquez of CIBC/Intria.

Forever thanks to the following corporations which believed in me early by sponsoring the first edition of this book: Canada Post Corporation (Ottawa, Canada), Cebra Inc. (Toronto, Canada), CommerceNet (Palo Alto, CA), Hewlett-Packard Company (Cupertino, CA), IBM Canada Ltd. (Toronto, Canada), and Oracle Corporation (Redwood City, CA).

I am indebted to CommerceNet and its affiliate organizations around the world, as my association with them has truly opened new horizons and doors that I wouldn't have tapped otherwise. Special thanks to Peter Keen, my coauthor along with Tracy Torregrossa of *The Business Internet and Intranet: A Manager's Guide to Key Terms and Concepts.* As a well-seasoned author, Peter showed me discipline and process. And to my editor at McGraw-Hill, Scott Grillo, thank you for your guidance and diligence throughout our journey.

Finally, my deepest appreciation goes to those currently involved in making Internet commerce a reality and a success for their organizations. Let us be reminded that we constantly owe them our collective understanding of doing business in this new world.

*There's wind and then there's a typhoon. In this business you always have winds. But a 10X force is a change in an element of one's business of typhoon force.*

*Is the Internet a typhoon force, a 10X force, or is it a bit of wind? Or is it a force that fundamentally alters our business?"*

ANDREW GROVE
Chairman
Intel Corporation
(From *Only the Paranoid Survive*, Doubleday, 1996)

# INTRODUCTION

So, where is Internet commerce in your corporate agenda? Are you thinking about the problems of the year 2000 date compliance instead, or is European monetary unification keeping you awake at night? The reality is that these global issues, day-to-day firefighting, and other important concerns are competing with Internet commerce for a share of the executive mind or budget, therefore the corporate agenda.

This book is about strategy. This book is about learning. The stories, cases, and examples demonstrate how electronic commerce is really changing everything in our business approaches and lifestyles.

The complexity of a journey into Internet commerce really depends on the complexity of the organization. The Internet is about exploration as much as it is about exploitation. Just as in the mining industry, there are uncertainties awaiting every gold or diamonds researcher. The ROI models are a moving target, full of what-if scenarios that keep changing.

Today we are still in the early stages of Internet commerce development, and only a few business cases can be completely documented. This book attempts to clearly articulate the strategies, trends, and where possible, lessons learned to date. Even though the book surveys Internet commerce technology, it is primarily focused on how technology is strategically applied in light of the Internet phenomenon. Keeping with the current trends, we will have a "live" Web site to allow readers to maintain an Internet linkage to the content.

The best way to see a big picture is by standing back from it. If you are currently involved with a given Internet project, and hence are close to it, maybe you are missing a part of the picture. If, on the other hand, you are an executive, somehow immune to the effects of the Internet phenomenon, maybe you are missing a deep understanding of its potential. Alternatively, you may be vacillating between using the Internet as a competitive advantage and using it to increase profits and revenues. Or maybe you are split in the middle and are using it safely—namely, to reduce costs. In all these cases, this book will guide you.

The content of this book will appeal to business and technology executives interested in exploring how Internet commerce is destined to change the way they do business, now and in the future. The assumption is that most organizations recognize that emerging Internet markets (iMarkets) are opening up, but they may not know how the change is going to affect them specifically. Or perhaps they are unsure of the approach to take, requirements to consider, critical success factors to target, or implementation methods to follow.

What is the most expansive viewpoint on electronic commerce, as seen by the advent of the Internet? How different is Internet commerce from traditional electronic commerce? What is the management framework required to allow a structured strategic approach to it? What are the challenges and drivers affecting Internet commerce? How do you develop an electronic commerce strategy driven by the Internet? How do you uncover new types of business opportunities that take into account the major changes affecting your industry? How do you build virtual marketplaces to protect your future? How do you participate in the intermediary game, without being disintermediated? What are the major functional building blocks and requirements of information technology (IT)? What are the wired consumer requirements? How do you continue to manage and measure the evolution of your strategy? What lessons have we learned from which we can derive models? These are the main questions this book tries to answer, based on research, assessment, analysis, and ongoing interaction with key industry users, vendors, and other influential organizations.

The "management" field of electronic commerce is quite immature, since we are still gaining experience in applying the new possibilities. This book contains original ideas regarding various approaches to Internet commerce. The focus is the "management" aspect of understanding it, and applying it. In many organizations, executive buy-in and understanding are common barriers to implementing new ideas. Internet commerce is no different. The answer lies with greater management awareness and education on the subject. The greater the scope you have and the more of an open mind you keep, the more opportunities you will see, after reading this book. Even if you are now an avid surfer, what you have seen on the Web is not really indicative of how the Web is transforming the way we do business. You have to understand the implications of what you see and don't see, and think about how they may affect you and your organization.

Today there is more technology than we know what to do with. Companies face the risk of having it surpass management's ability to comprehend it and act on it. So, let's assume there is no more new technology, and let's begin to implement what we have, by focusing on getting our organizations and people ready for the change.

As a business executive, you face several questions yearning for your answers. If you just ignore them, they will come back to quiz you again. For example, do you know what will happen if your entire business gets disintermediated by other new intermediaries you have never heard about before? Are you competing (without knowing it) with a new type of organization that is constantly reinventing itself every six months? Do you know how much market share you are susceptible to losing, not in the physical marketplace, but in the new electronic marketplace? Do you know how to change the nature of your products and services to take advantage of new Internet markets? How do you create or participate in these new virtual marketplaces? These are some of the questions that must be burning in the minds of Internet-aware executives. They represent real possibilities for changes bound to occur, with or without your willingness. The greatest risk lies in not knowing what you don't know. In a fast-changing marketplace such as the Internet, this trap seems to be so open and so wide.

The march toward an increasingly open electronic marketplace has already reached the point of no return. Every day the electronic commerce market gets bigger and bigger, and every day a new Internet-related business begins to threaten an existing traditional business. Market size predictions abound, as every market research firm attempts to get a headline by releasing a number, every so often. Whether the size is several billion dollars or one trillion by the year 2020 is irrelevant. The critical point that often gets missed is that no matter what the number is, it will be a very high percentage of the traditional trade business. So, if the relative size of traditional markets continues to get smaller and smaller, and if you are not planning to generate a larger part of your revenue from electronic markets, you will be left with only a much smaller market to compete in!

Digital markets are emerging as the next battleground for market shares and market dominance. Old or existing market shares in the current physical space we live in may soon become irrelevant and outdated, in favor of digital markets. Whereas traditional marketplaces rely on known value chains, digital markets will rely on "virtual" and "unpredictable" value chains made up of a plethora of new digital values created and re-created between buyers and sellers.

One of the main features of this book is that it presents a complete strategic perspective on what has to be done to fully exploit the Internet commerce marketplace by tying the various pieces together. The suggested process presented is a structured and methodical approach to dealing with electronic commerce. It includes the following four stages: (1) evaluation and understanding, (2) strategy formulation, (3) technology implementation, and (4) business management. Here are the major elements of these four phases.

**Phase I: Evaluation and Understanding**

- Expanded definition and meanings of Internet commerce (Chapter 1)
- EDI perspective and its evolution to the Web (Chapter 1)

- Business-to-business versus business-to-consumer characteristics (Chapter 1)
- Key business drivers (Chapter 2)
- Key technology drivers (Chapter 3)
- Challenges and issues, and how to address them (Chapter 4)

**Phase II: Strategy Formulation**
- Positioning electronic commerce within the organization (Chapter 5)
- Dealing with the new value chain and its implications (Chapter 5)
- Executing on key strategy actions (Chapter 6)
- Uncovering new types of intermediary functions and businesses (Chapter 7)
- Creating new virtual marketplaces (Chapter 7)
- Understanding the evolution of wired consumer requirements (Chapter 8)
- Knowing the ideal characteristics of consumer-based electronic commerce (Chapter 8)

**Phase III: Technology Implementation**
- IT strategy (Chapter 9)
- IT architecture for Internet commerce (Chapter 9)
- Internet computing, Intranets, and Extranets (Chapter 9)
- IT/Internet technology trends (Chapter 9)

**Phase IV: Business Management**
- Marshall Industries case study (Chapter 10)
- Lessons from Marshall Industries (Chapter 10)
- Management issues and principles (Chapter 11)
- Business value and measures for electronic commerce (Chapter 11)

By following the previously outlined four stages, organizations are able to progressively plan and evolve their levels of sophistication and participation in electronic commerce.

We all know that the Internet and electronic commerce will be with us for a long time. The Internet is destined to become a part of the success of all organizations in the future. As a manager, you have to continuously think about how the Internet will affect your business. Overall, we have only begun to understand the actions required to seize this once-in-a-lifetime opportunity.

This book contains condensed observations and actions that will guide your thinking to wider possibilities. So far it seems that some organizations "get it," and others don't (yet). My hope is that we all "get it," so as to simplify our business and personal lives at the same time!

# INTRODUCTION TO INTERNET COMMERCE

*[The term] electronic commerce is the same as everything else. As soon as someone latches on to the definition, it spreads. Within three to four days, the term is misused.*

JIM MANZI

*Chairman and CEO of Nets Inc. (formerly Industry.Net)*

The meaning of the term *Internet commerce* is becoming so big that it is now almost impossible to define it in a few concise words. Maybe in 1995 or 1996, when the term was new, it could have been defined in a few words. But today, dozens of concepts are being labeled with the catchall phrase "electronic commerce on the Internet" or "Internet commerce." Does anybody know how many times these terms are misused, just to get attention or perhaps to claim being part of the newest business trend?

The terms *Internet commerce* and *electronic commerce* will be used interchangeably throughout this book, because the future of electronic commerce is really in the hands of the Internet, whereas its past rested with EDI. Before the Internet (B.I.), EDI (electronic data interchange) was traditionally associated with electronic commerce. EDI focused mostly on the exchange of data and forms between computers. But after the Internet (A.I.), electronic commerce took on a much broader role, and a more profound one that has directly affected the heart of corporate business strategies. A.I. electronic commerce is really allowing organizations to recast their market power and corporate profits in an entirely new universe.

So, what is electronic commerce, from a business perspective?

One answer that points to its versatility is: "What would you like it to be?" Think about what would happen if several people were asked to describe a very large and complex object that they couldn't see, but could only feel. They would obviously argue about its characteristics, based on their own particular experience.

Attempting to respond to "What is electronic commerce?" is similar to responding to "What is information technology?" It would take a long time to depict a complete picture; furthermore, the responses would be as varied as the people answering.

Point made, electronic commerce is BIG and still getting BIGGER.

Internet commerce is clearly becoming an imperative for the internetworked enterprise. It can be characterized as an evolution of international trade. From a technology perspective, the Internet is the catalyst for yet another new computing paradigm: Internet computing (also referred to as network-centric computing or internetworked computing). The marriage of the Internet with electronic commerce represents the cutting edge in business today.

Implementation of an Internet commerce strategy can take different forms, depending on the business and the approach used. Every firm that wants to stay in business beyond the turn of the century should be reevaluating its strategy and operations, from customer service to marketing to product development to merchandising, logistics, and distribution. The tremendous scope of activities that must be reengineered makes Internet commerce a fascinating field, so hungry for implementation and practical knowledge.

Executives who doubt that Internet commerce could radically affect their businesses are urged to evaluate the amount and quality of research, investments, implementations, and success stories that are taking place in this area. They should quickly realize that Internet commerce will lead to significant, innovative ways of doing business. The Internet and electronic commerce will be with us for a very long time.

This introductory chapter focuses on defining a broader and newer meaning to electronic commerce. It explains why Internet commerce is different from traditional electronic commerce, and outlines the characteristics of the new electronic commerce world.

## THE BIG PICTURE

Electronic commerce is a big-picture phenomenon destined to change business habits in more than one way. Driven by the Internet, electronic commerce is rapidly emerging as an entirely new method to conduct business and interact with suppliers, partners, and clients. Applying all elements of this new model brings new dimensions of speed, efficiency, spontaneity, interactivity, pervasiveness, and cost reduction if you target the following areas:

- Approaches to marketing, sales, and distribution channels
- General, selling, and administrative processes
- Product generation process
- Digital content creation and manipulation for the purpose of adding value
- Manufacturing and procurement processes
- Relationship with trading partners
- Supply chain management

Jay M. Tenenbaum, chairman and founder of CommerceNet, defines electronic commerce as "the opportunity for companies to electronically *exchange information and services* that are important to their business. It doesn't have to involve money. Electronic commerce includes the *creation of an open marketplace*—in contrast with EDI, which doesn't. The Internet is synonymous to a vast marketplace."

Randall Whiting, president and CEO of CommerceNet (and previously Hewlett-Packard electronic sales and marketing manager), has a slightly different definition. He states that "electronic commerce is about a *global electronic marketplace* that enables *all members of a value chain* to interact spontaneously for mutual benefits. It provides an environment where *customers are empowered* to control the buying process more effectively, receiving and accessing personalized information. It provides a platform for *complete relationship management,* not just a one-time transaction."

The key words in italics encapsulate the essence of these definitions. Stop now and ponder the significance of each one for your own organization:

- Exchange of information and services
- Creation of an open (global) marketplace
- Spontaneous interaction among members of a value chain
- Empowerment of customers
- Platform for relationship management

Contrast the above *open-ended* definition terms with the following *narrowly focused* ones that have been publicized by the press:

- Secure payment transactions
- Selling in cyberspace
- Electronic shopping
- EDI
- Home banking
- Electronic publishing
- Interactive marketing
- Electronic catalogs

The above list represents valid issues and activities by which electronic commerce is manifested. However, they are not indicative of the vast and open-ended realm that electronic commerce really encompasses, especially when you add the Internet factor to it.

# NEW MEANINGS FOR A NEW WORLD

We won't embark on theoretical and boring definitions of electronic commerce. But we have to look at this big-picture phenomenon from more than one angle. Understanding the several meanings of Internet commerce is probably the most fundamental part of the book. It is not just important; it is essential. After all, how can you deal with something so strategic if you know only a part of it?

There are several definitions of electronic commerce, some of which are valid, others limiting. The terminology has not yet matured, and we are still searching for a common ground to rest on. However, the fact that we are still discovering new applications for this concept makes it all the more exciting. The following represents a logical process for discovering electronic commerce while we examine its possibilities.

## BUYING AND SELLING

One of the most common definitions of electronic commerce is "the buying and selling of products and services over the Internet or other electronic networks." At first sight, it appears that the definition refers to the placement of a product or service on the Web, followed by the enablement of a payment mechanism to capture the buy transaction. Several businesses wishing to get a slice of Internet markets are basing their implementations on this most boring definition of Internet commerce. During 1996 the definition still generated excitement among those interested in taming the dragon, but today there is little creativity involved and assured failure in just duplicating a part of the buying/selling process on the Internet. Why? Because duplicating only a fraction (perhaps just 5 percent) of the buying/selling process does not change enough of the entire process to produce a significant economic outcome. This is where first-generation Internet malls fell into the trap and stayed there.

Whether you are dealing with customers or suppliers, the buying/selling process really consists of several steps, chained one after another. (We will dissect the buying/selling process in Chapter 5.) These steps can be categorized in three pivotal parts: before the buying/selling, during, and after. The point that most organizations miss initially is that each and every one of these steps presents an opportunity to utilize the Web for replacing, adding to, enhancing, or changing what's already been done today. The payment transaction is only a small piece of it. So, the first definition of electronic commerce relates to all transactional aspects surrounding (and including) the buying/selling cycle. With the Internet, it is becoming obvious that, for the first time, there is a comprehensive and pervasive infrastructure available to support the entire buying/selling cycle via electronic means.

Let's push the concept even further and think about what changes in this picture. Two key elements change. The first one relates to "what" is being bought and sold. It is no longer the products and services that we see and touch or even currently have; it is the new ones that we haven't even dreamed about yet. The changing nature of products and services is covered in more detail later, in Chapter 6. The second element relates to "how" we buy and sell—that is, how the relationship between buyers and sellers changes every step of the way where *value* is created along the value chain. This *value* is not about the same set of value propositions that organizations have been used to attracting customers with. Internet markets no longer regard these values as worthwhile. The new value on the rise takes the shape of its transformed equivalent: the "digital" value.

## (DIGITAL) VALUE CREATION

The second most important way to define electronic commerce is by pointing to the creation of digital value, a new production process, and one that is emerging as an essential element to electronic commerce that hasn't been as widely depicted yet. It is best described by Ravi Kalakota, professor and electronic commerce author, as *the process of converting digital inputs into value-added outputs.* This definition is complementary to the first one, and may offer a more dominant view of electronic

INPUT                    PROCESSING            OUTPUT

**FIGURE** 1-1.   Digital value creation is a "production process." (*CYBERManagement Inc.*)

commerce, primarily because of the far-reaching impact on the way that value is created. The digital value creation process involves taking information as raw material and producing higher added-value information-based products or services from the original raw information (Figure 1-1). So, electronic commerce refers to an on-line production process. New value can be created in one of two ways: (1) by adding digital value on top of old value or (2) by turning old value (or products) into new digital value replacements.

The key question here is: Who is going to deliver this added value to your customers? Is it you? Or is it somebody else? The answer is *you,* only if you do it quickly enough.

## NEW INTERMEDIARIES' ARRIVAL

If you don't begin to add digital value quickly enough, this value can also be delivered to your customers by other new types of organizations, called intermediaries. They will come out of nowhere, hijack your potential new value by adding new value on top of your old value, aggregate it, and resell it with other value—therefore, in essence, stealing your customers.

At the heart of the new intermediaries' strategy is the digital value creation process which they own. Intermediary organizations interact with the producers of information and generate a resulting output, which takes the form of a digital product, service, and other processed information, such as a sales order, a payment, or a specific action.

If you think that this is theory, consider the new businesses that are inserting themselves between banks and their customers, between retailers and their customers, between publishers and their customers, and so on. Almost every industry has already been threatened to a certain degree by the arrival of intermediaries that ease their way into traditional buyer/seller channels, and begin to redirect buyer traffic themselves. There are also other types of intermediaries that cater to the demands of the new electronic marketplace and have no direct equivalent that they are replacing in the physical space. These include certification authorities, electronic payment gateways, electronic directories, and a range of others which are covered in Chapter 7.

The situation now looks like this. You have new types of companies called intermediaries that are adding digital value in a newly redefined value chain that has no boundaries. You have a number of organizations electronically linked together in ways that redefine the entire buying/selling process. What happens when you put all of this together?

## OPENING DIGITAL MARKETS

One result of this ongoing brouhaha is fueling the exploitation of new digital markets. These digital markets include the creation of a large number of electronic trading communities, virtual marketplaces, virtual companies, and new types of intermediary services that compete by building and rebuilding new forms of value on top of one another. Welcome to the world of digital markets!

It can be argued that a primary goal of Internet commerce is the relentless creation of tumultuous electronic markets. Electronic markets (or digital markets) are complete new virtual marketplaces that mimic certain characteristics of physical marketplaces, but at the same time exhibit very different behaviors. These marketplaces consist of a constellation of electronic buyers and sellers that come together within the confines of trusted virtual environments to conduct business spontaneously and efficiently. New market players arise daily, and they contribute to building these markets by interacting openly but unpredictably sometimes, while competing vigorously to exploit the markets in ways that are still being discovered. They include various choices of Web presence, such as storefronts, private Intranets,* bid/ask marketplaces, virtual order centers, agent-based intermediaries, and other yet-to-be-invented ways of reaching customers electronically.

In essence, the new Internet-driven electronic commerce is not about a one-time transaction, not just EDI, not about building a Web site, and definitely not a walk in the park either. It resembles a long journey more than a given destination. Electronic commerce is about businesses and consumers adopting a new process or methodology in dealing with each other. These processes are supported by electronic interactions and relations that replace close physical presence requirements or other traditional means.

## THE INTERNET EFFECT

The Internet with its World Wide Web facade is bringing a fresh new set of capabilities to electronic commerce. It is a new infrastructure composed of new technologies and new applications, with a new set of rules and technical requirements, some of which are still a challenge to resolve. The Internet, as a novelty or a new tool, is destined to radically change business models, deal with issues of disintermediation, and force us to rethink where we have to add or change value, throughout the value chain.

Today, several developments are focused on the commercialization of the Internet and corporate Intranets. Developers and builders are rushing to create and market content and services in four areas (Table 1-1).

This book is focused on the electronic commerce aspect of the commercialization of the Internet. It can be argued that electronic commerce is the killer application for the Internet, which is a positive development.

---

*Intranets mimic the Internet within an organization.

TABLE 1-1.  Four Major Areas for Commercialization of the Internet

| 1. COMMUNICATIONS/ COLLABORATION | 2. NETWORKED APPLICATIONS | 3. REAL-TIME MULTIMEDIA | 4. ELECTRONIC COMMERCE |
| --- | --- | --- | --- |
| Gathering/ processing information | Distributed Internet applications | Distance learning and education | Buying/selling |
| Communicating | Linked corporate and legacy data | Entertainment | Digital value creation |
| Publishing | Web-enabled and live applications | Virtual reality | New intermediaries |
| Collaborating | Object-oriented applications | Video/audio conferencing | Virtual market-places |

SOURCE: CYBERManagement Inc.

The Internet is exhibiting more and more promise to become the trusted forum for conducting electronic commerce. It presents several characteristics desired in an open information superhighway framework, such as shared accessibility and broad availability. It is, however, still maturing in other desired capabilities such as ease of use, pervasiveness, high integrity and availability, guaranteed grades of service, privacy and security, mechanisms for detecting and preventing fraud and abuse, usage and measures suitable for billing, quality of multimedia capabilities, and universality of gateways to the financial services required for many commercial applications.

## THE EVOLUTION OF ELECTRONIC COMMERCE

If we regard traditional electronic commerce as what EDI (electronic data interchange) promised, the current evolution of electronic commerce referred to as *Internet commerce* is what the Internet is promising, beyond EDI. Internet commerce is giving a new life to electronic commerce, with different characteristics from EDI. Internet commerce is not a "repeat of EDI," but rather an evolution from EDI.

## BUSINESS-TO-BUSINESS VERSUS BUSINESS-TO-CONSUMER ELECTRONIC COMMERCE

It is generally accepted that there are three sectors for electronic commerce: business-to-business, business-to-consumer, and intraorganizational (Figure 1-2). Even though they have basic differences and characteristics, companies must approach all three sectors in a holistic manner in order to exploit and leverage the synergy that can be derived from the common aspects of implementation. The intraorganizational side of electronic commerce can be associated with Intranets working for the corporation, whereas the business-to-business and business-to-consumer aspects are Intranets working for trading partners and consumers. As Intranets begin to interact externally, among different organizations, they can also be called Extranets.

The business-to-consumer market focuses on the consumer as the end user or buyer (Figure 1-3). The business-to-business market relates to (1) businesses selling products or services to

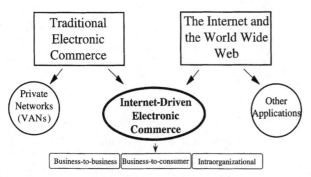

**FIGURE 1-2.** Internet commerce is about the convergence of the Web with traditional electronic commerce. (*CYBERManagement Inc.*)

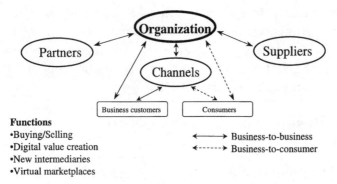

**FIGURE 1-3.**    Business customers and consumers represent different segments of Internet commerce. (*CYBERManagement Inc.*)

one another, with a given organization serving as either buyer or seller, or (2) transactions and information relating to back-end processes between suppliers, partners, or channels, such as ordering, paying, EDI, basic and advanced procurement services, distribution support, and logistics management. For consumers, the term *buying* means shopping, whereas for businesses, it means procurement.

The differences between business-to-business and business-to-consumer Internet commerce suggest that the business-to-business sector will develop more rapidly, because a higher percentage of businesses are connected to the Internet. However, the speed at which consumers begin to adopt certain technologies is not to be underestimated, especially when contrasted with the relative shortage of business-to-business Internet applications (Table 1-2).

## COMPARISON OF TRADITIONAL ELECTRONIC COMMERCE WITH INTERNET-DRIVEN ELECTRONIC COMMERCE

What Internet commerce offers, which EDI commerce does not, are four important characteristics that make it so appealing for the expected rapid growth. These are:

TABLE 1-2. Differences between Business and Consumer Characteristics for Internet Commerce

| CHARACTERISTIC | BUSINESS | CONSUMER |
|---|---|---|
| Percentage on-line | High | Low |
| Total potential value of transaction | High | Medium |
| Value/price sensitivity | Low | High |
| Known relationship? | High | Low |
| Number of customers | Low | High |
| Time required to "get in or out" of relationship | Long | Short |
| Motivation to improve efficiency of transactions | High | Low |

SOURCE: CYBERManagement Inc.

- *Interactivity.* One can interact with a remote person in a variety of ways, such as by e-mail, voice, or video, while doing a transaction.

- *Spontaneity.* There is no need for establishing lengthy predetermined procedures in order to engage in a relationship or transaction.

- *Pervasiveness.* Because of the spread of Internet access, it already has many potential ready users, both as consumers and as businesses.

- *The creation of a marketplace.* The Internet is both a marketplace and a delivery vehicle. By reaching these markets, you make them available.

Organizations should assess how the above four characteristics can affect the relationship with existing or new trading partners. Trading partners can be categorized in three categories:

1. Customers (including distribution channels to reach them)
2. Suppliers of goods and services to your organization
3. Other partners such as health care and insurance entities, banks and financial institutions, external information sources of recipients, government departments, and transportation carriers

TABLE 1-3. Comparison of Traditional Electronic Commerce versus Open Electronic Commerce

| FACTOR | TRADITIONAL ELECTRONIC COMMERCE | OPEN ELECTRONIC COMMERCE |
|---|---|---|
| Implementation dynamics | Value proposition is biased toward a predetermined relationship; otherwise the transaction can't happen. | The consumer of services decides and initiates the request to buy in a one-to-many relationship. |
| Business case | You develop the transaction capabilities only after you know there is a market or willingness to use the channel. | You develop content and make it ready for a critical mass of buyers to get connected. |
| Financial transactions | Financial transactions can take place over existing networks. | Internet gateways to financial networks, new instruments, and micropayments become important. |
| Effect on business processes | Any transaction has a direct effect on internal business processes. | Transactions should mirror reality or should dramatically simplify a business process. |
| Frequency of transactions | There is smaller frequency, but higher dollar value per transaction. | Mass market, infrequent usage, and lower dollar value per transaction are acceptable. |
| Choice of products | Comparison shopping is difficult. | Comparison shopping is essential. |
| Level of trust | High. | Low to medium. |
| Duration of relationship | Long. | Short to medium. |
| Cost | Higher. | Lower. |

TABLE 1-3. Comparison of Traditional Electronic Commerce versus Open Electronic Commerce (*Continued*)

| FACTOR | TRADITIONAL ELECTRONIC COMMERCE | OPEN ELECTRONIC COMMERCE |
|---|---|---|
| Reliability | Higher. | Lower (but getting better). |
| Flexibility | Lower. | Higher. |
| Effect on distribution channels | There is no conflict of distribution channel, because primary focus is on the uniqueness of transactions. | Channel conflict is on-line, as the transaction becomes the "back end" and the customer interface becomes the "front end." |

SOURCE: CYBERManagement Inc.

Table 1-3 highlights fundamental differences between traditional (EDI-led) electronic commerce and *open* (Internet-led) electronic commerce.

# THE FUTURE OF EDI: OPEN, LIGHTER, AND CHEAPER

Today, EDI is largely associated with the software technology for formatting electronic messages, data, and forms among computers, as well as with the actual value-added network (VAN) services that support them. One of the challenges for EDI has been its lack of widespread usage with small and medium-size organizations, mainly because of implementation cost and complexity. But today organizations have to learn and accept that modern electronic commerce goes well beyond EDI.

It is perceived that EDI is going through a rebirth potential because of the Internet's ability in determining its future. The future of EDI will really depend on how "open" it becomes. Open EDI refers to several aspects of the evolution of EDI as it becomes more integrated with the Internet. I foresee the rise of a "light EDI" phenomenon. Light EDI is easier to implement

and more user-friendly because it relies on forms-based transactions and other Web interfaces that hide the behind-the-
scene complexities. Light EDI relies on the Internet as the
"network," or uses the Internet as a gateway to existing value-
added networks (VANs).

Open, lighter, and cheaper EDI holds the promise of finally
allowing EDI transactions to reach small to medium-size businesses, a goal always missed by traditional EDI. The marriage
of EDI with the Internet will have the following elements:

- Web-based transactions that map information seamlessly
  into the back end of EDI systems. The initiation of the EDI
  transaction will be through a Web-based form, instead of
  directly from a computer. This means that forms-based gateways become the drivers of the transaction.

- Traditional EDI transactions that utilize the Internet as the
  network, otherwise known as Internet EDI. This means that
  existing EDI-type transactions will be using the Internet as
  the transport network, instead of using a VAN.

- EDI integrated with business-to-business virtual trading
  communities with end-to-end services that cover the entire
  buying/selling cycle. This means that EDI is one of the components, and an invisible part of a greater picture.

- Order entry, purchasing, procurement, and other applications that are built on top of EDI and utilize the Web as a
  delivery mechanism.

- The shift of VANs to VAINs, or value-added Internet networks. The Internet becomes an integral part of EDI, and
  EDI embraces the Internet in order to get its share of the
  renewal potential.

- Increased interoperability among EDI vendors' products in
  the areas of integrity, confidentiality, digital signature, and
  nonrepudiation when conducting EDI transactions over the
  Internet. (The EDI-INT standard addresses this issue.)

- Marriage of EDI with XML (eXtensible Markup Language) as
  a powerful combination to allow a variety of Web-based data

sources to be accurately handled by EDI dictionaries (e.g., a health care claim, a payment order, an invoice).

*Actra Corporation: The Future of EDI?*
A partnership of Netscape and GE Information Services called Actra Business Systems is providing tools and applications that facilitate the use and rapid adoption of EDI via the Internet and Intranets, for both large and small corporations. According to Actra Business Systems, their mission is to develop software applications with an initial focus on two key areas:

- A business document gateway to facilitate the exchange of EDI and messages between a business and its trading partners
- A suite of server software products focusing on purchasing and supplier management, EDI, electronic product catalogs, and Internet client software technology to streamline sourcing, ordering, purchasing, and the payment process from the buyer, agent, and seller sides, such as electronic product catalogs, procurement services, ordering, purchasing, and payments

Question: Could this mark the beginnings of "interactive prospecting," with businesses truly searching for new opportunities on-line?

The rise of the Internet as a viable catalyst for electronic commerce is prompting VANs to extend and expand their offerings into Internet-related products and services, as well as striking new alliances with emerging Internet partners. Here are two examples that illustrate the rise of Internet EDI.*

Bell Atlantic is providing a more secure way for its large customers to send their phone bills. Bell allows them to use Internet-based EDI to transmit their phone bills with an Internet-based EDI approach, where authentication of customer site is essential. The approach incorporates encryption technology to messages that are signed with the receiver's public key, which is a unique number used for coding/decoding information.

Diamond Shamrock is sending financial EDI transactions over the Internet to its banking partner Chase Manhattan. Both trading partners

---

*CommerceNet Research Note #97-01, Business Applications of Digital Authentication, February 1997.

are using a combination of two public and two private keys. Shamrock began with about 25 percent of its 300 trading partners, mainly utility and freight-handling companies, over the Internet. EDI files sent via the Internet reach their destination in real time.

# THE ROLE OF INTRANETS

Otherwise known as "the Web goes inside," Intranets have gained a lot of attention from large to small organizations. For many organizations, Intranets are regarded as an extension of client/server networks, with new flavors of information technology standards, infrastructure, tools, and applications that rely on the Internet as the network and the development platform. The strength of a company's Intranet infrastructure and applications can serve as an important launching ground for inter- or intra-organizational business-to-business electronic commerce.

Several companies are getting their Intranet "house" in order, so that they can compete more effectively in the marketplace, and interact efficiently with their partners, suppliers, and customers. The richness of Intranet functionality is increasing rapidly, and almost anything one can think of might have an Intranet application.

Large organizations needing to engage in Internet commerce must base their future information technology strategies on the development of rich Intranets. Rich corporate Intranets will be necessary to raise the organization's readiness for electronic business interactions. The current rush to build Intranets is a strong signal for increased open Internet commerce activity. The business-to-business side of Internet commerce will have to rely on Intranet-to-Intranet applications interchange.

Intranets are needed to fully integrate the supply chain electronically within the organization. For example, at Marshall Industries, a customer order automatically triggers a scheduling order for the warehouse, an order acknowledgment for the customer, and a shipping status when the order ships, and ends up managing the bill of materials for the customer in real time.

When compared with the rigidity of EDI, Intranets are much easier to implement with business partners. To enable electronic commerce with its independent dealer network, Michelin efficiently and quickly rolled out Bib Net™, a private Intranet linked to its legacy systems. Bib Net includes order/inventory management, claims processing, accounting status, marketing and sales information, dealer bulletin board, and other business-to-business functionality.

Here are two other solutions of business-to-business commerce, backed by Intranet-to-Intranet communications via the Internet. These focus on streamlining internal and external workflow processes.

Through the technologies of Internet-based electronic commerce, Ariba's Operating Resource Management (ORM) automates the acquisition of operating resources (the goods and services required to operate companies, such as industrial supplies, office supplies, capital equipment, and services). This is done through the effective use of aggregate buying, volume discounts from vendors, lowered transaction costs through the use of electronic communications, and decision support techniques to identify vendor discount operations. Since nearly 95 percent of all goods and services purchased by corporations are purchased with paper-based processes, the electronic automation, consolidation, and leveraged buying processes present a significant opportunity for companies to directly lower purchasing costs, and therefore improve their bottom line. For example, Octel Communications and Cisco are using Ariba's applications across several thousands of desktops to streamline global procurement within their Intranet and over the Internet.

Automating business processes between enterprises and their key partners by connecting enterprise systems over the Internet is CrossRoute's vision. The company allows the business information behind a process to flow seamlessly within an enterprise and externally with its business partners over the Internet. For example, to implement vendor-managed inventory, CrossRoute automatically forwards a release or purchase order to the supplier. The supplier returns an advanced ship notice once the delivery is scheduled. Another example involves linking a customer's purchasing system to a supplier's quote or pricing system, while maintaining security and privacy for internal processes. As requests for quotes are received, quotes can be automatically calculated, routed for internal approvals if necessary, and then returned to the customer.

## DO-IT-YOURSELF MARKET SIZE ASSESSMENT

You may be asking yourself: What is the size of the market for all these opportunities? Various market research reports abound weekly, touting different numbers for the size of the electronic commerce market, cutting it and slicing it in several ways. From millions it grew to billions, and is expected to approach a trillion by 2020, according to some analysts. The macrolevel view is useful for researchers and statisticians, but you'll need to get a handle on the specific segment size within your own industry. For example, if you are in the travel industry, you will be interested in knowing specifically the percentage of transactions or customers that are shifting to the on-line world, coming directly from that specific industry. If your industry is growing faster than the average growth of the market, keeping an eye on the macrolevels will give you a distorted view and lead to missed opportunities.

Following is a simple approach for estimating the size of the commerce market, based on a generic view of the marketplace. You can apply the same process to your own segment by inserting your own assumptions and numbers. Let us start with the business-to-consumer market, using an example with Canadian data.

Table 1-4 indicates that the size of the business-to-consumer market in Canada should be $50 million in 1997 and $1.5 billion in 2000. If you live in a country where the Internet is not as developed, you can apply different ratios to the number of people who might buy over the Internet, or to the average amounts they represent. But you have to start by knowing approximately the total number of Internet users.

TABLE 1-4.  A Do-It-Yourself Exercise to Estimate the Size of
Internet Commerce in Your Segment

| PARAMETER | 1997 | 2000 |
|---|---|---|
| Number of users over the age of 16 on the Internet | 2.5 million | 6 million |
| Percentage of those who buy on the Internet | 20% | 50% |
| Total eligible buyers | 500,000 | 3 million |
| Average buying value per year | $100 | $500 |
| Total value purchased over the Internet | $50 million | $1.5 billion |

SOURCE:  CYBERManagement Inc.

Let us assume that you are interested in a particular segment of the industry—for example, flowers. We will use the following fictitious assumptions, based on the Canadian data. If 3 percent of all Internet users (75,000 people) spend an average of $40 per year on flowers, the total size of that segment is $3 million (75,000 multiplied by $40).

How about the business-to-business market? It is generally accepted and assumed that the size of the business-to-business market is about 7 to 10 times the size of the business-to-consumer market. This consists of all business-to-business applications, including the value of goods and services exchanged during procurement processes among organizations. This gives Canada $500 million for 1997 and $15 billion for 2000.

You do the math now.

Since you are excited about the size of these opportunities, let us move along to the other chapters!

# BUSINESS CATALYSTS

*We're already selling on the Web. Our sales have tripled in the last three months, and we're going to be making from $2 to $5 million [this year (1996) on Web sales].*

RICHARD THALHEIMER
*Chairman, Sharper Image Inc.*

Many factors are driving the growth of electronic commerce. Each industry or organization is eventually affected in a different manner; therefore, each one of the following catalysts should be evaluated accordingly. The potential revenue generated by the Internet commerce market will probably exceed the value of traditional EDI-based services before the end of the second millennium. It is important to note that it is the business drivers, not the technology drivers, that should be paramount in the decision to address Internet commerce within your organization.

## DISTRIBUTION COSTS AND VALUE CHAIN INEFFICIENCIES

Any given product or service travels down a distribution channel that may or may not add value to it. Ultimately, a distribution channel's role is to reach the customer at a price that includes the inherent distribution costs—in addition to other benefits it may carry, such as ease of location and a knowledgeable salesperson. In general, for most retail products, a 40 to 60 percent markup from the most immediate handling channel is normal. By the time the product reaches the user, this markup could total 135 percent in many cases. Both manufacturers and

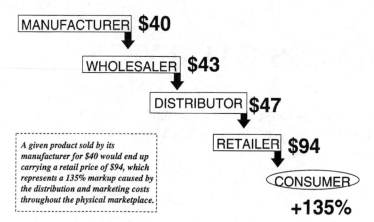

**FIGURE 2-1.** The typical distribution channel has several intermediary layers. (*CYBERManagement Inc.*)

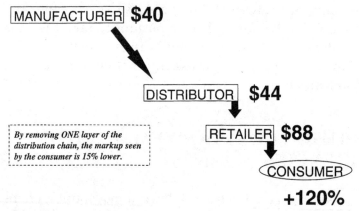

**FIGURE 2-2.** Delayering the distribution channel—Step 1. (*CYBERManagement Inc.*)

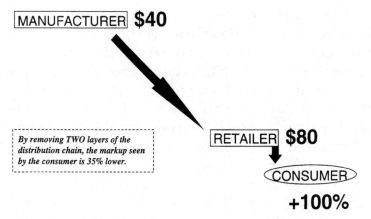

MANUFACTURER $40

By removing TWO layers of the
distribution chain, the markup seen
by the consumer is 35% lower.

RETAILER $80

CONSUMER

+100%

FIGURE 2-3. Delayering the distribution channel—Step 2.
(*CYBERManagement Inc.*)

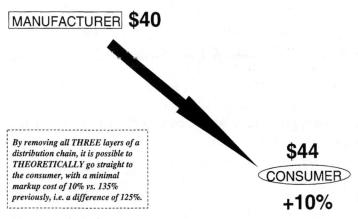

MANUFACTURER $40

By removing all THREE layers of a
distribution chain, it is possible to
THEORETICALLY go straight to
the consumer, with a minimal
markup cost of 10% vs. 135%
previously, i.e. a difference of 125%.

$44

CONSUMER

+10%

FIGURE 2-4. Delayering the distribution channel—Step 3.
(*CYBERManagement Inc.*)

consumers have reasons to worry about the perceived lack of value offered by the distribution channels.

Manufacturers are becoming concerned that more customer revenue is being left with their distribution channels, and less with them, as they watch their profit margins get squeezed. On the other hand, customers are realizing that a large part of what they are paying is actually staying with the distribution channels. Because of the presence of the Internet as a marketing and product selection vehicle, customers are beginning to question the value offered by the distribution channels, when they can theoretically obtain the same products directly from the manufacturer. If manufacturers are able to connect directly with consumers and shorten the traditional distribution chain they used to depend on, it is theoretically possible to get rid of the inefficiencies of the current structure. *Welcome to the emerging trend of disintermediation!*

Disintermediation is a new term that refers to the removal of organizations or business process layers responsible for certain intermediary steps in a given value chain. A logical alternative to disintermediation is reintermediation, which actually points to the shifting or transfer of the intermediary function, rather than the complete elimination of it.

Current models of doing business in the marketspace indicate that the costs are much lower than in the physical marketplace. Chapter 5 elaborates on how the current distribution model can evolve with Internet commerce. The storyboard (Figures 2-1 to 2-4) illustrates the potential benefits of theoretically delayering certain parts of the distribution channels.

## COSTS OF BUSINESS TRANSACTIONS

The cost of doing business with traditional paper-based and human-intensive processes continues to grow, whereas the electronic processing of transactions can be done at a fraction of the original cost. The generally accepted examples in Table 2-1 illustrate this point. They relate more accurately to a large enterprise.

TABLE 2-1.  Cost Differences between Paper and Electronic
Processes

| PROCESS DESCRIPTION | PAPER/HUMAN COST | ELECTRONIC PROCESSING COST | SAVINGS FACTOR |
|---|---|---|---|
| Producing and processing an invoice* | $100 | $10 | 10 |
| Average retail banking transaction | $1.50 | 15–25 cents | 6–10 |
| Answering a customer service request | $15–$25 (call center) | $3–$5 (Internet self-service) | 5 |
| Mortgage application† | 1% of value | .2% of value | 5 |

*Price Waterhouse 1996 Technology Forecast Report
†Cebra Inc.

## SEARCH FOR GROWTH MARKETS

Retail markets are barely expanding. Many large retailers are
still posting declines in sales and earnings. It is becoming
increasingly difficult to expand market share in the traditional
marketplaces. By shifting attention to new "open markets,"
such as Internet-driven marketplaces, organizations have a
chance to redefine market shares in the *marketspace*. This is an
opportunity for companies to recast their marketing savvy in
order to capture these new markets, otherwise known as electronic markets. Growth could come from:

- The creation of new on-line markets for existing products
- The creation of new products specifically designed for the
  on-line markets
- The opening of international markets via the electronic marketplace

However, having global reach is not the same as being a
global competitor. For example, Amazon.com, with its 2.5 mil-

lion titles of subvirtual inventory, has global reach for English books only. It is not able (as of this writing) to compete in other markets serving French or Spanish titles, for example. The reason is not a lack of technical infrastructure, which Amazon.com could expand easily. The reason is of a business nature: The company does not have the same relationships with foreign publishers, nor has it integrated its process with regional fulfillment/logistics of books to and from publishers to its warehouse. Inasmuch as most employees are currently located in Seattle, it will undoubtedly have to move some employees out of Seattle in order to compete globally.

## COMPETITIVE PRESSURES

Any serious corporate planning takes into account what the competition is doing. In the electronic marketplace, old leaders are challenged simply because the value demanded by customers changes. There aren't many cases of current market leaders that have lost their position because of electronic markets, yet. However, presumptive dominance is challenged continuously.

The tricky part about competitive pressure is that after you have copied what your competition has done, you are both on an equal footing again, and just moving along. That was the case with the reengineering trends of the early 1990s and with other previous innovations, such as just-in-time inventory and (even before that) total quality programs. The difference with the Internet is in the speed of implementation. Whereas it took perhaps up to three years for a reengineering program to come full circle and prove its benefits, we are now witnessing entire processes being reinvented around the Internet within months. It has been reported that Hanes, which competes with Fruit of the Loom, copied Fruit of the Loom's Internet supply chain management system within a six-month period. Even though being first pays dividends, the differential time required to catch up is narrowing.

Another competitive factor that is often understated is competition from customers kicking old habits away. When I asked

Terry Jones, president of Travelocity, the on-line travel business, who his competition was, he replied: "They tell me it's Microsoft's Expedia or Preview Travel. In reality, my competition is the telephone—people picking up the phone to call their travel agent, rather than coming to us."

*German Exporters Lose Sales because of Internet* *
German exporters, battling against a strong currency and high labor costs, have found another cause for their declining share of international markets: the Internet. Mr. Michael Fuchs, the president of Germany's wholesale and foreign trade association, said that companies were losing lucrative niche markets because the worldwide computer market network made it easier to compare prices and thus was making competition tougher.

Where once a German company would offer to supply goods abroad at a given price and be fairly sure of winning the order, it was now likely to find the potential customer quoting more competitive prices from perhaps five other suppliers and putting the German company under pressure to improve its terms. The information used by a potential customer with such devastating effect has been garnered by surfing the Internet.

This microlevel representation outlines the effects of global sourcing, led by Internet markets. By extrapolating this scenario at a macrolevel, you can begin to imagine how global reach can now affect the competitive landscape of any industry, in any country.

## DEMANDS OF THE ELECTRONIC CONSUMER

Finally, as consumers become increasingly wired and aware of the implied convenience of electronic interactions with sellers of products and services, they will begin to demand more and more services on-line. Soon, consumer choice will be driven by the richness and depth of the on-line services offered by vendors or service providers, such as banks and retail stores. The same applies to suppliers and partners that will favor each other only if the on-line exchange capabilities are in place.

---

*Excerpted from an article in the German press by Peter Norman, Bonn, April 1996.

In today's physical world, sellers seek out consumers by advertising and promoting their products and services. Consumers respond by seeking these sellers and buying correspondingly. With electronic commerce, once the channel is open between buyers and sellers, the novelty is that it becomes a bidirectional channel that empowers consumers to a new level of sovereignty.

The electronic consumer wants:

- Easy and comprehensive comparison shopping
- The ability to bid out a request to the Web
- Self-service control

We will look at consumer requirements in more detail in Chapter 8.

## GLOBALIZATION ISSUES AND LOCATION OPTIMIZATION FOR COMMERCE

Hansa.net Global Commerce Inc., a part of the Span-Hansa Group of companies which is based in Anguilla, has coined the term "location-optimized commerce on the Internet" (LOCI). According to Hansa.net's Web site, "where to locate a business' electronic commerce has become a critical factor in today's global environment. The choice of jurisdiction affects economic, regulatory compliance, supply source, tax, and many other elements. Companies that choose their locations wisely will have major price and competitive advantages over those that do not." The footnote to the statement is that the tax rate in Anguilla is 0 percent.

Tax haven locations have always attracted certain types of sophisticated businesses because of the fiscal benefits they provided them. They have also attracted criminals. The issue is that tax haven countries can allow companies to set up Web sites that would be treated under the same secrecy laws as those extended by their traditional banks. The practice would encourage the following scenario: A company wishing to sell downloadable products sets up a Web site in a tax haven country, allowing anybody around the world to order its products without being charged a sales tax, therefore undercutting other non-tax haven companies that sell the same products. It is still, however, unknown whether a tax haven environment would guarantee a company's competitiveness in this area without due regard to other issues. Countries and industry organizations around the world are studying international tax implications for electronic commerce, including the impact of tax haven countries on the potential drain of taxes.

Another variation on the concept of Internet commerce globalization and reach is the following scenario. Company X is successful within its own country, but would like to expand globally, as it senses a demand for its products or services worldwide. The problem is that it would have to translate its Web site contents into several languages and study the various processes needed to do business in foreign countries, including currency conversions and fulfillment services.

Enters the picture a company based in Hawaii, called WorldPoint™. WorldPoint offers a complete turnkey, multilingual commerce and hosting solution for companies worldwide. It has developed the technology and worldwide processes that allow a company to effectively market and sell its products and services over the Internet to users in several English and non-English countries at the same time, overcoming traditional language and cultural differences. One element of the service is the creation of an on-line catalog that features a multilingual interface. WorldPoint also builds the capacity to price products and accept credit cards and other forms of payment in several currencies, and offers localized customer support and worldwide fulfillment services.

## GOVERNMENT ROLE AND COMPETITIVE POSITIONING OF NATIONS

On July 1, 1997, President Clinton announced to the world a historical document, rightfully entitled *A Framework for Global Electronic Commerce*. Available as a draft since December 1996, it reads more like a progressive manifesto, and a wake-up call for nations around the world to cooperate and become part of this new economy whose forces of change are greater than what any single nation can sustain. The principles behind this document, spearheaded by Ira Magaziner, senior policy adviser to President Clinton, are brilliantly articulated and are serving as a model for other countries that are drafting their own. Japan and Europe have released similar documents, with their own viewpoints on similar issues. All three documents ultimately aim at achieving international cooperation and harmonization, as their respective positions serve to demonstrate to each other that there is substantial common ground.

Says Magaziner: "We have likened the Internet's impact to that of the Industrial Revolution, because of its transformative effect. We believe that by the turn of this century, electronic commerce on the Internet will bring a new unparalleled economic vigor to our nation." Transformative is an understatement. The framework's opening statement is: "The Internet has the potential to become the United States' most active trade vehicle within a decade, creating millions of high-paying jobs." This point can apply to any nation that is willing to seize the opportunity and treat the Internet as the catalyst, and not the enemy.

Here are the five key principles outlined in the *Framework for Global Electronic Commerce*. They are powerful and far-reaching and are intended not just for a U.S. audience, but for the world as well.

1. The private sector should lead. The Internet should develop as a market-driven arena, not a regulated industry. Even where collective action is necessary, governments should encourage industry self-regulation and private sector leadership where possible.

2. Governments should avoid undue restrictions on electronic commerce. In general, parties should be able to enter into legitimate agreements to buy and sell products and services across the Internet with minimal government involvement or intervention. Governments should refrain from imposing new and unnecessary regulations, bureaucratic procedures, or

new taxes and tariffs on commercial activities that take place via the Internet.

3.  Where governmental involvement is needed, its aim should be to support and enforce a predictable, minimalist, consistent, and simple legal environment for commerce. Where government intervention is necessary, its role should be to ensure competition, protect intellectual property and privacy, prevent fraud, foster transparency, and facilitate dispute resolution, not to regulate.

4.  Governments should recognize the unique qualities of the Internet. The genius and explosive success of the Internet can be attributed in part to its decentralized nature and to its tradition of bottom-up governance. Accordingly, the regulatory frameworks established over the past 60 years for telecommunication, radio, and television may not fit the Internet. Existing laws and regulations that may hinder electronic commerce should be reviewed and revised or eliminated to reflect the needs of the new electronic age.

5.  Electronic commerce on the Internet should be facilitated on a global basis. The Internet is a global marketplace. The legal framework supporting commercial transactions should be consistent and predictable regardless of the jurisdiction in which a particular buyer and seller reside.*

Governments around the world can and should take a positive step in depicting a compelling vision for the future of their country and its role within global electronic commerce. Then they should stand back and watch their digital economy grow.

## UNITED STATES VERSUS EUROPE VERSUS JAPAN: LESSONS FOR THE FUTURE

The entrepreneurial explosion of Internet technology developments and Internet businesses is largely led by the United States, judging by the flow of venture money that has created

---

* Reprinted from http://www.whitehouse.gov/WH/New/Commerce/summary.html.

some of the most innovative applications and opportunities. A single most important differentiating factor has been the availability of venture capital to fund all these initiatives, in addition to an efficient public offering vehicle, guaranteed to give a chance to those who have done their homework. For the United States, the venture capital process results in a huge independent laboratory environment that sparks the economy every time a successful idea goes to market.

The question is: Where does this leave the rest of the world? Whereas the United States owns the majority of Web technological innovations, any other country in the world should be able to excel at the application of this technology for its own advantage. Here is a synopsis of the situation in Europe and Japan.

Despite reaching close to perfection at formulating electronic commerce policies, Europe seems to be handicapped owing to several factors. First, the European monetary unification agenda is consuming a lot of resources in planning and implementation. This is a distraction from electronic commerce. Some believe that the complexity of the European endeavor makes the year 2000 date compliance issue pale in comparison. Second, Europe does not have the venture capital mentality or process that is driving most American innovations focused on the Internet. In Europe, most large R&D investments and ventures seem to be driven by the large national industrial organizations, and lack the entrepreneurial spirit of the American system.

Consider the following additional differences between Europe and the United States. Europeans are known for their inclination to study, analyze, and discuss theories before deciding to jump into trials. They quickly bring the cultural, sociological, human, and philosophical debates to the forefront of technology issues, an approach that tends to paralyze actions while the debate goes on. Americans have an urgency to embrace technology, do not consider their cultural heritage as a barrier, and work on dealing with problems later, whether they are of a technology nature or not. Europeans like to analyze the past and reflect on it. They quote philosophers and litterateurs (Molière, Montesquieu, Socrates). Americans are quick to forget past failures, and learn from them, going forward. They prefer to quote technologists, entrepreneurs, and billionaires (Gates, Forbes, Walton).

Even though a little late at the start, Japan is taking the Internet very seriously. At home, a number of government-sponsored initiatives are well funded and they are addressing key issues in Internet commerce. These include conducting small- and large-scale pilots that have the potential of an explosive rollout. Abroad, the Japanese are investing in American ventures, which are considered a great source of learning as well as of potential financial return.

There is another critical factor that the Japanese seem to have addressed better than any other country. They have articulated a burning platform scenario for their economy, and linked its resurgence to their ability to exploit the new wealth and prosperity behind electronic commerce. In a 1997 work entitled *Towards the Age of the Digital Economy: For Rapid Progress in the Japanese Economy and World Economic Growth in the 21st Century,* Japanese experts write:

> ...Anxiety still remains, concerning the future of the economy. Meanwhile, in the 1990s the economy of the United States has recaptured its ability to compete, and has shown continuous powerful and stable growth. Certainly one of the reasons for this difference in economic performance is the difference in the application of information technology in the two nations. That is to say, after the bursting of the economic bubble in Japan, investment in information technology fell greatly, and as a result efforts to reform the economic structure with the application of information technology have lagged behind; and it is believed that this is one of the reasons for the low pace in the economic recovery in Japan....Electronic commerce has the potential of greatly changing the ideal situation of our economy.

Let the Japanese approach serve as a compelling example for other countries to paint a positive future for electronic commerce. In *The Power of Vision,* Joel Barker says: "The positive vision of the future has generated the impetus for individuals, organizations, and even societies to shape their own destinies."

In summary, there are five general areas that governments should focus on:

1. Develop and communicate a compelling vision for electronic commerce

2. Clarify and communicate related policies and regulatory issues

3. Promote and develop electronic commerce–enabled businesses that create new jobs and new export potential

4. Become a role model for the application of electronic commerce inside and outside their own jurisdiction

5. Publicize and document success stories and best practices to accelerate knowledge and experience levels

# TECHNOLOGY DRIVERS AND TRENDS

*Revolutions aren't made by gadgets and technology. They're made by a*
*shift in power, which is taking place all over the world. Today,*
*intellectual capital is at least as important as money capital and probably*
*more so.*

WALTER WRISTON

*Past Chair and CEO of Citicorp/Citibank*
*(during an interview with* Wired, *October 1996)*

Technology is an enabler of change and a catalyst. Change has to be driven by business drivers that take advantage of the technology. Today there is enough technology for electronic commerce to prosper on the Internet. What is lacking are more applications of the technology infrastructure, and our ability to implement it and practice it widely.

## CONVERGENCE OF TECHNOLOGIES AND CAPABILITIES

Convergence creates new forms of capabilities by combining two or more existing technologies to create a new one that is more powerful and more efficient. Three areas of convergence are positively impacting Internet commerce: infrastructure components, information appliances, and vendors/services.

### CONVERGENCE OF INFRASTRUCTURE COMPONENTS

Thanks to various switching and data conversion techniques, we now have confidence (as users) that information will make its way through the various hybrid components of the information highway, such as the telephone, TV, satellite, and wireless networks. The Internet benefits as a result, since it ties to all of them in a way that is seamless to the user.

## CONVERGENCE OF INFORMATION APPLIANCES

The marriages of several information-access appliances are giving birth to more sophisticated devices. These will become the *point-of-sale* devices that can be used to conduct electronic transactions, retrieve information, authenticate users, and perform other functions related to electronic commerce. Some of these marriages are:

Personal Computer + Television = INTERACTIVE TV or WEB TV

Television + Internet = INTERCASTING

Palmtop PC + Wallet = WALLET PC

Telephone + Internet = WEB PHONE

Internet + Wallet = ELECTRONIC WALLET or DIGITAL WALLET

Internet + PC = INTERNET PC or NETWORK COMPUTER (NC)

Internet + Video streaming = NETCASTING or WEBCASTING

Information kiosks + Internet = INTERNET KIOSKS

## CONVERGENCE OF VENDORS AND INDUSTRY SERVICES CAPABILITIES

Most technology-related vendors are recasting their marketing savvy and product plans on the Internet. Existing capabilities are merging with new ones that target the emerging Internet market from every possible angle. For software companies and others alike, the Internet is the new "energy pill." This is creating a temporary confusion, until market forces determine which market leaders will emerge.

For example, *Internet service providers* (ISPs) are targeting Internet commerce services, *IT vendors* are positioning themselves as end-to-end electronic commerce solutions providers, *telephone companies* are becoming ISPs and aiming to capture new types of electronic transactions, *financial institutions* are aiming to protect their current financial networks while capturing new Internet financial networks, and *software vendors* are becoming content providers. As digital TV reshapes the TV industry, and more content is coming at us from information highways other than the Internet, the term *ISP* takes on a new meaning: Does it become your cable company, or telephone company, or satellite company? Table 3-1 illustrates the current "musical chairs saga."

## COST OF TECHNOLOGY

Whether you start with Moore's Law—which assumes that every 18 months the power of semiconductors doubles—or whether you track the price/performance of any hardware technology, the cost factor cannot be ignored as a direct contributor to widespread usage. Table 3-2 shows the major key costs that are coming down and that are contributing to the widespread usage of Internet commerce.

> *Cisco's Micro Web Server: The First Web Server Appliance?*
> For $1000 and a footprint equivalent to the book you are holding, you can have a plug-and-play Web server appliance that allows your organization to get an Internet presence quickly and cost-effectively. It is ready to be installed out of the box within minutes, and is ideally suited for kiosk-types of applications. For example, once you have designed your Web commerce application, you transfer it to the Micro Web server, and install it as a kiosk in a mall or other public locations. The appliance weighs 2.5 pounds.

## CONTENT LIQUIDITY

Since almost everything is being digitized, a new content liquidity is arising. *Content liquidity* refers to the ease with which

TABLE 3-1. The Convergence of Industry Services Capabilities Is Creating New Opportunities

| TYPE OF VENDOR | NEW INTERNET OPPORTUNITIES |
| --- | --- |
| *Software vendors* e.g., Netscape, Microsoft, Oracle, Open Market Inc. | Limitless array of new software requirements and extensions to current capabilities. Some of them are getting into the "digital content business." |
| *Hardware companies* e.g., Sun, IBM, HP, Intel, DEC, Cisco, US Robotics | Non-PC devices that need to connect to the Internet, wireless information appliances, domestic appliances. |
| *Large Internet service providers* e.g., UUNET, PSI-Net, iStar | Expanding into VAN-type Internet commerce services and virtual private networks for businesses. |
| *Telephone companies* e.g., Deutsche Telekom, AT&T, France Telecom, Bell Canada, MCI | Becoming ISPs to "get their feet wet" in the marketplace. Enabling Internet malls, capturing new financial transactions, and adding new Internet services. |
| *EDI VANs* e.g., GEIS, Sterling Software | Opening Internet gateways and becoming VAINs: value-added Internet networks services. |
| *Systems integrators* e.g., EDS, Andersen Consulting | Handling large projects, while standards get harmonized. |
| *Financial institutions* e.g., Wells Fargo, Bank of America, Royal Bank of Canada | Capturing new Internet financial networks, intercepting commerce transactions, facilitating trusted electronic services, and exploiting new commerce infrastructure. |
| *New types of organizations* e.g., iCAT, Ariba, Cebra | End-to-end Internet commerce services and solutions. |

SOURCE: CYBERManagement Inc.

information is obtained, processed, searched, encrypted, classified, converted, disseminated, and reused.

Content liquidity allows the commercialization and proliferation of information and removes transport inefficiencies. Beneficiaries of this liquidity include products like books,

## TABLE 3-2. Cost Factors Affecting Key Internet Technologies Are Going Down

| TECHNOLOGY | COST TREND |
|---|---|
| Internet access | Both for residential and business services, the cost to get connected and stay connected to the Internet has been going down steadily. Examples: For consumers, flat-rate programs for $20 to $30 per month are common; for businesses, a T1* connection to the Internet is now more affordable (approximately $2000 to $3000 per month). |
| Internet-based secure virtual private networks (SVPNs) | Instead of connecting various worldwide office locations with private wide area networks, companies are using the public Internet as a virtual network. A recent study commissioned by Sun Microsystems showed that savings resulting from building an SVPN could be as high as 50 percent of the cost of building a private network. |
| Internet firewalls | Not that they are the only solution to security, but firewalls represent a necessary piece of the puzzle. International Data Corporation (IDC) predicts that the firewall market will go from an average price of $16,000 in 1995 to $650 in 2000. |
| Internet Web servers | Another necessary but not sufficient element is the Web server. The price of basic commercial Web server software declined from $5000 in 1995 to less than $1000 in 1996. Furthermore, we are seeing the bundling of plug-and-go secure Web servers (with firewalls and routers) for $1000 (see Cisco's Micro Web Server on page 45). |
| Internet PCs and appliances | From Internet PCs, touted at under $500, to other mundane domestic appliances that become connected to the Internet, the cost of access devices is going down, and will no longer be limited to PC users with at least a $1500 configuration. |

*(Continued)*

TABLE 3-2.  Cost Factors Affecting Key Internet Technologies Are Going Down  (*Continued*)

| TECHNOLOGY | COST TREND |
|---|---|
| Internet-based EDI | Whatever form Internet EDI takes, it will be cheaper than over private networks. |
| Internet e-mail | Still considered a luxury in 1995, e-mail is now a necessary condition for communicating with the business community. For $10 per month, it is possible to obtain an e-mail account that pays for itself in just a few minutes of usage. |

*T1 denotes a network connection speed of approximately 1.5 million characters per second.
SOURCE:  CYBERManagement Inc.

movies, music, business documents, videos, and sound that take new forms as they become digitized.

## THE INTERNETWORKED ENTERPRISE

The proliferation of networks is allowing many more electronic connections between various businesses and their external trading partners. As businesses get connected and Internet-enabled, they begin to demand the same from the business constellation they interact with. This should lead to more coordinated business processes and workflows between any two parties interacting. Chapter 5 covers this area in more detail.

## A HUMAN DIMENSION TO TECHNOLOGY

The advent of the World Wide Web, with its user-friendly and appealing hyperlinkage interface, brings a human dimension to electronic commerce through its interactive multimedia capabilities. *Interactive multimedia* are defined as including sound, video, pictures, images, animation, and bidirectional communications between any parties engaged in communicating or collaborating.

Interactive multimedia provide a much *richer* experience for communicating and collaborating, both important aspects of electronic commerce. The richness relates to the dynamic environment offered, which attempts to mirror and re-create reality. This environment will be popularized, thanks to the Virtual Reality Modeling Language (VRML). VRML had been used by graphic designers to represent three-dimensional objects on computer screens. It has since evolved, with motion added to it. Motion allows users to simulate and participate in interactive behavior. The future of VRML will see its entry into "social computing," where the sociality factor includes multiuser interactions in virtual worlds and spaces.

# RAPIDITY OF SOFTWARE DEVELOPMENT

Rapid software development and deployment are becoming the norm with Internet applications, including electronic commerce. Object-oriented software is becoming more widespread, and the advent of applets,* component software, and reusable objects helps in the deployment of electronic commerce solutions. Electronic commerce toolkit vendors such as InterWorld, Connect, Inc., and OneWave adhere to object-oriented frameworks to speed up the deployment of Internet electronic commerce applications and their integration within enterprise systems.

---

*An applet is a highly mobile small computer program that is downloaded to your PC only when it is needed. Applets transparently migrate across networks. When invoked through a browser, they could extend its functionality with new multimedia effects or transaction capabilities.

# CHALLENGES AND SOLUTIONS TO INTERNET COMMERCE

*Digital ID is not optional for electronic commerce on the Internet.*

SENIOR ANALYST

*at Piper Jaffray*

One of the common errors that corporations make is to underestimate the realities of challenges facing Internet commerce deployment. Yes, the march is on, but the road is bumpy, and there are detours and hidden traps. Several surmountable barriers exist. So, what is really holding back the exponential growth of Internet commerce? In this chapter, we examine the major challenges and the factors surrounding them. Ignoring these challenges will directly affect the realistic expectations you may have had. A warned person is worth two. What is important here is the approach to be taken.

## CHARACTERISTICS OF INTERNET COMMERCE CHALLENGES

Before approaching these challenges, we need to consider a number of general observations.

- *Divide and conquer.* You have to recognize how to divide the challenges into different categories, and address them accordingly separately.

- *It's not the technology.*   Once you get past the technical challenges, the nontechnical challenges will often be more difficult to resolve. The technical challenges that used to be the
  most prevalent, such as security, have received the highest
  priority and resources from technology vendors and large end
  users. Therefore, the range and choice of solutions have
  accelerated such that this is no longer perceived to be a difficult issue.

- *Internal versus external factors.*   Whereas several challenges
  are internal to the organization, and therefore within your
  control, many others are rooted in external factors that are
  beyond the reach of individual organizations. Either you
  have to wait for them to be resolved (e.g., critical mass) or
  you have to work collectively on resolving them (e.g., PKI
  infrastructure).

- *Tell me who you are, and I'll tell what your challenge is.*
  Depending on your role in the marketplace, you will have a
  different view of the priorities that matter to you the most. If
  you are a content provider, issues of content security and
  copyrights may be the most important, whereas if you are a
  consumer, trust and privacy may top the list of your concerns. And if you are a merchant, the issue of payment
  instrument universality is one that you'd like resolved as
  soon as possible.

## CATEGORIZING CHALLENGES

Following the "divide and conquer" strategy outlined earlier, let
us start by dividing the challenges into an organized set of
issues. In reality, the objective is to clearly organize not just on
paper, but also in your mind how to handle each one of these
challenges (Table 4-1).

## TABLE 4-1. Categorizing Challenges to Internet Commerce

| TECHNOLOGICAL | ORGANIZATIONAL AND BUSINESS |
| --- | --- |
| • Strength of security | • Lack of business process integration |
| • Availability/interoperability of payment instruments | • Lack of understanding of potential value (i.e., perception of "no need to do anything different about it") |
| • Interoperability of technologies and applications | |
| • Comparative buying capabilities | • Not enough proven business models |
| • Richness and depth of content | • Not enough best practices documented |
| | • Unpredictable cost justification |
| • Lack of reliable network infrastructure services | • Corporate structures as barriers to change |
| • Lack of standards | • Not enough qualified individuals within the organization |
| • Deployment of public key infrastructure (PKI) | • Initial and ongoing costs of implementations |
| • Technical integration with existing applications | • Channel conflict on-line or off-line |
| | • Not all members of value chain on-line |
| • Bandwidth costs | • IT management vs. business management: Who is the barrier? |
| | • Limited executive vision |

| LEGAL AND REGULATORY | BEHAVIORAL AND EDUCATIONAL |
| --- | --- |
| • Lack of consistent rules and policies | • Trust and privacy |
| | • Complexity of PKI |
| • Customs and tax uncertainties | • Fraud |
| | • Hype |
| • The role of governments and nations | • Awareness about availability of services |
| • Other regulatory issues | • E-money laundering |

| OTHER CHALLENGES |
| --- |
| • Channel conflict |
| • Critical mass |
| • Fulfillment process |

SOURCE: CYBERManagement Inc.

# TECHNOLOGICAL CHALLENGES

The list of technical challenges appears to be a long one, but this is also the area where the quality and quantity of solutions are increasing dramatically.

## STRENGTH OF SECURITY

During 1995 and early 1996, security was one of the most popular Internet barriers, grabbing perhaps the greatest number of headlines. The positive reverse effect was to force technology vendors and large users to apply an unprecedented level of resources aimed at addressing the various pieces for security. Today there is a growing confidence in solving the same security issues that had been negatively publicized. Yes, the original Internet was not conceived with electronic commerce in mind; however, its robustness and reliability have been dramatically increasing over the last two years. Overall, the Internet has been adapting very well to the increasing challenges of security, judging by the multiplicity of security solutions addressing a variety of requirements, and the number of business-critical applications that are moving to it.

More specific security requirements are covered in a subsequent section on the IT building blocks to electronic commerce (Chapter 9). This book doesn't attempt to fully explore all security aspects, since many of them are continuously evolving. Furthermore, the field has a lot of existing coverage. Even though security is a challenge, it should not be regarded as a barrier to electronic commerce. Security is fairly new to the Internet, so it is still maturing. However, corporate security professionals have known and applied computer security for many years to safeguard their private networks. They are now beginning to apply similar principles to Internet security.

One view on security is that it is somehow like insurance. The type, cost, and coverage really depend on the choices made by the stakeholders. From a management perspective, security is nonetheless a multifaceted issue. The following security areas must be addressed simultaneously:

- User access
- Data, application, and database security
- Transaction and payment security
- Network and systems security
- Security maintenance and management

## AVAILABILITY/INTEROPERABILITY OF PAYMENT INSTRUMENTS

When was the last time you were in a restaurant or retail store that refused to accept your American Express or Diner's Club credit card? Even though nonacceptance is rare today, it does occur. On the Internet, this analogy is more than rare: it is common. With the multitude of Internet payment choices came a lack of universality, and interoperability standards to make one work with another, among users, merchants, and banks.

The result has been confusion over the availability and choice of Internet payment instruments, which have sprung up like zucchini. The banks' lack of early leadership in this area has contributed to the confusion. New payment instruments from small companies emerged while banks were standing by the side. Several banks and financial institutions were forced to realize that they have to work with these new methods, even though the instruments were not invented by them. For example, First Data Corp. and First USA Paymentech (large U.S. credit card processing companies) and GE Capital invested $12.5 million in First Virtual Holdings, Inc. This could potentially expand First Virtual's Virtual PIN™ method to 200 million cardholders, almost overnight. DigiCash had to team up with the Mark Twain Bank to test its digital cash management concept. The National Bank of Canada has teamed up with CyberCash to allow Canadians to conduct payment transactions over the Internet. Mondex, which started as a technology-minded venture, is now owned by MasterCard International and 17 other financial institutions from various parts of the world. In Europe, KLELine is both a technology vendor with an electronic wallet solution and a financial institution that takes the risk for clearing Internet payment transactions.

In an ideal world, only four parties are involved in the initiation and settlement of a given financial transaction (Figure 4-1). In reality, the actual model is not as simple, because of the presence of other transactional intermediaries and the combination of manual and electronic processes that complicate the appearance of what should be seamless transactions. Perhaps the Internet has a chance to simplify this process.

Even though it is obvious that the Internet is infiltrating the customer-merchant links and those links with banks, there is even today the possibility of opening existing financial networks to the Internet with secure gateways that are widely accepted.

The proof that this is happening was in the June 1997 announcement by the Financial Services Technology Consortium (FSTC) to form the Bank Internet Payment System (BIPS) project, a cooperative effort among several major U.S. banks, technology firms, government agencies, and industry trade organizations that aims to encourage corporations to initiate payments via the Internet and other open public networks by increasing system security. This group will work to demonstrate the robustness of these new capabilities that link existing back-end payment systems with customers. It will focus on developing the following key components: an architecture, an open specification, a secure method for spontaneously initiating payment instructions over public networks, and a standard interface to existing bank payment systems.

Recently, three organizations have decided to jointly attack the Internet payments interoperability issue. They are providing a forum for collaboration among multiple organizations. This joint alliance is called the Electronic Payments Forum (EPF). It includes the Financial Services Technology Consortium (FSTC), the Cross Industry Working Team (XIWT), and CommerceNet. The current working project of this alliance is called the Join Electronic Payments Initiative (JEPI), and is sponsored by the W3C Consortium, an international industry consortium, jointly hosted in the United States, Europe, and Asia.

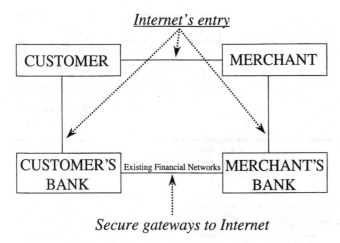

FIGURE 4-1. How the Internet is infiltrating existing financial networks. (*CYBERManagement Inc.*)

The EPF describes the new world of payments as composed of

> a variety of devices, both hardware and software, and digital representations of both paper and plastic instruments that will have to interoperate safely, reliably, and globally. They also include enabling technologies such as payment protocols and public key encryption. A legal and regulatory framework, a reference architecture, and standards for external interfaces must all be defined for this environment.

The main goal of the JEPI project is to enable a successful transparent negotiation of originally incompatible payment protocols. Users will then be able to select the most appropriate payment system for both parties during a given transaction (Figure 4-2).

What payment systems and choices does one use? To avoid being overwhelmed by the apparent array of choices, I suggest that you analyze your needs and select only the Internet payment instruments and choices that you require, keeping in mind the two most important factors: interoperability and universality. (See Appendix A for more coverage of digital payment options.)

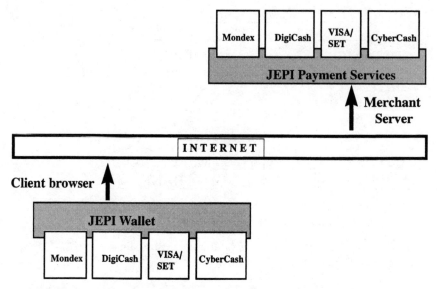

**FIGURE 4-2.** The Joint Electronic Payments Initiative will allow the universality of payment instrument from a user's and a merchant's perspectives. (*CommerceNet*)

## INTEROPERABILITY OF TECHNOLOGIES AND APPLICATIONS

Interoperability, interoperability, interoperability. These three magic words mean a lot in the emerging field of Internet technologies. Conceptually, as more and more technologies interoperate, a larger and more open environment becomes available, which results in a growing number of users converging to it. The competitive nature of the Internet technology marketplace has resulted in a multiplicity of solutions that do not take one another into account very well. On the technology side, for example, a digital ID given to a user will likely work only with the certificate authority that issued it. This limits the range of available applications and users. On the software applications side, there is a need to integrate various functional pieces, in addition to choosing multiple vendors often. This is allowing the software integration side of electronic commerce to prosper.

## COMPARATIVE BUYING CAPABILITIES

Consumers or corporate buyers need to conduct comparative shopping before deciding to buy. The promise of the Internet is to virtually bring forward the vast array of choices directly to users' desktops. However, comparative buying on the Internet is still very primitive, especially since we are relying on search engines that return 12,453 choices to a given query. What is lacking are tools and capabilities that allow comparative shopping and querying to occur in a vendor-neutral fashion seamlessly and efficiently.

Whether for businesses or consumers, the trend will favor Web locations that offer a cross-sectional view to a given marketplace, and that allow comparative shopping or choice of procurement to occur transparently for users. Two types of comparative buying are required:

1. Competitive (across other vendors of the same product)
2. Noncompetitive (within the same vendor, but for different products)

Today, certain Web sites are beginning to cater specifically to the comparative shopper. They include CompareNet, ConsumersEdge, and NetBuyer. The positive aspect is that these types of Web sites offer a very thorough search process, which means that the results returned are accurate, since they are coming directly from a well-maintained database. One popular method, called the parametric search technique, allows the user to drill down into the available choices by using a process of quickly narrowing down possibilities. This type of front end relies on a sophisticated database cataloging of products. The only inconvenience of the parametric method rests with the time it takes to be entirely satisfied with the results, since the user has to assist and participate in the search process.

Under another method, the user initiates a search straight from the browser by relying on an intelligent agent to fetch across Web sites, databases, catalogs, manufacturers, and local distributors. NetBot, a Seattle start-up, has an automated agent product called Jango that allows the user to initiate a search that returns information from a multitude of different Web sites, truly enhancing the comparative shopping experience. The inconvenience of this method is tied the possibilities of incomplete data or missed data, since the user is at the mercy of the agent. If the agent doesn't find it, the user doesn't know about it.

Ideally, what is needed is an approach that combines the accuracy of a closed Web-centric system and the convenience of an open-ended user-centric system that does the work while you wait or sleep.

## RICHNESS AND DEPTH OF CONTENT

The Web is certainly about quantity of information, but not evenly about quality. In the context of electronic commerce, *content* refers to products, services, and capabilities that can be traded between buyers and sellers. Content is the inventory of the Web, and it is a key aspect to gaining success in the marketplace. In 1995, when Amazon.com opened its Web site, it had 1 million titles in its virtual inventory—from day 1.

## LACK OF RELIABLE NETWORK INFRASTRUCTURE SERVICES

Without a lot of enhancements, the plain old public Internet as a network cannot be trusted for a 100 percent uptime, or to run mission-critical applications. The next-generation version of the Internet protocol, called IPng or IPv6, will have more built-in controls and reliability features. In addition, we are beginning to see vendors offer a higher degree of trust in secure transaction services that can be applied to any application. Several companies are placing more and more business-critical applications on the Internet.

## LACK OF STANDARDS

It has been said that the good thing about standards is that there are so many of them to choose from. Too many competing or overlapping standards are as detrimental as a lack of them. Significant Internet commerce standards are still few, but the typical alphabet soup of acronyms is making its way into this area with a new list: SET, OBI, OTP, JEPI, OFX, and more. These standards are covered in more detail in Chapter 9.

What is different with the Internet is the rapidity at which technology vendors are coming together to propose and agree on standards. Whereas in the early 1990s client-server/open systems standards took a long time to mature and develop after several competing periods, the Internet is bringing competitors together much more quickly, as they realize the size of the opportunities that await them, once standards are agreed on. They are realizing that companies should not compete on standards, but rather exploit their existence into the marketplace.

## DEPLOYMENT OF PUBLIC KEY INFRASTRUCTURE (PKI)

In the real world, we are used to driver's licenses, photo IDs, passports, birth certificates, and other forms of identification to prove our identity, when asked to. These various forms of papers achieve the necessary authentication to perform a transaction or gain access somewhere. They were issued by a granting authority, or trusted organization such as a government office, a bank, or a public notary. Let us call them certificate authorities (CAs). It is generally accepted that they did their job in verifying your identity and credentials before issuing you the ID.

The problem with the Internet is that across the distance it becomes practically impossible to check the identification of the originator by looking at a photo card. So different forms of remote identifications are needed to authenticate the identity of a user. These are the digital certificates which are equivalent to an ID. Digital certificates are issued by certification organizations. During transmission of electronic transactions, the digital certificate is sent along with the encrypted message to verify that the sender is truly who it is claiming to be. Every digital certificate is unique, and so is a driver's license or passport. A digital certificate is encrypted with the owner's private key (a lock that stays with the owner), and is decrypted with the owner's public key (which is widely available to anybody). This public/private key process is also referred to as public key cryptography.

Because of the need for certifying a wide range of users on an unlimited number of transactions possibilities and credentials granting, there is currently an explosion of certificate authority businesses. CAs issue, register, generate, manage, and revoke digital certificates for consumers and organizations. This complete authentication infrastructure—which includes the people, technology, services, and processes behind it—is referred to as the public key infrastructure (PKI).

The following list summarizes what features are needed as part of a secure and trusted infrastructure:

1. *Authentication.*   No one can pretend to be someone else.
2. *Privacy.*   Only authorized people and systems can access information. This includes privacy both during transport on the network and against unauthorized insiders.
3. *Nonrepudiation.*   Users are prevented from denying that they authorized the transaction.
4. *Transaction integrity.*   This ensures that the transaction is not tampered with so as to avoid a situation where the buyer is saying: "I ordered two pounds of chocolate, not 200."
5. *Nonrefutability.*   This ensures that users can verify that the actual exchange took place by providing a digital receipt or similar proof of payment.
6. *Time stamping.*   This is especially important for responding to requests for proposals with a submission deadline.

The above six requirements appear to be technical goals. The translated business goals are confidence, trust, efficiency, effectiveness, and cost containment.

It is commonly agreed that a full deployment of successful Internet-driven electronic commerce will not be possible without a public key infrastructure in place. In a multiuser environment, it becomes very complex to distribute and manage secure keys. Public key cryptography was developed to address the issue of managing digital certificates. Given that public and private keys are needed to properly engage in trusted transactions, remotely, the PKI's role is to provide a framework for managing this process. A fully deployed public key infrastructure may have a hierarchical structure with several players in it (Figure 4-3).

So it appears that public key management is an important (but cumbersome) factor in the growth of digitally secure transaction environments. The challenge today is the deployment of a business infrastructure that supports this concept on a wide scale.

New players are needed for each one of these levels. New roles are emerging for trusted authorities that are able to set up secure environments where buyers and sellers can meet and conduct business safely. This is a business opportunity for organizations able to collect fees for generating certificates and public keys, and for developing businesses that depend on the certification process itself. Who are the candidates that are stepping in to fill this role? There will be a wide range of certificate-granting authorities, including ones we are familiar with, but also some new ones. These are the banks, post offices, licensing agencies, large corporations, financial processing brokers, telecommunications companies, cable companies, universities, large retailers, and publishers.

**FIGURE 4-3.** The hierarchical structure of a PKI includes several players. (*CYBERManagement Inc.*)

*CyberSource Uses Digital Certificates to License Software Distribution*

CyberSource License Clearing House Services facilitate electronic software distribution by issuing passwords, unique product ID numbers, or digitally signed and encrypted end-user license agreements (EULAs). The passwords, IDs, and EULAs provide security and accountability and are used to unlock and open a digitally encrypted container which holds the software for electronic distribution. License Clearing House Services are for companies that wish to distribute software electronically over the Internet and ensure the secure transmission of products to the customer.

*VeriSign, Inc., Builds a Business Based on Security Management Services*

VeriSign, Inc., is a provider of digital authentication services and products for electronic commerce and other forms of secure communications. It has set up its business to benefit from the need for trusted certification authorities and processes by issuing different classes of certificates and managing them for various vendors and markets.

## TECHNICAL INTEGRATION WITH EXISTING APPLICATIONS

Technical integration is an IT implementation challenge. The problem is aggravated if existing software applications are one or two generations behind in the current technology. Most organizations have a wealth of values in their existing information systems which they need to interface to the Internet or Intranet. For example, Internet commerce applied to supply chain activities or to support business-to-business interactions will need to interface with these existing systems. This is an important area for chief information officers (CIOs) to focus on, since they must think of Internet commerce as an extension of what is currently done on the inside.

## BANDWIDTH COSTS

Bandwidth costs are more of a problem for small to medium-size organizations, but this is becoming less and less of an issue in developed countries. It is nonetheless still a challenge in geographical areas where the Internet is not yet well deployed. However, most electronic commerce applications do not impose heavy bandwidth requirements, except where multimedia are utilized (e.g., distance education/training and pay-per-view multimedia applications). Developments in broadband connectivity linked to Internet content are bringing new affordability levels to high-speed access with rich interactive multimedia. Two examples of such services include the @Home Network in the United States, and New Brunswick Telephone's *Vibe* service in Canada.

# LEGAL AND REGULATORY FRAMEWORK

From electronic copyright issues to electronic cash policies, tariffs, privacy, digital offers, and receipts enforcement, the Internet is still largely unregulated. The following capsule of problems is presented:

1. *The Internet is global.* There are no territorial limits, so whose rule would apply and when? A regulatory regime becomes more difficult to enforce. If the boundaries are difficult to see, how can you control or police them? You need other types of control than "crossing the boundaries."

2. *The Internet is electronic.* There is no "writing." Whereas written documents have been legally binding for years, what happens now with electronic documents?

3. *The Internet is digital.* Perfect copies can be made almost instantaneously and repetitively, with little or no costs. So, how do you ensure copyrights?

## LACK OF CONSISTENT RULES AND POLICIES

In the May–June 1996 issue of the *Harvard Business Review,* Debora Spar and Jeffrey Bussbang state that "commerce will migrate to areas where rules will prevail and responsibility can be assigned."

What happens if something goes wrong in cyberspace? Will traditional laws be able to deal with it, or will it be new laws that are still in the making? If a company does business over the Internet, does it automatically become exposed to the laws of other countries? Who is going to police the actions of users? Will we get fined if we don't obey certain rules? Does government need to know about our buying habits in cyberspace? Is this like the real world, where if you want to drive, you have to know the rules of the road and practice in private before getting a driver's license? Where are the road signs, if any exist? Or do we have them constantly memorized?

These and other difficult questions remain to be answered. If we go back in history to the evolution of the transportation industry, when the first roads were paved, the signs weren't automatically prevalent. Later the code of conduct was established, and now it is being enforced. The same analogy may apply with the rules of conducting business over the Internet. The "western style" of relaxed rules may soon be supplanted by more strict business guidelines and practices that help to instill more confidence for all participants in this marketplace.

Here is a sample regulation imposed by the state of California, regarding all sales taking place over the Internet when the buyer is in California. The following is an excerpt from the California Business and Professions Code Section 17538(d), showing the increasing potential complexity of regulation that may govern Internet businesses. It also prompts us to wonder about the complexity of monitoring and enforcing such laws.

Effective: January 1, 1997

(d) A vendor conducting business through the Internet or any other electronic means of communication shall do all of the following when the transaction involves a buyer located in California:

(1) Before accepting any payment or processing any debit or credit charge or funds transfer, the vendor shall disclose to the buyer in writing or by electronic means of communication, such as E-mail or an on-screen notice, the vendor's return and refund policy, the legal name under which the business is conducted and, except as provided in paragraph (3), the complete street address from which the business is actually conducted.

(2) If the disclosure of the vendor's legal name and address information required by this subdivision is made by on-screen notice, all of the following shall apply:

(A) The disclosure of the legal name and address information shall appear on any of the following: (i) the first screen displayed when the vendor's electronic site is accessed, (ii) on the screen on which goods or services are first offered, (iii) on the screen on which a buyer may place the order for goods or services or (iv) on the screen on which the buyer may enter payment information, such as a credit card account number. The communication of that disclosure shall not be structured to be smaller or less legible than the text of the offer of the goods or services.

(B) The disclosure of the legal name and address information shall be accompanied by an adjacent statement describing how the buyer may receive the information at the buyer's E-mail address. The vendor shall provide the disclosure information to the buyer at the buyer's E-mail address within five days of receiving the buyer's request.

(C) Until the vendor complies with subdivision (a) in connection with all buyers of the vendor's goods or services, the vendor shall make available to a buyer and any person or entity who may enforce this section pursuant to Section 17535 on-screen access to the information required to be disclosed under this subdivision.

(3) The complete street address need not be disclosed as required by paragraph (1) if the vendor utilizes a private mailbox receiving service and all of the following conditions are met: (A) the vendor satisfies the conditions described in paragraph (2) of subdivision (b) of Section 17538.5, (B) the vendor discloses the actual street address of the private mailbox receiving service in the manner prescribed by this subdivision for the disclosure of the vendor's actual street address, and (C) the vendor and the private mailbox receiving service comply with all of the requirements of subdivisions (c) to (f), inclusive, of Section 17538.5.

## CUSTOMS AND TAX UNCERTAINTIES

The area of Internet taxation is a hot one, because of government interest in all parts of the world. Some countries see it as a "tax heaven" and have started to impose new Internet-related taxes; others are studying the situation carefully, not wanting to rush in with policies that might dampen the growth of electronic commerce in their region. It is tempting to apply existing tax rules and systems to the Internet world, but it is not the answer to the needs of this marketplace. The United States has sounded the alarm bell on this issue in its *Framework for Global Electronic Commerce* ("no new Internet taxes"), and the world seems to be listening.

The issue of customs or tariffs is an easier one to tackle. The worldwide trend has been to remove tariff barriers on IT-related products. In November 1996, the World Trade Organization adopted a Ministerial Declaration on Trade in Information Technology Products (ITA) which commits the European Union and 13 other countries with over 80 percent of the world trade in information technology to eliminate all tariffs on these products beginning now and culminating in 2000. Internet trade tariffs should follow the same trend.

One key aspect to resolving the taxation issue of Internet commerce is to keep tax policies universal, uniform, and neutral. Otherwise, it will become impossible to manage the inconsistencies and buyers and sellers will become confused, leading to a lower degree of overall tax compliance. To get a small taste for this potential global anarchy, consider the fact that as of 1997, about half of the states in the United States were imposing a sales tax on soft goods downloaded via the Internet, and the other half were not. If you extend this situation to the global level, you start to realize the negative effects such differences could have on Internet world trade. Governments should also focus on growing global commerce that originates from their countries. As companies increase their revenues from these new methods, governments can reap the benefits of collecting further corporate taxes. The summation of the tax issues lies in answering these five questions for the Internet environment: (1) what gets taxed, (2) what doesn't get taxed, (3) who taxes, (4) who gets taxed, and (5) how it is done.

## THE ROLE OF GOVERNMENTS AND NATIONS

The legal and regulatory aspects of the Internet have emerged in 1997 as critical challenges being addressed by a number of governments and nations. Governments around the world have started to politicize the Web, as they become sensitized to the effects that explosive Internet commerce could have on their economies. Consider the following four spheres that are shaping the landscape of global electronic commerce:

1. National frameworks similar to the ones of the United States, Japan, and Europe
2. Policies and politics addressing specific internal (within a country or set of countries) or external directions
3. Global organizations with traditional roles of regulating or benchmarking global trends to influence governments around the world
4. Various industry associations that represent the technology sector, interest groups, or other public forums that work on lobbying any one of the other three forces (Figure 4-4)

What Internet commerce needs is a predictable, open, and efficient legal and regulatory environment that allows it to prosper without undue regulation. But when it comes to regulation, two avenues are possible: (1) self-regulation or (2) imposed regulation. The United States is clearly advocating industry self-regulation as a strong cure and catalyst necessary to the prosperity

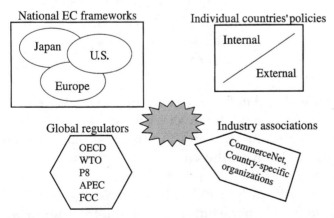

**FIGURE 4-4.**   The global landscape for electronic commerce. (*CYBERManagement Inc.*)

of electronic commerce around the world. Ira Magaziner, senior adviser to President Clinton on electronic commerce policy and author of the *Framework for Global Electronic Commerce,* says: "This is happening faster than government can control it. Enforcing it would be a nightmare. Industry self-regulation will allow electronic commerce to prosper."

## OTHER REGULATORY ISSUES

Other issues that we will not cover in detail, but that are potential challenges to Internet commerce, include cryptography export, copyrights, intellectual property, and domain name to business trademark linkage. These issues are developing and will be further clarified as time goes on.

# BEHAVIORAL AND EDUCATIONAL CHALLENGES

Another general category of barriers relates to consumer attitudes: Consumers simply do not like to change their current habits quickly, or they may not be very well informed about the impact that the Internet could be having on their lives. Says Scott Cook, chairman of Intuit: "We're asking people to change their habits. And we've got to convince them that it's not hard." So, it is the responsibility of organizations to lower the barriers of entry by using various approaches such as offering something for free or lowering the price of a service.

## TRUST AND PRIVACY

Trust and privacy go hand in hand. Just as only a small circle of friends have earned our confidence, it is likely that only a few organizations will gain our trust in cyberspace initially. These organizations will probably be the same ones that we have trusted in the physical world. Resistance to trust is sometimes also tied to perception. In early 1997, when Manitoba Telecom Services first introduced phone bill review on the Internet to all subscribers, it received complaints from citizens citing privacy concerns. This forced MTS to pull out the service and reintroduce it a few months later, under a different scenario. The service is now available only to those who request it and register accordingly off-line, not on-line. This solution addresses the concerns of those fearing that their private information will be in the open. So, the lesson here is also that trust and privacy go hand and hand: People will trust only very few organizations that claim to safeguard the privacy of information.

To help alleviate the concerns of consumers and users of electronic commerce and allow them to trust a larger number of organizations, over 100 vendors around the world, including Netscape and Microsoft, announced their unprecedented cooperation to advance the implementation of the Open Profile Standard (OPS). OPS is a framework with built-in privacy safeguards for the trustworthy exchange of profile information between consenting individuals and Web sites. Under the auspices of the W3C consortium, this project is also referred to as the P3 project, or Platform for Privacy Preferences. This development has obvious positive ramifications for electronic commerce and advertising on the Web, as it allows businesses to create personalized services to each of their customers, while also respecting their customers' privacy. The OPS will use a combination of digital certificates and the vCard concept, which is standard for sharing business card information among electronic users.

## TRUSTe

The TRUSTe initiative, spearheaded by the Electronic Frontier Foundation (EFF), is an effort to increase the level of trust between merchants and consumers in electronic communications, and especially the Internet. TRUSTe was founded on the belief that "the greater the level of trust among the participants in a transaction, the lower the transaction costs."

The key principles that govern the TRUSTe program are:

1. *Informed consent.* Consumers have the right to be informed about the privacy and security consequences of an on-line transaction *before* entering into one.

**2.** *No privacy without appropriate security.*   Privacy and security are inexorably linked in an on-line transaction. There is no privacy without appropriate security measures.

**3.** *Privacy standards vary according to context of use.*   No single privacy standard is adequate for all situations. Three levels of privacy for commercial transactions have been delineated, all of which fall into the realm of "best business practices," but which offer varying levels of privacy to the end user.

TRUSTe has partnered with CommerceNet, which brought the ability to commercialize the project and a channel for reaching companies already involved in producing electronic commerce best practices. A pilot launched in November 1996 focused solely on privacy issues: creating a reasonable, effective, and enforceable system to ensure that personally identifiable information is not abused. It included a contractual agreement that details the rights and responsibilities of a site, gives the guidelines a site must follow, and licenses the TRUSTe service marks for use on a pilot member site.

Some companies are posting extensive privacy policies on their Web sites to help educate and reassure users. Of notable mention is The McGraw-Hill Companies Customer Privacy Policy. McGraw-Hill prominently displays links to this policy on its home page. This is a great example of corporate self-regulation, which is the preferred trend on the Internet. Web sites will have to explicitly display their practices in the areas of privacy, security, integrity of transaction, and overall business conduct. Many of them will augment this process with several trust marks they might have earned from organizations such as TRUSTe and others in the business of certifying these Web sites. A critical aspect of any privacy process is to clearly communicate with the consumer what information is being collected, and its exact intended usage. Says Joseph L. Dionne, chairman and CEO for The McGraw-Hill Companies: " Our information and analysis is credible because we have earned the trust our customers over the more than 100 years of our existence, and we must continue to earn that trust in the Information Age."

## COMPLEXITY OF PKI

Another challenge associated with the public key infrastructure (PKI) process is simply an educational one: We are still not accustomed to operating in, and understanding, the complexities of the certification process and its management requirements. It is not yet known whether better education will lead to better adoption, or whether we are still awaiting simpler solutions. Simpler solutions will have to be transparent to users, including transparent key generation and distribution.

Given that a variety of digital IDs will be required to become a full-fledged digital consumer or digital producer, our knowledge level and behavior about making them a part of our usual life is a change that is challenging us. Average consumers will probably end up with a handful of various digital IDs in their wallets, and the change needs time to get used to.

## FRAUD

In real life, fraud could happen almost everywhere. The key is to minimize its occurrence and therefore minimize the risks for users. The main question is: Will fraud be higher or lower in electronic markets? Everybody is working to ensure that it ends up being lower, but there isn't yet enough historical data about it. The types of possible fraud areas include fictitious company, no product, and customer with wrong identity and stolen credit card. In France, where 30 million smart cards are in use with a personal identification number (PIN), the rate of fraud is almost zero.

## HYPE

Is hype a barrier or catalyst to electronic commerce adoption on the Internet? The frequency of Internet-related stories has galloped all over the world. The result is an increased number of reported inaccuracies, overestimates, generalizations, and misconceptions to be planted in the minds of readers. Early get-rich-quick evangelists turned out to be misleading users and early adopters. Hype is accompanied by an increase in expectations. And obviously, the greater the expectations, the greater the fall if they are not met. This lesson is valid for internal corporate expectations for what the Internet commerce opportunity can deliver.

## Awareness about Availability of Services

If nobody knows about your service, there is a problem. On the Internet, every organization inherits this problem at inception. As soon as a new service is being introduced, what immediately looms in the minds of the marketers behind it is: "How do I let my customers know about it quickly?" Or "How do we let all 60 million Internet users know about this from day 1?" This is why companies are working hard at establishing their brand identity on the Web, which draws more traffic to them. Companies are working hard at tightly integrating their customers and trading partners to their Intranets, in order to streamline the effectiveness of communications with them. This is intricately tied to having a captive audience, to educate it constantly, and to increase the adoption rate for new capabilities. The acid test is when your customers begin to treat your Intranet as if it were theirs, and start to depend on it on a daily basis. The issue of awareness, which leads to adoption, is also important for governments that are migrating a variety of their services to the Internet. They will have the challenge to educate citizens about their new services. Therefore, they have to include education and awareness as part of their rollout endeavors.

## E-money Laundering

The reality of electronic money laundering is still questionable, since it is argued that traditional money laundering mechanisms are still done more easily without the Internet. This threat is nonetheless echoed by governments around the world. Even though electronic cash mechanisms of any type are expected to represent a large number of the daily financial transactions, that still represents a small number today. In addition, new payment instruments such as Mondex and CyberCash have built-in efficiencies to deter would-be criminals. Another unanswered issue is whether Internet gambling will draw potential e-money laundering, in the same way that physical casinos have traditionally attracted this type of activity.

## ORGANIZATIONAL AND BUSINESS BARRIERS

The organizational obstacle is often overlooked as the whole industry focuses on the technology developments that keep coming at us. Senior executives are asking several valid questions about business models, cost justifications, ROI, and so on. These types of challenges, listed below, are covered in great depth in the reminder of the book. There are 12 organizational and business barriers to electronic commerce on the Internet. For answers on how to meet them, read the rest of this book.

1. Lack of business process integration
2. Lack of understanding of potential value (i.e., perception of "no need to do anything different about it")
3. Not enough proven business models
4. Not enough best practices documented
5. Unpredictable cost justification
6. Corporate structures as barriers to change
7. Not enough qualified individuals within the organization
8. Initial and ongoing costs of implementation
9. Channel conflict on-line or off-line
10. Not all members of value chain on-line
11. IT management versus business management: Who is the barrier?
12. Limited executive vision

# OTHER MISCELLANEOUS CHALLENGES

## CHANNEL CONFLICT

If we look at the PC software industry, theoretically most software applications could be purchased and delivered electronically. Actually, Forrester Research expects that by 1998, 34 percent of all software sales will be via electronic delivery. The on-line software delivery channel could present a channel conflict with existing physical channels. Producers of software are careful in testing the Internet as an alternate delivery channel in order not to alienate their distribution partners. However, in the long term, if the physical distribution function itself is no longer perceived as added value, the Internet will become a preferred delivery channel.

There are two types of market segments that the on-line marketing medium addresses:

1. Replacement or alternative to the existing physical channel for existing products
2. New channel for niche products that would not have made it in the physical retail space for various reasons

Organizations need to look at the changing role of the sales representative amid the possible channel conflicts that may arise. The sales representative's role becomes dependent on the role of the company's Web site in how it supports and informs customers. Whereas traditionally, there was value in the sales representative offering information about products, this value is diminishing rapidly, as most information is now available on the company's Web site, and can be viewed and reviewed only minutes later. So, the sales representative's role has to evolve quickly beyond information presentation and dissemination.

*AMP Industrial Catalog Substitutes Sales Representative's Role*

AMP is a leading supplier in the development and manufacture of 150,000 different electronic/electrical interconnection devices. Because of the thousands of products available from AMP, many customers had found it difficult to determine the right product for their application without assistance from a salesperson.

Consequently, AMP (along with SAQQARA Systems, Inc.) has developed an industrial catalog, where virtually from anywhere in the world at any time, customers can search alphabetically or by product picture or part number and find up-to-date information on their products. The electronic catalog is available in several languages, including English, French, German, Italian, Spanish, Japanese, Chinese, and Korean. Purchasing agents and engineers can quickly locate the products they need by using features such as graphical search, comparison tables, and 3-D viewing.

The electronic catalog was designed to minimize the tremendous costs associated with paper catalogs. AMP wanted to increase the effectiveness and profitability of sales engineers by equipping them with tools that minimize trivia and maximize their ability to sell systems solutions. The AMP sales team is immediately advised of catalog traffic, sample orders, and prospects in their territory. They follow up with prospects accordingly.

## CRITICAL MASS

A critical mass of buyers of information and services is needed for electronic commerce to survive and sustain its own financial model. The demographics are still not at the point of reaching the desired economies of scale, but the growth is spectacular. On the consumer side, the 25 million users connected to the World Wide Web in 1995 still represented a very small market. Compare that with the 1.1 billion cable TVs in use worldwide, or 700 million telephones.* Overall, less than 15 percent of worldwide office workers have PCs, and less than 1 percent of the world population has any kind of Internet access (e-mail included).†

However, you must not be misled by the above macrostatistics, even if you apply the most recent numbers. You should also look at the microlevel segmentation of the market you are trying to reach. For example, if your target market segment is not the average consumer, the percentage on-line may be much higher, therefore affording you a larger critical mass factor. On the consumer side, the reason PCs and PC-related equipment have

---

* ITU World Telecommunications Indicators Database, 1995.

† *The Internet Report*, Morgan Stanley, 1996.

been popular items for Internet sales is that most PC users have a much higher rate of Internet connectivity than the rest. On the business side, if we take Cisco Systems and Marshall Industries as prime examples, for both of them, their primary customers (network specialists and electronic engineers) have traditionally been Internet users longer than have any other professionals. Regardless of whether it is for businesses or consumers, another challenge will be to retain *electronically enabled* customers once you have attracted them.

Finally, at the global level, a critical mass of electronic commerce-enabled nations is required. Canada, for example, has a goal to be recognized as an electronic commerce-friendly country to attract international investments and business to it.

## FULFILLMENT PROCESS

Fulfillment presents a different challenge whether it applies to hard or soft goods. For hard goods, once you have an order that has been approved and acknowledged, you have to activate a shipping transaction to complete it. This can be accomplished in a variety of ways, including local store delivery, integrated logistics, or a third-party outsourced process. Organizations should focus on the following guidelines to move to a more efficient process using the Internet to speed the actual fulfillment of goods to customers:

- Integrate electronic orders with current shipping, logistics, and other supply chain elements (some of this could be via EDI).
- Partner with transportation organizations that can offer efficient fulfillment in areas not well served.

The fulfillment area is often overlooked, and could represent a challenge for small to medium-size businesses that are not used to handling the increasing shipping activities for their products. It is, however, an opportunity for the transportation industry, which is benefiting from increased traffic and integrated Internet access to shipping information.

A recent example that illustrates the importance of the fulfillment integration as a possible control point for Internet commerce is Federal Express Virtual Order$^{SM}$.

### Federal Express Virtual Order

With FedEx Virtual Order, businesses have the capability to electronically integrate the ordering of products on-line with the ability to fulfill and deliver them anywhere in the world. This solves one of the key limitations of electronic commerce by linking the automated order and fulfillment system to the delivery of the product to the end customer. Thus a company of any size can quickly become a global marketer and create new sales channels without the need to invest in additional customer service and warehousing.

FedEx is working with qualified merchants to host their commerce Web sites, create electronic catalog templates, and even input their inventory for them. When an order is placed, FedEx receives it, initiates a shipping order, and updates the catalog inventory. A customer confirmation number is linked to a FedEx tracking number to give the merchant and the buyer instant real-time access to package order and tracking information from pickup through delivery. Companies such as Cisco, Monorail, Sun Data, and Insight Direct are benefiting from FedEx's integrated ordering and logistics approach. Says Mike Janes, vice president of marketing logistics, electronic commerce, and catalogs, at FedEx: "Logistics are the flip side to electronic commerce. To do sophisticated virtual commerce, you need sophisticated virtual logistics management."

# EMBARKING ON INTERNET COMMERCE

*It must be considered that there is nothing more difficult to carry out,
nor more doubtful of success, nor more dangerous to handle, than to
initiate a new order of things. For the reformer has enemies in all those
who profit by the old order, and only lukewarm defenders in those who
would profit by the new order.... This arises partly from the incredulity of
mankind who do not truly believe in anything new until they have an
actual experience of it.*

NICCOLÒ MACHIAVELLI
*The Prince*

The history of modern commerce can be traced back to 1000
B.C., as the Phoenicians established the first trading system
along the Mediterranean Sea. They were the first society known
to have ventured outside of its geography to effectively conduct
commerce with other peoples. They had perfected the technology to build ships with a keeled hull (an evolution from flat-bot-
tomed barges that hugged the shore), which were made from
the famous cedars of Lebanon. The Phoenicians were not only
adventurous merchants but expert sailors and navigators as
well. The Mediterranean Sea allowed them to wander, explore,
and to discover. It was their link to a world that awaited their
skill and their art. These fine merchants brought their dye, fab-
ric, ceramics, glass, metals, wine, crops, and oil from port to
port. Their skill allowed them to sail the open seas, and as a
result the Phoenicians developed a flourishing sea trade. At the
height of their trading empire, they imported copper from
Cyprus, linen from Egypt, ivory from India, tin from Spain,
horses from Anatolia, and peacocks from Africa.

There is a striking resemblance between the birth of trade as just described and the rise of Internet commerce. In some ways, the early days of the Internet have generated the same excitement as that experienced by the Phoenicians in discovering new ways to trade among nations and peoples. The Internet as a market can be likened to the Mediterranean Sea. Only if you navigate it with the right ships are you able to reach your new trading partners. Exploiting its powers allows you to create wealth for your organization by trading products and services with entities you have never met before.

Electronic commerce requires an evolutionary approach that addresses each piece of the puzzle both separately and as part of an overall strategy. Few organizations are handling the electronic commerce phenomenon as a whole. Rather, they are breaking it into pieces, and implementing different areas separately or in a fragmented manner, mainly because of a lack of understanding of how to manage the complexity of issues and barriers.

## APPROACHING THE STRATEGY

By tackling only individual elements of electronic commerce without a comprehensive electronic commerce strategy, organizations may never fully realize its synergistic potential. A planned approach is needed now that several concepts are maturing, and now that the marketplace has gained enough experience.

A strategy should include:

- A clear view on how an organization will use the electronic marketplace. Since the electronic channel is destined to become the primary vehicle to conduct business in the future, companies must learn how to attract and engage customers in it, take orders and payments, distribute products and services and support their customers in this new business environment.

- An ability to transform internal business processes according to the requirements imposed by the new types of electronic interactions. For example, Intranets designed to keep up with the external speed of Internet information dissemination may not be enough if they fail to address the complete internal business automation process.

- An organizational framework led by a senior-level person whose role is to develop the overall Internet commerce strategy, coach senior executives to initiate calls for actions, and educate employees throughout the organization.

## YOUR VIEW OF THE INTERNET

The Internet has five multiple identities, and each one must be taken advantage of by developing and applying a different strategy. It is important to understand and accept the unique potential of each one, as a sign of Internet organizational maturity. The synergistic effect realized by addressing all five faces of this identity enables organizations to take maximum advantage of electronic commerce capabilities. Successful large organizations are addressing every one of the five identities (Figure 5-1).

### IT'S A NETWORK

Large organizations have for years relied on the Internet structure and mixed it with their own private networks. Only now is it becoming more affordable for smaller companies to do the

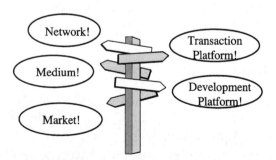

**FIGURE 5-1.** The many faces of the Internet each require a strategy. (*CYBERManagement Inc.*)

same. With proper security, organizations can use the Internet as a virtual private network to link employees and offices. The link could form the basis for valuable intracompany human collaboration and corporate information publishing and sharing, as a starting point.

## IT'S A MEDIUM

The Internet augments the traditional marketing mix as a new channel. This venue is primarily being touted by advertising, PR, and marketing departments or agencies. From corporate communications and service information to product marketing, the Internet serves as a communications channel.

## IT'S A MARKET

The Internet has been likened to a vast, open marketplace where your next customer may not even know you yet. The Internet is a market only if it directly generates new or additional revenue for your business. If the Internet just provides you with leads or referrals, then it is still a medium.

## IT'S A TRANSACTION PLATFORM

This is the Internet's newest and most exciting business face. Imagine a magic black box that allows you to complete your business transactions in the marketspace. Completing all your financial transactions on line, while linked directly to your suppliers, customers, and financial institutions, is the most challenging new opportunity for business.

## IT'S AN APPLICATIONS DEVELOPMENT PLATFORM

The Internet is a growing development platform. Organizations are running existing client/server applications on it and developing new network-based applications (e.g., using Java technology). In this case, organizations are jumping into the new Internet-centric computing paradigm.

# THE BUYER/SELLER MODEL

The buyer/seller model is at the heart of what needs to be transformed electronically. We need to look at each one of these steps, and investigate their sequential and nonsequential relationships. The goal here is threefold:

1. Replace as many steps as possible with an electronically enabled capability that brings the cycle closer to a closed-loop process.
2. Start to tie various steps together as it becomes logically or financially feasible.
3. Begin to measure the value derived from the new processes.

The following steps have been identified, and they include the presales interaction, product/service delivery, and postsales interaction. It is interesting to note that the burden for providing most of these capabilities rests on the sellers. Buyers are in a situation where they will be provided with what they need from suppliers that want to increase their sales volume (Figure 5-2).

We need to think about how each one of these steps can be affected by end-to-end electronic commerce. Tables 5-1 and 5-2 explain how Internet commerce affects the seller and the buyer.

## SELLERS      BUYERS

|  | SELLERS | BUYERS |
|---|---|---|
| **PRE-SALE** | Distribution | Search/Inquire for product |
| | Promotion | Discover product |
| | Display | Compare products |
| | Pricing policy | Negotiate terms |
| | Receive order | Place order |
| | Authorize payment | Receive acknowledgment |
| | Schedule order | Initiate payment |
| | Build or retrieve from inventory | Receive product |
| **POST-SALE** | Ship product | |
| | Receive payment | |
| | Support products | Request support |
| | Market research | Give feedback |

**FIGURE 5-2.** The buyer/seller model includes several steps that must be studied. (*CYBERManagement Inc.*)

TABLE 5-1. Mapping Traditional Selling to Internet Commerce Selling

| TRADITIONAL SELLING STEPS | INTERNET COMMERCE SELLING |
|---|---|
| Distribution | Treat the Internet as a distribution channel where you directly reach either the end user or your resellers. |
| Promotion | Advertise both on the Internet and outside the Internet about the specific products or the organization. Also become present in other forms of electronic distribution channels on the Internet, including search engines, directories, and other communities of interests. |
| Display | Focus on the visual interface that your customers will interact with. Think of how 3-D and multimedia will enhance the buying experience of your customers. |
| Pricing policy | No major changes except that customers can be notified more immediately. |
| Receipt of order | This can happen in two ways: (1) by receiving the order electronically or (2) by interfacing the receipt of the order to the order entry system, therefore automating this function. |
| Authorize payment | Payment can be authorized by enabling a back-end interface to the financial institution's authorization processes, or to your own credit-granting policies. |
| Schedule order | This requires a business-to-business process integration, where the receipt of the order can trigger the scheduling of the order. |
| Build/retrieve from inventory | If the product has to be built or retrieved from inventory, the same order can trigger a bill-of-materials order or an inventory retrieval order. |
| Ship product | Integrating the shipping logistics or fulfillment process is an important part that sometimes gets ignored. If the product is "soft," the appropriate on-line distribution has to take place. |
| Receive payment | Ideally, payment receipt is integrated to reach your financial institution in a seamless way. |

Table 5-1. **Mapping Traditional Selling to Internet Commerce Selling** (*Continued*)

| Traditional Selling Steps | Internet Commerce Selling |
| --- | --- |
| Provide support | This is an easy area to begin with, because support does not require you to sell electronically as a prerequisite. You can start supporting customers immediately for your existing products. |
| Perform market research | Once you have customers electronically engaged in a relationship with you, you can continue to obtain feedback from them about their needs. This information produces real-time market research benefits. |

source: CYBERManagement Inc.

## THE NEW VALUE CHAIN

What happens to the old value chain? How does it really change? Where do you add digital value? Following are three possible scenarios, each with various degrees of complexity and requirements.

### Scenario 1: It Gets Smaller

One obvious scenario is that the old value chain gets smaller and therefore more efficient. This means that manufacturers can now reach customers by bypassing one or two layers of the old value chain (Figure 5-3).

An example of this scenario includes the financial services marketplace for buying and selling equities. The old model forced customers to go through a broker who would take the order and place it on the stock exchange. Today the advent of a multitude of Internet brokering businesses is allowing customers to place these orders themselves, thereby eliminating a step in the process. In fact, when one such business was launched, its ad headline was "Your broker is now obsolete."

TABLE 5-2. Traditional Buying versus Internet Commerce Buying

| TRADITIONAL BUYING STEPS | INTERNET COMMERCE BUYING |
|---|---|
| Search/inquire for products | Aided by intelligent agents and interactive directories, buyers can search or inquire for products across various sources without really visiting their Web sites. |
| Discover products | A search would have yielded the targeted product, or an agent would have brought to your attention the availability of a product you were waiting for. |
| Compare products | The same directories which you have consulted with allow you to compare competitive products. |
| Negotiate terms | You can negotiate either by interacting with the vendor or by calling. |
| Place order | The order is placed directly on the Web. |
| Receive acknowledgment | Through the Web, acknowledgment is received directly from the sellers' Web site or from their Intranet. |
| Initiate payment | The user chooses from one of several Internet payment instruments. These may vary depending on whether the user is a business or a consumer. |
| Receive product | If the product is soft, it is received on-line. If it is hard, shipping logistics information is expected. |
| Request support | Support starts on-line, since that is more efficient. This could include live video or audio links to a customer representative. Support should include the ability to review a detailed transaction history on-line. |
| Give feedback | Once the electronic relationship is established, feedback becomes ongoing. |

SOURCE: CYBERManagement Inc.

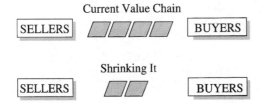

**FIGURE 5-3.** The value chain shrinks: players move out. (*CYBERManagement Inc.*)

## SCENARIO 2: IT GETS REDEFINED

In several cases, as old intermediaries get disintermediated, newer types of intermediaries arise in several new areas, and become an integral part of the new value chain. They begin to take their place between buyers and sellers. Understanding this disaggregation is at the heart of realizing Internet commerce's potential for your organization (Figure 5-4).

The cost of distribution through new intermediaries is assumed to be lower than with old ones.

## SCENARIO 3: IT BECOMES VIRTUAL

Before there was predictability in the flow of goods. Today the behavior of intermediaries is really unpredictable, and will be subject to dynamic market forces. Old intermediaries get disintegrated and reconstructed. Everything is up for grabs. What goes on inside is beyond the control of buyers and sellers, especially sellers. Certain behaviors include a dynamic allocation of

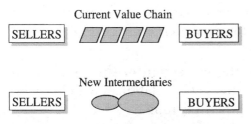

**FIGURE 5-4.** The value chain is redefined: players are replaced. (*CYBERManagement Inc.*)

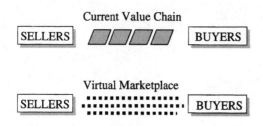

FIGURE 5-5.  The value chain goes virtual:
players are invisible and dynamic.
(*CYBERManagement Inc.*)

intermediaries, based on the needs of buyers (Figure 5-5).
Some of this is really invisible!

## THE THREE SPHERES OF CONNECTIVITY

Every organization interacts on a daily basis with three major
entities: customers, suppliers, and partners. With the advent of
digital markets, electronic supply chains, and virtual partnerships, organizations must now look at these entities through a
virtual cloud of subentities. Often referred to collectively as the
"new Net connections," this cloud becomes like a junction box
for reaching customers, suppliers, and partners. The junction
box permits an amplified and simultaneous entry to these new
marketplaces. We shall call them CustomerNet, SupplierNet,
and PartnerNet. Each one has a certain focus which is at the
core of its existence (Figure 5-6).

- CustomerNet focuses on the expansion of electronic distribution channels to reach targeted electronic customers in several types of segments.
- SupplierNet focuses on the perfection of the supply chain
  management process. It affects the relationship and processes between suppliers and their customers.
- PartnerNet is set to exploit virtual partnerships with all kinds
  of trading partners that are not suppliers or customers.

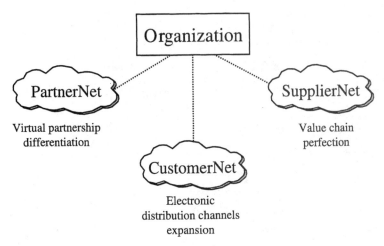

**FIGURE 5-6.** The three new "Net" connections clouds of influence and their primary goals. (*CYBERManagement Inc.*)

## THE MAIN WEB SITE IS DEAD: STRATEGIES FOR EXPANDING MULTIPLE ELECTRONIC CHANNELS

Several companies are basing their entire strategies on their main Web site. However, the Web site is only one of several segments that must be utilized. Electronic marketplace segmentation is still in its infancy, and we are still learning how best to utilize all possibilities. The trend could be likened to the history of the retail industry, when the first "mom and pop" stores opened. After the first store, several store chains appeared, then buying clubs opened, then large multipurpose stores happened, then malls grouping several stores were built, then mail-order became popular, and other forms of indirect selling prospered. A parallel can be drawn with the electronic marketplace in order to stimulate the diversified evolution that is necessary.

Figure 5-7 identifies three different major strategies, each one including two separate segments, therefore yielding a total of six separate segments. The key here is to maximize your participation in all of them by developing new products or services,

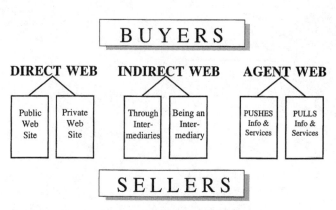

**FIGURE 5-7.** The multiple segmentation of electronic distribution channels. (*CYBERManagement Inc.*)

new alliances, or new capabilities in order to get in all the "nooks and crannies" of the electronic marketplace. It is important to leverage what you can across the various segments, but at the same time exploit the unique aspects of each independently.

## DIRECT WEB

*Segment 1: The public main Web site.* In this case, the objective is to post all products and services on the company's Web site, and to attract buyers and partners to it.

*Segment 2: The private Web site.* A part of the Web site becomes restricted, and it is only accessible to selected customers, partners, or even employees. On the consumer side, examples include any of the news retrieval services. On the business side, this can also be referred to as private Intranets. Examples include Cisco, Dell, and Silicon Graphics, all of them allowing restricted access to a captive audience of their own.

For the public Web site, you have only to give your Web address. For the private Web, you give your address and a password, with a note that says "Welcome to our Intranet!"

## INDIRECT WEB

*Segment 3: Through other intermediaries.* In this case, you are part of another Web site, which we shall call the intermediary. A section of your Web site becomes a part of another Web business, and this allows you to expand your electronic distribution channels. Several early electronic mall models operated under this concept by allowing several storefronts to coexist under their Web roof. This is also the America Online (AOL) model. It is the marketplace. Omaha Steaks, for example, is one of its tenants, but Omaha also has its own public site. Amazon.com is the exclusive bookstore for Excite and AOL, and it relies on 15,000 sales associates which are all indirect Web channels for it.

*Segment 4: Being an intermediary.* Another variation of the indirect Web model is that you are the intermediary, therefore taking the responsibility for drawing traffic to your Web site, and then redirecting it to others. A certain part of your service offering may lend itself to this model. Microsoft's Sidewalk is a great traffic collector. It redirects some of this traffic to other services, including potential competition. For example, it can direct a service inquiry to fetch an event ticket from the Ticketmaster Web site. By doing so, Microsoft has achieved two objectives: It has served its customer, and it has given some business to Ticketmaster. Going back to the Amazon example above, if you are one of its 15,000 sales associates, you are in fact the intermediary for Amazon, and you benefit too by collecting your sales commission on orders that emanate from your site. Intermediaries and intermediary strategies are covered in depth in Chapter 7.

## AGENT WEB

*Segment 5: Pushing information to customers.* Pushing information to prospects and customers is considered as agent-based commerce. From BackWeb and Marimba to the PointCast Network, what is being pushed includes services and products. Your strategy here should be to decide how to exploit push technology either to sell something or to support your customers.

*Segment 6: Ready to be pulled.* The reverse process of using push technology is to ensure that your Web site is "open" to agents that will fetch its contents on the request of one of your prospects. This area is an emerging one, with several examples of agent technology able to perform these tasks, which then leads to increased commerce activity for your products.

*Redefining the Role of the Automated Banking Machine (ABM)*

The Canadian Imperial Bank of Commerce (CIBC), Canada's second largest bank, is giving a face-lift to its 3000 ABMs. Recognizing the ABM's changing role, CIBC is enhancing its 3000 ABMs with a simple browser-like interface to allow it to function as a multipurpose kiosk. Says Brian Cassidy, executive vice president of electronic banking: "With the increasing utilization of digital cash and smart cards, we expected a decreasing usage of the automated bank machines. However, to offset this trend, we decided to gradually introduce specialized services to be delivered via the ABM, with a browserlike interface." For CIBC, the ABM is the point-of-sale device which is becoming a special-purpose Internet appliance, therefore increasing the reach of CIBC's electronic distribution with new Internet content. These new Web ABMs will include services such as dispensing money orders, gift certificates, discount coupons customized to your profile, airline tickets, and show tickets. They will also allow you to pay taxes, and more. Says Cassidy: "When we conducted our initial market trials in 7-Eleven locations that had our ABMs, we dispensed personalized discount coupons, and found out that the rate of in-store immediate utilization jumped from 1.5 to 7 percent. That is value added!"

# THE INTERNET COMMERCE VALUE CHAIN

The following model describes how the various components of Internet commerce can form a new value chain that links producers (vendors and businesses) and consumers (developers and users). Vendors are developing capabilities in network infrastructure, commerce infrastructure, and commerce applications. Developers exploit these capabilities to build applications for intermediaries, agents, or appliances. Businesses commercialize specific commerce applications, become intermediaries, or exploit the usage of agents and appliances. Users (corporate users or consumers) interact with agents, appliances, intermediaries, and commerce applications (Figure 5-8).

*Producers*                                        *Consumers*

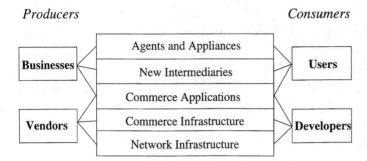

**FIGURE 5-8.**   The new Internet-driven value chain links producers to consumers. (*CYBERManagement Inc.*)

## NETWORK INFRASTRUCTURE

The infrastructure covers the physical networking requirements
that make the Internet what it is, as well as the computer and
communications equipment to support and operate it. Broadly
speaking, this includes cable TV networks, wireless transmission, satellite systems, current telephone infrastructure, and
future private and public information highways. It also includes
various electronic commerce-related services that make the
network infrastructure mission-critical and transaction-ready
for the Web.

## COMMERCE INFRASTRUCTURE

The Internet commerce infrastructure required is different from the
(more known) physical networking infrastructure. This infrastructure
consists of a set of services that are needed to support the building and
interoperation of commerce businesses.

As the commerce infrastructure matures and gets harmo-
nized, we will be able to think of it as a utility, in the same way
as network access has become one. The day will come when we
will have the "OSI seven-layer equivalent"* of an Internet com-

---

* Open Systems Interconnection (OSI) has defined a standard seven-layer networking ref-
erence model to facilitate the internetworking of incompatible computers and networks.

merce infrastructure defined as a standard. This will allow virtual trading entities to coalesce and cooperate as "free floating" communities of interests, creating digital wealth for their players. We have identified the major infrastructure services that need to interoperate seamlessly. Table 5-3 shows only examples of players in this segmentation.

## COMMERCE APPLICATIONS

Commerce applications consist of new or existing companies that have a successful Internet-based business. These businesses were created either by extending the existing business and market model into the Internet or by creating an entirely new company that competes within this new model. Some of these Internet businesses may contain a "new intermediary" flavor. These companies sell (1) hard-goods products, (2) information-based products, (3) services, and (4) token-based products. They address consumer content or business content (Table 5-4).

It is interesting to note that entering a new Internet commerce business may be more appealing to entrepreneurs than to existing businesses, because of different business models. Whereas entrepreneurs have "nothing to lose" as they enter markets that didn't exist before, new businesses have to continuously ask themselves how their new Internet ventures affect their current models. For most of them, it will be business as usual, until most questions have been answered. The ROI model is different depending on whether you are entering Internet marketplaces as a separate business or are extending your existing model into it. In the latter case, you can rely on existing revenue while electronic revenues slowly increase. For example, NYNEX is extending its current business to the Internet.

NYNEX, a U.S.-based global communications and media company, has extended its established business into the Internet by introducing BigYellow in 1995. BigYellow has more than 16.5 million businesses listed nationwide. It has become one of the largest advertiser-supported sites on the Internet,

**TABLE 5-3. A Sample of Commerce Infrastructure Services**

| SECURITY | REAL-TIME MULTIMEDIA | SOFTWARE APPLICATIONS AND DEVELOPMENT ENVIRONMENT | PUBLISHING/ AUTHORING | EDI SERVICES AND GATEWAYS | PAYMENT INSTRUMENTS AND WALLETS | METERING AND MEASURING | DIRECTORIES AND CATALOGS | DIGITAL IDs AND CERTIFICATION MANAGEMENT | ELECTRONIC PAYMENT SERVICES |
|---|---|---|---|---|---|---|---|---|---|
| Security Dynamics | VocalTec | InterWorld | NetObjects | Premenos | CyberCash | I/PRO | SAQQARA Systems | Verisign | First Data Corp. |
| Technology | Camelot | OneWave | Haht Software | GEIS | Checkfree | NetCount | iCat | GTE Cybertrust | PayLinx |
| Certicom | IDT | Connect, Inc. | Adobe | Sterling Commerce | VISA Cash | Intersé | Cadis | Entrust Technologies | IBM's eTill |
| RSA | Dimension X | Open Market | Microsoft | Advantis | KLELine | PC Meter | Trilogy | IBM's Net.Registry | VeriFone |
| HP's Virtual Vault | Worlds, Inc. | BroadVision | Netscape Communications | Harbinger | First Virtual | Andromedia | | Keywitness Inc. | InternetSecure |
| | Xing's Stream Works | Oracle | | Open Market | Mondex | Inverse Network | | InterTrust Technologies Corp. | BlueMoney |
| | Progressive's Real Audio | Vantive | | MPACT Immedia | GCTech | NetGravity | | | *(Financial Institutions)* |
| | Earth Web | Speedware | | | | | | | |
| | Intel | Square Earth Smart Technologies | | | | | | | |

SOURCE: CYBERManagement Inc.

TABLE 5-4. Examples of Commerce Businesses on the Internet

| NEW COMPANIES CREATED ENTIRELY DUE TO THE INTERNET | COMPANIES SUCCESSFULLY EXTENDING INTO THE INTERNET WITH OR WITHOUT THE SAME BRANDING |
|---|---|
| CouponNet | NYNEX: BigYellow |
| Gamelan (by Earth Web) | Desktop Data: NewsEDGE WEB |
| The Internet Shopping Network | Ziff-Davis: ZD-Net |
| PCQuote | CUC International: netMarket |
| Quote.com | Intuit: Quicken Financial Network |
| Security First Network Bank | Marshall Industries: Marshall on the Net, @Once, NetSeminar |
| PAWWS | AMP: AMP-Connect |
| Amazon.com | SABRE: Travelocity (with Worldview Systems) |
| Enews | Mecklermedia: Meckler Web |
| E-Stamp™ | c|net: cnet |
| ONSALE | PhotoDisc: PhotoDisc |
| pcOrder | |
| The PointCast Network | |

SOURCE: CYBERManagement Inc.

with more than 5000 advertisers. BigYellow includes a database of more than 75 million nationwide White Pages listings, and a directory of 7.5 million e-mail addresses. In addition, BigYellow links users to the on-line directories of 32 other countries, which include complementary content in about 12 other categories, including travel, weather, dining, and health care. BigYellow is quickly increasing its market share in the on-line directory services. It claims to have more advertisers on-line than all its Yellow Pages competitors combined, and nearly twice the usage of it nearest competitor. For NYNEX, BigYellow creates an entirely new business that begins as an extension of its current competencies, but actually goes much further. It has the following characteristics:

- Allowing the company to reach markets outside of its previous geographical boundaries, both in the United States and internationally
- Providing new revenue from a channel that did not exist before
- Providing existing NYNEX customers with access to national and international information
- Putting NYNEX on the ground floor of the evolving directory industry into electronic services
- Allowing NYNEX to move into Internet commerce transactions by selling processed information

This segment also includes generic commerce applications—such as shipping, order management, inventory, supply chain management, and logistics—that can be applied to a variety of businesses. For example, Ironside™ Technologies has an order entry system that allows corporations to give their customers access to real-time order entry capability and up-to-the-minute host access for pricing, inventory availability, promotions, and order status inquiries via the Internet. This order management subsystem could be part of an overall solution, and it could be applied to a variety of vertical industries.

## NEW INTERMEDIARIES

The most important common denominator for companies in this new segment is that, in all cases, they replace an existing business or method that was done differently in the physical marketplace (Table 5-5).

## COMMERCIAL AGENTS AND INFORMATION APPLIANCES

Agents and information appliances are positioned at the highest levels of user interaction, because they utilize all other lower levels of the hierarchy to accomplish a specific task. In the future, agents will contribute to making many Web sites increasingly "invisible." Additional information on agents and their impact is presented in Chapter 9.

TABLE 5-5. **Examples of New Intermediary Businesses**

| THE NEW INTERMEDIARIES | |
| --- | --- |
| Electronic auctions | Marketplace concentrators |
| On-line software delivery | Product/service brokers |
| On-line support and service | Fulfillment and logistics support |
| Outsourced professional services | Van-less EDI and procurement services |
| Multimedia content delivery | Virtual trading communities |
| Financial transaction brokers | Digital rights management |
| Marketplace aggregators | Customer information resellers |

SOURCE: CYBERManagement Inc.

The relationship between agents and appliances is as follows. Information appliances with specific agents embedded in them will become highly specialized point-of-sale devices for a variety of products and services. Some information appliances will be assembled with these agent technologies built-in, and others will have more flexibility in adapting to a variety of agents functionality.

Agents have been labeled the "cholesterol" of the Internet, because of the multiplicative effect they have on draining resources from various sources. The threat is that any Web site that wants to be accessible to potential business opportunities has to make itself available to potential agent technology that will bring prospective customers to it. This chapter highlights a few examples of emerging agent technology that is definitely metamorphosing the way we interact with the Web. What agents are doing for electronic commerce could be likened to what search engines did for the Web.

**Have Agent, Will Go Anywhere.**    Agents will take us places we have never been before, or have never even thought about finding on the Internet. The following sample of agent technologies gives a view on what is coming at us very quickly.

Identify is a tool for finding products and pages that use IDML to identify themselves. IDML is an extension of HTML that tags products and pages on a Web site to make it easier for people to find them. When the Identify robot encounters IDML, it uses it to categorize a page more precisely than any search engine could. So, Identify is like a virtual catalog on the Internet that connects qualified customers with merchants. Merchants control their own listings by inserting IDML tags. Shoppers refine queries in steps to get what they want. The result is that multiple companies are tied in an open virtual Internet market. Merchants participate in Identify with no prior relationship and no special technology beyond the IDML tags.

AGENTics is a company that develops what it refers to as "electronic commerce facilitation products." Its software technology allows the integrated viewing and automatic accessing to remote on-line catalogs. AGENTics' technology allows a user to receive an intelligent integrated view of a set of remote on-line catalogs, enabling the user to interactively describe and identify his or her requirements. Then, depending on the user's exact requirement definition, it accesses the relevant on-line catalogs and obtains up-to-date and pertinent product information. This presents applications for Internet marketplaces, purchasing departments, and buying organizations, since they provide end users with an intelligent, unified view of the commercial on-line catalogs of their choice.

Tesserac Information Systems (TIE) provides universal information integration of legacy information sources on an Intranet or the Internet (Web pages, databases, programs) in a heterogeneous, distributed, and dynamic environment where the integrated data may be queried in familiar business terms. The result for users is a unified view of an entire corpus of information that is literally glued together in real time. TIE allows users to construct specific requests and is able to translate these requests intelligently. For example, a user may ask for used "automobiles," while the information sources have information about used "cars." Given that TIE knows that an automobile is a car, it can translate the request into a form that can be handled.

NetBot's Jango works in concert with a user's browser. A user enters the name of a shopping product and Jango automatically determines which stores and information sites are relevant. Jango then automatically consults those sites and quickly prepares reports for the shopper, including such things as detailed product information, comparative reviews, product pricing, and manufacturer's specifications. When a shopper is ready to buy, Jango accelerates the process by automatically filling in order forms with information provided by the user during the original registration process. Jango is based on a new Web technology navigation approach called "Parallel Pull." With Parallel Pull a user types a high-level request, such as a product name, and is brought information in parallel from 20, 30, or more relevant sites.

**The Next Generation of Agents and Agent Technologies.** The next generation will play a key role in allowing us to transition from "eyeball" searching to automated and efficient ways to find information and act on it. Table 5-6 gives a list of enabling technologies. The key for you is to investigate how you can utilize them to enhance your Web commerce capabilities or your personal Web lifestyle.

**The Future of Agent-Based Competitive Analysis: Infiltrating Enemy Lines Invisibly.** Imagine the following scenario. A salesperson needs to gather quickly the most recent competitive analysis information in order to develop his or her own counterstrategy in a given sales situation. There are two ways to do so. If the person works for a large company, the corporate Intranet will likely have a section on competitors which may or may not be up to date. Another option is to search a multitude of Web sites, including the company's own Web site, newswires, financial information sites, and so forth. This is usually a tedious and long process. Enters a Web automation capability (such as webMethods). Imagine now that the same salesperson is able to receive all this competitive information without personally visiting any Web site. Rather, the Web automation software does. It is automatically programmed to contact relevant Web sites for up-to-the-minute competitive information. Welcome to automated competitive tracking!

# THE ROLE OF COMMERCENET

CommerceNet is a unique industry organization dedicated to accelerating the transformation of the Internet into a viable open marketplace. CommerceNet's efforts focus on market and business development, technology research, industry pilots, education, and advocacy in legal and regulatory issues for its

**TABLE 5-6. A Survey of Key Agents and Agent Technologies**

| COMPANY | PRODUCT | DESCRIPTION | APPLICATION |
|---|---|---|---|
| Agentics | CatalogExpert™ | Unified classification and access technology which enables integrated view and automatic access to remote on-line catalogs | Purchasing departments, buying organizations |
| Identify | IDML tags | Tags products and pages on a Web site to make it easier for people to find them | Finding narrowly defined information, products, locations, subjects |
| Junglee | Canopy™ | Virtual database technology that allows automatic aggregation of data from the Internet, Intranets, and legacy data sources and delivers the data to business applications | Finding a movie and show times near you, an apartment, a job |
| NetBot | Jango | Parallel pull agent that automatically consults sites and prepares reports for the shopper | Finding information and products in categories such as books, wines, clothing, PCs |
| OnDisplay | PageAgent™ CenterStage™ | Enables Web data to be dynamically accessed, extracted, and seamlessly integrated with a software application | Multisourced information from newswires, financial data, competitive data, suppliers |
| AgentSoft | Live Agent Pro | Scripts that provide automation of data retrieval and data entry activities | Gathering investment information, news collection, competitor investigation |
| Autonomy, Inc. | Agentware | Intelligent management of unstructured data and personalized information delivery | Combining content from several newspapers |
| Epistemics | Infomaster | Integration and management of distributed, heterogeneous databases | Housing rental from different listings, virtual cookware catalog |

*(Continued)*

**Table 5-6. A Survey of Key Agents and Agent Technologies (*Continued*)**

| Company | Product | Description | Application |
|---|---|---|---|
| Tesserae | Unifind | Universal information integration of legacy or heterogeneous information sources | Finding an apartment, integrating diverse customer information |
| webMethods | Web Automation Suite™ | Software that integrates Web data into applications allowing businesses to automate their transactions with one another by using the Web | Order tracking, multisourcing, competitive analysis, manufacturing, purchasing |

SOURCE: CYBERManagement Inc.

500 member organizations worldwide. Since its inception in 1994, in the Silicon Valley of California, CommerceNet has expanded internationally and locally in other parts of the United States with affiliates and chapters. CommerceNet is now considered the most respected industry association for Internet commerce.

CommerceNet has shaped the Internet commerce landscape, and will continue to do so, by binding together key players and contributors worldwide. They have been the incubation ground for several Internet business ideas such as CyberCash, I/PRO, Internet Shopping Network, Netscape, Open Market, SAQQARA, Terisa Systems, and Tesserae, as well as other important Internet-related industry initiatives such TRUSTe and JEPI.

## THE VISION

Because of CommerceNet's increasing influence on the worldwide Internet commerce scene, this section offers a snapshot of CommerceNet's vision. Understanding it provides you with a view of the future, as implied by this vision. As an action item, try to imagine how your business will be affected, as various pieces of the CommerceNet vision become more and more a reality.

The following is an excerpt from CommerceNet's vision, as depicted by its chairman and founder, Jay M. Tenenbaum.

> Today, Internet commerce is at a critical juncture. After an exhilarating start-up phase, further development hinges on bridging "the chasm" between early adopters and a true mass market. CommerceNet has identified four synergistic goals to ensure a successful transition:
>
> - Developing the infrastructure to support mass market Internet commerce on a global scale
> - Jump-starting key vertical markets
> - Engaging businesses in many more industries and geographic regions
> - Creating a conducive legal and regulatory environment
>
> The CommerceNet vision calls for the next-generation infrastructure to support a seamlessly integrated set of E-commerce services, including security, payment, directories, collaboration, and EDI. This infrastructure must be robust, easy to use, scalable, trusted, and open. And it must support advanced capabilities such as micropayments, microcredentials, and agents. CommerceNet is helping the industry converge on a standard architecture by endorsing key protocols and application programming interfaces (APIs), and certifying the conformance and interoperability of its members' products.
>
> CommerceNet calls this architecture E-co System (as in E-commerce), and expects it will play a major role in facilitating communications between vendors and end users, as CIOs struggle to navigate the Internet commerce jungle. CommerceNet is also organizing global "Communities of Interests" around important vertical markets.
>
> CommerceNet will focus primarily on large international service industries such as finance, retail, publishing, and shipping, as well as manufacturing industries such as electronics, automobiles, and software, with international supply networks.
>
> An essential tenet of CommerceNet's vision is that Internet markets should be open—not just to all buyers and sellers—but to

the numerous providers of software and value-added services that support and lubricate the marketplace. Industry pilots will build on the E-co architecture, and utilize commercial software wherever possible. Over time, CommerceNet anticipates adding application layers to the architecture, to accommodate reusable modules for common functions such as catalog search, order fulfillment, brokering, and shipping. The goal is to create a generic open market framework that can be quickly replicated across many industries.

The creation of regional and industry chapters is an important complement to CommerceNet's infrastructure and market development activities. Historically, industries have congregated in geographical regions—autos in Detroit, publishing and finance in New York, and high tech in Boston and Silicon Valley, for example. Chapters enable CommerceNet to reach many more of these end-user companies, particularly the smaller ones, creating new business and networking opportunities.

The combination of a robust Internet infrastructure, open markets, and local chapters opens awesome new possibilities. For instance, we can envision communities of interest, created dynamically by companies that transcend traditional industry and geographic boundaries, to pursue specific market opportunities.

Whether such possibilities actually materialize depends in large part on the existence of a conducive legal, regulatory, and policy environment. CommerceNet will work proactively with agencies at all levels of government around the world to create a lawful environment where consumers and corporations alike feel comfortable doing business. We will also continue to respond reactively to ill-conceived attempts by local authorities to pass preemptive legislation that fragments or limits growth of the Internet market.

CommerceNet members cooperate to build the iMarket, then compete vigorously to exploit it. The result is an entrepreneurial explosion of products and services, building on and adding value to each other, that no proprietary on-line marketplace can hope to match.

Tenenbaum's concluding words—"no proprietary on-line marketplace can hope to match"—envision the Internet as a truly open marketplace that will thrive when various pieces begin to interoperate in true open systems fashion. Making this happen goes beyond the scope of an individual company. Hence, CommerceNet's efforts in developing the E-co system architecture are probably one of CommerceNet's most important contributions. E-co represents CommerceNet's vision of an open market architecture—in other words, a "marketecture."

## THE E-co ARCHITECTURE: RESPONSE TO DIGITAL ANARCHY

Jay M. Tenenbaum, founder and chairman of CommerceNet, is really the father of the E-co vision. His comments encapsulate the situation:

> The E-co System project addresses the interoperability of E-commerce applications, services, and platforms—arguably the most important and vexing issue in realizing the vision of a global Internet marketplace. The good news is that these are proliferating at an astounding rate from vendors all over the world. The bad news is that no one talks to each other, or builds on each other. For example, we have about 20 members who have developed proprietary payment solutions, and another dozen with incompatible security solutions. What consumers want, by contrast, is a universal wallet that can hold any payment instrument, as well as a digital identity card or two that they can use to obtain many additional credentials, such as credit cards, licenses, and membership cards. Similar interoperability issues exist at every level—directories, catalogs, collaboration tools, EDI protocols, shopping agents, shipping services, markets, etc. We are well down the path toward digital anarchy.

So, the promise of the E-co vision is to move us away from the "proprietary" days of Internet commerce. Several solutions and components do not interoperate well without special interface requirements. E-co's objective is to allow the various technologies and services to interoperate in two ways:

1. Interoperability between components of similar function (e.g., one certification authority to support user authentication, signing EDI messages, and paying for transactions)

2. Interoperability between components of complementary functions (e.g., an interactive catalog that interfaces with a trading service that accepts any payment instrument and any certificate authority)

The E-co vision may become a critical foundation for building successful Internet markets around vertical electronic commerce marketplaces. E-co is an open architecture for the global Internet marketplace—the iMarket. CommerceNet believes that by applying all E-co components to a specific marketplace, it is possible to jump-start a given vertical market and create a constellation of open market players. Welcome to the new world of "component-based" commerce, where the vision consists of building new virtual enterprises on top of existing services.

The development engine covering this new paradigm is CommerceNet's Global Partners program, which includes regional chapters in the United States and international affiliates in Japan, Canada, Korea, Australia, Sweden, Malaysia, China, India, Norway, Germany, Italy, and several other industrial and emerging countries. According to Tenenbaum, "These partners will engage their local businesses and governments, jointly creating global trading networks for key vertical markets. The strength of CommerceNet chapters and affiliates around the world will bring a new global business development paradigm—one that exploits the Internet's unprecedented ability to link business organizations across traditional company, industry, and national boundaries."

CommerceNet is pioneering the definition and creation of this standard, open architectural framework for building and integrating electronic commerce components. E-co is a road map that helps define (1) the major Internet commerce building blocks and (2) the required interfaces between them.

From a technology implementation perspective, E-co is an open, object-oriented framework that consists of reusable Java-class libraries and Interface Definition Language (IDL) interfaces. The Java-class libraries provide the building blocks for the electronic commerce components. The IDL is used for specifying integration among various electronic commerce components. In addition, the E-co framework includes a registry service for users to register their needs, a notification service to notify users of the availability of their needs, and a standard taxonomy of the various types of content, which CommerceNet refers to as "taxonomy of everything" (TOE). To make all this work, E-co will rely on XML, a new HTML extension that provides a more structured way to identify the data types in any given Web site, so that agents can retrieve information accordingly (Figure 5-9).

To prove the E-co architecture model, CommerceNet has spun off a consulting services arm called CNgroup. CNgroup is bringing the various pieces of the E-co architecture to the market by creating developers' toolkits and by testing the overall architecture with targeted vertical applications.

An application model for putting the E-co architecture to work as an end-to-end commerce virtual market is depicted with the COIN concept.

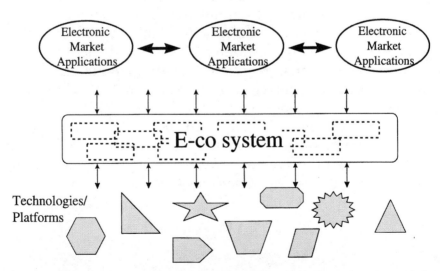

**FIGURE 5-9.**   E-co architecture for component-based commerce. (*CommerceNet*)

## COINs: Internet Commerce Applications at Work

Bringing together communities of interests around a common value chain is not a new concept on its own. However, now that value chains depend on the Internet as the underlying service infrastructure, it becomes a new concept. This new concept has been "coined" by CommerceNet as COINs, or community-of-interest networks.

COINs enable the creation of new markets by leveraging virtual trader/partner business models to create new companies, products, and service opportunities as a result of the open iMarket and based on the E-co architecture. New opportunities are also created to implement these models around important vertical markets. Companies that leverage the business opportunities enabled by the community-of-interest business models will become leaders and command positions of authority as the electronic commerce marketplace expands.

COIN applications bring businesses and consumers together and allow them to securely initiate and settle electronic commerce transactions on the Internet. All business and consumer participants in the COIN have a common interest and derive benefit from the completion of the transaction.

For example, one COIN prototype is being developed for the real estate industry to bring together buyers and sellers with numerous third-party organizations such as multiple-listing services, lenders, appraisers, title companies, termite inspectors, roofing inspectors, and closing attorneys. Jim Dills, director of market creation at CommerceNet, says: "The COIN model will enable new business paradigms and create new sources of revenue for a wide range of organizations. Those who understand and prepare for this evolution will be best positioned to capitalize on Internet-based electronic commerce."

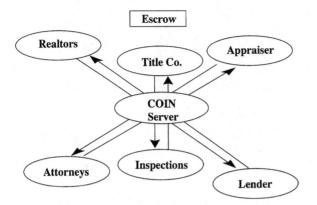

**FIGURE 5-10.**   A real estate community-of-interest network (COIN) prototype. (*CommerceNet*)

New markets and services are created almost daily. The COIN business model creates a productive environment for all participants as they concentrate now on leveraging their primary strengths and business contributions within the local COIN. The prototype model is depicted in Figure 5-10.

# STRATEGY ACTIONS

*Cyberspace is a topology, not a topography. There are no physical constructs like "beside," "above," "to the north of."*

NICHOLAS NEGROPONTE

*Director, MIT's Media Laboratory*

Where do you start to introduce and develop electronic commerce capabilities into the organization? From a planning viewpoint, Internet electronic commerce has the following characteristics:

- It is *multidisciplinary* from a job perspective, *cross-functional* from an interorganizational perspective and *interindustry* from a broad market perspective.
- It requires a business management approach
- It has multiple starting points, each with a different angle.
- It requires a long-term approach to achieve a strategic impact.

## SETTING INTERNET'S EXPECTATIONS

A number of management-level issues must be addressed prior to deciding on the implementation steps. Since Internet commerce is a new methodology for doing business in the non-physical marketplace, its impact can be as strategic as you are willing to make it. Unfortunately, because of the challenges that were outlined earlier, there may be a nonlinear relationship on the return on investment.

Regardless of the approach taken, the need for a quick view on your investment is more important than an immediate return on the investment. Learning in this marketplace becomes the most important thing, and learning can be achieved only by early experience, so that you can see some results in less than three months from the start.

Sometimes, even if all the pieces are there, and implementation does not lack any resources, ultimate return on the investment may still be questionable.

## ANSWERING STRATEGIC QUESTIONS

At the end of your planning period, you have to answer the following questions very succinctly:

- *How is Internet commerce going to change our business?* This is a fundamental question, as it can set the stage for how deep you end up taking your strategy. You have to articulate at the strategic level the linkage between your current business objectives and your objectives in cyberspace by outlining clearly how they will change with the Internet. This must done with concrete expectations, not just wishful thinking based on marketplace approximation.

- *How do we uncover new types of business opportunities?* There are two types of opportunities: ones that allow you to extend your current model into the Internet, and ones that are entirely birthed with the Internet in mind. For either type, there will be more tempting opportunities than ones that need to be pursued. As much as this sounds like a cliché, with the Internet, it becomes even more difficult to accurately predict the market factors and parameters which you usually base decisions on. Many of my consulting engagements focused entirely on covering this aspect. With one client, we identified 10 possible ventures, 4 of which received funding for further research. The client ended up launching one of them.

- *How can we take advantage of new electronic linkages with customers and trading partners?*   If you already have a number of trading partners, the Internet allows you to expand the capabilities you currently have with current trading partners, and it allows you to link newer partners much faster than before by opening your Intranets to them. For example, Michelin with its independent dealer network, Fruit of the Loom with its distributors, and Cisco continuously pushing the limits of their Intranets with their distribution partners.

- *Will intermediaries be eliminated in the process? Or do we become intermediaries ourselves?*   By examining how each piece of your value chain may be affected, you can determine whether it is time to become an intermediary, or defend a position weakened by the rise of a new intermediary.

- *How do we bring more buyers and sellers together electronically (and keep them there)?*   Today it is a challenge to bring electronic buyers into your sphere of selling influence. However, once you have mastered this initial challenge, it becomes even more important to keep them. The old adage that "keeping a customer is cheaper than getting a new one" applies equally well in the marketspace. For your customer, your competitor is only a "click away" from you. It becomes too tempting to switch when it is so easy.

- *How do we change the nature of our products and services?* You have to evolve beyond hard goods, to soft goods and information-based products and interactive services. There is an evolution to be followed, even if it cannibalizes initially some of your existing offerings.

- *Why is the Internet affecting other companies more than ours?* You might be asking yourself whether you are immune to the Internet. It would be nice not to have headaches or anxiety associated with the uncertainties of electronic commerce. In reality, it is hard to imagine a large corporation not being affected by the Internet.

- *How do we manage and measure the evolution of our strategy?* Once you have identified where to focus your priorities, you have to ensure that you are following up with a sustained management and measurement framework for monitoring and refining your success in the marketspace.

# 10 STEPS TO CYBERMATURITY

In order to avoid some of the possible pitfalls, I recommend assessing the following 10 steps and acting on perfecting the outcome of each one, in order to maximize the chances of success. Your "cybermaturity" will increase when you are addressing all of them simultaneously.

1. Conduct necessary education.
2. Review current distribution and supply chain models.
3. Understand what your customers and partners expect from the Internet.
4. Reevaluate the nature of your products and services.
5. Give a new role to your human resources department.
6. Expand your current systems to the outside.
7. Track new competitors and market shares in the new digital marketspace.
8. Develop a Web-centric marketing strategy.
9. Participate in the creation and development of virtual marketplaces and intermediaries, *now.*
10. Instill electronic markets management style.

## STEP 1: CONDUCT NECESSARY EDUCATION

Education involves more than communication. Communicating an idea that is well understood is one thing, but communicating a new and perhaps complex way of doing business requires additional education. There are two sides to the education imperative. First, internally executives and managers must be educated. Second, externally customers, prospects, and trading partners must also be educated.

**Educate Internally, from the Top Down.**   The Internet has been labeled as probably the most important new tool for today's learning organization. In order to avoid having Internet technology surpass the ability of management to exploit it effectively, the proper executive education has to formally take place. Because of its newness and complexity, the Internet and electronic commerce represent a learning challenge that has to be met with a business education focus.

Education, education, education. When all levels of employees and managers are well educated about Internet commerce, they will each begin to discover their own business opportunities. Any implementation becomes much easier if it is understood that the pain of not doing anything is greater than the pain of doing something about it. After my seminars to executives, I always ask them: "What will you do next when you go back to your office?" The answer that is most frequently mentioned is: "Conduct more executive education."

By addressing the management training needs early, organizations can better understand and absorb how to take advantage of the Internet effectively. The best decisions are taken by the most informed managers. For example, organizations can start with a half-day executive education and awareness session that covers the following topics:

- Internet market segmentation: What is our strategy for each one of them?
- Inventory review of Internet applications (internal/external functions)
- Evolution of Internet deployment within an organization
- Strategic planning elements for the Internet
- Introduction to electronic commerce on the Internet (definitions and state of practice)
- Buyer/seller model and transactions
- Drivers and challenges to electronic commerce
- New Internet commerce business opportunities
- Major building blocks to Internet commerce
- Assessment of management readiness
- Case for action requirements on the basis of scenario planning

Executive education has nothing to do with "surfing the Net," but rather with understanding how it is going to change your organization. The audience should include selected senior managers and executives who will have an influence on how the Internet may be deployed within your organization. They will become the internal marketers and champions you will need later.

It is a logical step to start with executive education, since with a greater degree of knowledge, your organization will be better able to deal with the Internet and any implementation that may follow. This could give you an edge against your competition. As an action item, executives are encouraged to move Internet business education to the center of the corporate agenda.

Once the education awareness campaign has been kicked off, it is important to follow with an internalization of these concepts. While visualization helps you explain the strategy and vision, action starts to happen only when a large number of employees and managers begin to internalize the concepts and issues that affect them directly. You can test various aspects of this transition by specifically asking employees how the Internet is affecting their jobs, and how they interact with customers and trading partners. When employees have internalized and understood the forces of change within your vision, you can really begin to reap the rewards of employee Internet productivity. The burning-platform scenario helps to fuel the case for action.

The issue of executive education applies as well interorganizationally, in the context of what is necessary to move the whole marketplace forward. CommerceNet Southeast depicts it as shown in Figure 6-1.

**Educate Your Customers about Your Capabilities and Their Benefits.**  You must constantly and directly educate your customers and electronic partners about how to interact with you in this new marketplace. It is no longer enough just to give out your Web site URL address. You have to specifically explain and show to customers the benefits of using all Internet venues and features, including, but not limited to, your Web site.

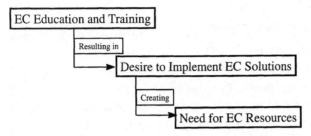

**FIGURE 6-1.** Linkage of Internet commerce education resources. (*CommerceNet Southeast*)

The Web site is the product, and it is becoming a complex one. Therefore, many of its features may not be obvious at first sight, and must be explained. What will attract customers to it will not be the user's guide, but rather the brochure. When you look at a product, you don't want to try to figure out its features. They have to jump at you. Keeping electronic partners and customers will be more challenging than getting them in the first place.

### Desired Outcome of Step 1

- Understanding the new meanings of Internet commerce leads to the creation of a common framework for action.
- Informed managers and executives are able to uncover opportunities for their own business functions.
- When employees have internalized the strategy, they are better able to act on it.
- When customers know about your new capabilities, there is a better chance that they will try them.

## STEP 2: REVIEW CURRENT DISTRIBUTION AND SUPPLY CHAIN MODELS

You need to examine the potential effect that Internet commerce will have on your distribution channels and supply chain management:

- Can you increase the number of electronic connections, simplify interorganizational processes, and at the same time discover ways to shrink, speed up, or virtualize the value chain?

- What is likely to happen with your wholesalers, distributors, or retailers? Are they going to be disintermediated or are they likely to survive by transforming their businesses into new types of intermediaries? Are you going to support their transition to electronic mediation, or do you plan on bypassing them?

*Fruit of the Loom Manages the Electronic Supply Chain and Serves Its Customers' Customers*

Fruit of the Loom is providing its Activewear distributors with branded Web sites, thus enabling interactive commerce via the Internet between the company and its Activewear business partners. The Web sites feature the distributors' entire inventory and operation, not just the Fruit of the Loom lines. The Web sites are preengineered and can be customized. As long as the distributors commit to using the system for one year, they pay nothing. According to Fruit of the Loom, distributors are saving $10 to $20 in order entry costs with each order. Each site also gives the distributors a new gateway to silk-screen printers in their areas. This improves their competitiveness, since they are now better able to respond to their customers' requests by quickly sourcing the silk-screen requirements they need. So, Fruit of the Loom has even thought of its customers' customers.

On-line customers of Fruit of the Loom distributors can order products around the clock, seven days a week. On-line customers of Fruit of the Loom distributors can also check order status, inventory availability, and price schedules using any desktop Web browser. Fruit of the Loom's Internet application is improving access by the distribution channel and providing real-time information on product availability, which is improving customer service.

Once you have analyzed the impact of the Internet on your distribution and value chains, you have to ask yourself: "Is the Internet a new channel or is it a new market?" A different strategy is required for each. As a new channel, the Web requires careful consideration, since it may be competing with your existing channels. As a new market, it gives you more freedom of action, since there is less at stake to start with. Sometimes the emergence of a new channel, which appears to be small at its onset, ends up becoming a real market.

However, by treating the Internet as just another channel, you may be missing some of the necessary nuances of electronic microchannel segmentation. The Internet is not just a third channel (assuming the other two are direct sales and indirect sales). The Internet is made up of a series of electronic microchannels that have to be evaluated simultaneously. Assuming that today most business is conducted via a company's main Web site (front door), more and more business will come from other Web sites or marketplaces where the company has to be strategically positioned. For example, Amazon.com is already deriving a percentage of its revenue from the 15,000 Web sales associates it maintains. By directing orders to Amazon's Web site, the sales associates are contributing to expanding a new electronic micro-channel for Amazon. Hypothetically, if the main Amazon site were to shut down, Amazon would still get a percentage of its revenue from its sales associates, since they are already entrenched with the company.

*American Greetings Would Like History to Repeat Itself*

With $2.2 billion in sales, and a presence in 100,000 retail outlets, American Greetings is aggressively entering the electronic cards business, an embryonic segment of Internet commerce for consumers. Some 15 to 20 years ago, over two-thirds of greeting cards were sold in specialty card and gift shops, whereas today, over two-thirds of sales are through the mass channels (e.g., Wal-Mart, Sears). Several years ago, American Greetings had sensed the changing shopping trend and capitalized on it, by growing its business accordingly. Today, it likens the Internet channel to the emergence of the new mass channel 15 to 20 years ago. And it is hoping that history will repeat itself as the consumer shopping trend turns to the electronic channel.

## Desired Outcome of Step 2

- Proactively, change the configuration of your value chain.
- Concentrate your electronic distribution strategy on the Internet as the primary electronic marketplace.

- Review and expand your entry in each one of the three channel segments outlined in Chapter 5: direct web (public/private), indirect Web (through an intermediary/being an intermediary), and agent Web (push/pull).

## STEP 3: UNDERSTAND WHAT YOUR CUSTOMERS AND PARTNERS EXPECT FROM THE INTERNET

Do you know how many of your customers are able and willing to interface with you via electronic networks and conduct transactions? Do you know what their readiness and behavior patterns are? The question applies equally well to businesses and consumers.

If you know where and how your customers are buying in electronic marketplaces, you can then be in tune with their level. This is good for setting expectations. For example, Marshall Industries and Cisco have had the luxury of starting with a captive audience, since their customers were used to the Internet well before it became known as the Web. Today, they can both tell their customers about new products, probably faster than anybody. Furthermore, their customers depend on their Internet capabilities, in the same way that a company's employees now depend on their Intranets for their day-to-day duties. The ultimate test of success is when your customers think of your Intranet as theirs.

Businesses are more sophisticated in their ability to interface their computer systems to transaction networks while effecting their internal processes, but consumers are really novices in using sophisticated data entry devices, encryption mechanisms, smart cards with a PC, and other promised add-ons. It is not enough just to have a PC at home connected to a 33KB modem. Overall, consumers are scratching the surface of their readiness for electronic commerce.

The necessary action is to target a focused segment of your customers that is open to this new channel and perhaps to help them get up to speed with what is required to meet your needs for efficient distribution and fulfillment. The day will come when sellers will give away modems, software, or free Internet access to specific customers, just to entice them to use an Internet self-service from the seller. Sellers will eventually save by converting more customers and more transactions per customers to a self-service mode.

You must also assess the economic potential of the new electronic community which is being targeted. Even if the sales generated by the new electronic channels came to only a small percentage of your total sales, at least you would have started a trend destined to keep going up. It is generally easier to scale the technical infrastructure than it is to change your business processes, so any early experience on how to do both will be beneficial when it becomes time to really expand your capabilities.

For example, in the first three months of operation, Fidelity Investments was receiving and fulfilling only 5 percent of its mutual funds information requests directly from its Web site. However, as this percentage grew, Fidelity was able to meet the demand, because its capabilities were already enabled.

## Desired Outcome of Step 3

- Take steps that reflect an accurate assessment of the sophistication level of your electronic customers and their segmentation.
- Open your Intranet to make Extranets by allowing customer and supplier access.
- Make your suppliers think of and depend on your Extranet as if it were their Intranet.
- Look at the entire buying/selling cycle process and decide where which services can be introduced.

## STEP 4: REEVALUATE THE NATURE OF YOUR PRODUCTS AND SERVICES

It is not enough just to sell hard goods over the Internet. You must aggressively develop other types of products and services to increase your revenues in the electronic marketplace, and solid-

|  | OLD World | NEW World |
|---|---|---|
| OLD Products & Services | KEEP | Selective Market |
| NEW Products & Services | PROMOTE | NEW GROWTH |

FIGURE 6-2. New products and services growth strategies for electronic markets. (*CYBERManagement Inc.*)

ify your position on several fronts. These include the addition of soft goods, interactive services, and information-based products and services. As a first step, make a grid that includes the four types of products, and place your current products appropriately. This helps you get a realistic view on your products and services inventory. Then, you can decide how to evolve them for the future, according to the criteria given in Figure 6-2.

Are any of your products and services conducive to electronic distribution via networks such as the Internet? The answer is probably yes for many products, but each with a different angle on implementation.

You need to evaluate how your current offerings map into the following four types of products or services in order to take full advantage of the electronic commerce capability of the Internet. There is a relationship to the evolution of these products and services depending on whether the Internet is used as a market only, or as a delivery medium. A greater affinity applies when it is used for both (Figure 6-3).

**Hard-Goods Products.**    Hard-goods products are usually sold in retail stores or catalogs or in face-to-face selling. On the Internet, the most popular hard-goods items have been books, flowers, wine, food, clothing apparel, cars, and office supplies. If your products have to be shipped, there are a number of added-value services that you can offer to your customers:

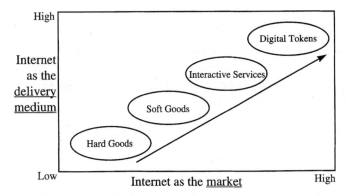

**FIGURE 6-3.** Evolution of products and services on the Internet. (*CYBERManagement Inc.*)

- *Integrated shipping information with order acknowledgment.* For businesses, integration seems to be the norm, but for consumers, it is still an added-value novelty, and certainly is a convenience. The Internet Shopping Network ties product advertisement to product information and integrates order acknowledgment with shipping status.

- *Place in-depth product and expert information on-line to make the buying decision easier.* For example, a manufacturer of drugs has an "asthma information center" that informs users about the topic for educational purposes. The expression "They have the most knowledgeable salespeople" will be replaced by "They have the most informative Web site."

- *If you offer a selection of products related to a similar purpose, you can provide "product comparison shopping" to enhance the shopping convenience.* Hewlett-Packard, IBM, Sun, and Apple have implemented parametric search capabilities that enable users to hone in on a product of choice, after narrowing their needs. The parametric search process allows buyers to converge on their needs quickly, instead of diverging with a multitude of choices.

**Soft-Goods Products.** Soft-good products such as information and other types of media-based products can be delivered instantly or regularly over the Internet. These could be in the form of published information, software, news items, publications, catalogs, videos, music, or customized design specifications. For example, Microsoft has decided to start selling certain software products electronically under a program it calls "electronic software distribution." After a six-month trial, Microsoft expects that by 1998, 10 percent of its unlicensed software revenue will come from third-party retail sales over the Internet. Microsoft intends to pass savings from electronic distribution directly to customers. The saving typically would be about 10 percent.

**Virtual Interactive Services.**    Virtual interactive services are based on new or existing services. Sometimes the service is extended as a self-service to the Internet user. Some examples: Federal Express InterNetShip software allows a user to schedule a package for pickup; Marshall Industries' on-line catalog leads to direct ordering; Silicon Graphics' or Cisco Systems' Intranets allow sales orders status updates for their business partners. Customers are usually familiar with these services, but now they are enjoying their convenience over the Internet. This area will become more and more a necessary requirement for organizations. The differentiation will be not just in offering the service, but in the depth and richness of services offered. The fields of entertainment services (such as gaming and gambling), travel, events ticketing, banking, trading services, and distance education/learning are also included in this area. The consensus is that substantial growth will come from travel, ticketing, and distance education areas, since they are expected to become major sources of revenue by the year 2000, and beyond.

*GeneraLife Extends Self-Interactive Insurance Services*

GeneraLife, a subsidiary of St. Louis-based General American Life, is enabling policyholders to go "live, on-line" to make changes in their life insurance programs. Via a direct access to personal policies, a policyholder can make policy changes to his or her name, address, or beneficiary on the Internet. When a policyholder conducts a transaction, the agent automatically is notified of the policy changes that are made.

**Digital Value Token Products.**    There are new types of digital tokens as information-based products, where the token received allows the user certain rights to access products or services in the physical marketplace.

You should continuously ask yourself: "How can we make more information-intensive products?" Ever since Nicholas Negroponte told us that bits travel better and faster than atoms, it has become increasingly necessary to begin to replace certain existing products with their information-based equivalent. The following are examples of possible usages of token-based products. These can be delivered over the Internet, and may rely on smart card technology as a storage vehicle.

- Smart telephone cards—making public telephones more convenient
- Electronic money/prepaid accounts—replacing coins and bank notes
- Ticketless travel—the card as the repository for tickets and vouchers
- Electronic access—control access to data and facilities
- Storage of security tokens—storage of security keys and access controls
- Medical records—repository of medical history and insurance information
- Single merchant incentives—cardholder storage of "points" for frequent-purchaser programs for single merchants
- Electronic wallet—repository of multiple financial, credit, debit, and merchant accounts
- TV-top terminals—key to unlocking and controlling in-home access to expanded TV facilities
- Multiple merchant incentives—cardholder storage of "points" for frequent-purchaser programs across multiple merchants
- Smart devices—control personality, operational profile, and access to the smart devices of the future

A factor that will fuel the development of information-based products is the advanced smart card that contains personal demographics and dynamic information linked to a remote database. This type of smart card will enable multiple applications, such as recently demonstrated by the ImagineCard alliance (Hewlett-Packard/Informix/Gemplus). A single card accommodated the following functions: electronic purse, conference evaluation, logical and physical access, and registration with full customer accessibility and owner-controlled authentication. This is giving rise to multiple operating systems for the smart card, such as Mondex's Multos and IBM's.

### Desired Outcome of Step 4

- Digitize old products where applicable.
- Introduce new information-based products.
- Develop a separate strategy to take advantage of smart-card products.

## STEP 5: GIVE A NEW ROLE TO YOUR HUMAN RESOURCES DEPARTMENT

Internet commerce requires a cross-functional focus, so it is important to cut through potential vertical layers within an organization. Internet commerce cannot be driven only by the technical abilities to implement information systems and handle the transactions and security requirements. Internet commerce must be totally integrated with the overall business strategy, and requires the same discipline as corporate planning.

The role of each employee may be changed with increasing penetration of electronic commerce capabilities: The role of the salesperson changes, marketing takes on a new meaning, customer support relies on how quickly an e-mail is answered, and other jobs begin to have an increasing "electronic value" component. The electronic marketplace is as important as the physical one, but internal processes must be simplified in it.

**The Role of the Human Resources Department.**   What is the role of the human resources department in the new and evolving

Internet world? In addition to providing content for the company's Intranet, three specific responsibilities have been identified.

**1.** *Establishing corporate Internet/Intranet policies.* Some organizations have no formal policies or guidelines for employee access to the Internet. Even though guidelines are usually written by a cross-functional group of employees, the initiative could be led by the personnel department with its knowledge of company policies, legal issues, and corporate communication guidelines, such as confidentiality, security, intellectual property, and other specific employment contract issues. Ideally, these policies are on the company's Intranet, with bidirectional hyperlinks to existing material.

**2.** *Acting as a companywide certification authority.* Innovative human resources departments are acting as the certification authorities for their own companies. They are responsible for issuing digital IDs to their employees, renewing them, revoking them, and managing their proper usage. For example, Hewlett-Packard has a project to provide each of its employees with a unique digital ID to allow the worker to conduct several paper-based corporate processes on-line. Employees can use their digital identity to obtain disbursement vouchers for petty cash, reimbursement of travel expenses without waiting for an expense check, and even for direct payroll disbursements. For employees working at home or on the road, a digital ID means gaining remote access to the corporate Intranet. HP plans to make its human resources department responsible for issuing and revoking the digital ID, in effect functioning as the corporate certification authority.*

**3.** *Formalizing new job descriptions.* Contrary to what is rumored about the Internet taking away traditional jobs, the Internet is in reality doing more than its fair share by returning a variety of jobs that didn't exist even six months ago. High-growth companies are barely keeping up with finding the right

*CommerceNet Research Note #97-01, Business Applications of Digital Authentication, February 1997.

talents. Formalizing the job descriptions helps in attracting the right experience and skills.

Major categories of Internet jobs include (1) creative development, (2) software development, (3) Java, (4) marketing and sales, (5) networks and security, (6) Webmasters, (7) Intranets, and (8) content management.

The Internet is no longer providing technical jobs, but it is rather spinning off entirely new types of business-related jobs and creatively oriented positions. Similar job titles have very different descriptions and expectations.

In support of Internet commerce, an increasing number of professionals are now focused on "selling" Web content, advertising, and services. As content increases, it becomes a valuable inventory that needs to be treated with the same respect as traditional products. In addition to the creation of "purely new" Internet jobs, a few others are traditional jobs that now have a new Internet angle and requirement. This indicates how the Internet is infiltrating current positions. The Internet is giving birth to strange job titles, such as Web technical guru, cyberdog engineer, Internet guru, cyberjournalist, Web spinner/Web weaver, Internet content evangelist, Java beans engineer, Web advertising traffic cop, and Internet concierge. These are all valid positions with formal job descriptions, and they exist in a variety of organizations, from start-ups to large corporations.

### Desired Outcome of Step 5

- Determine how to increase your Internet professionals in all departments, not just the technical ones.
- Develop and hire new positions for producing, selling, marketing, and supporting new content for the Internet marketplace.
- Establish Internet and electronic commerce knowledge within the HR department to allow it to proactively add value to your strategies.
- Copy organizational models and functions of companies entirely dependent on the Web for your Web-related initiatives (e.g., Yahoo!, InfoSeek, Excite, Amazon.com).

## STEP 6: EXTEND YOUR CURRENT SYSTEMS TO THE OUTSIDE

Your Web site may have been the first beachhead you built to mark your entry into cyberspace. However, with the trend toward user-centric inquiries and intermediated marketplaces, it becomes important to link your products and services with other on-line catalogs, directories, and trading communities as well as integrate back-end business to your partners and suppliers' Intranets. The Web site got you there, but it won't keep you there. In the near future, it will be theoretically possible to engage in Internet commerce without even having a visible Web site! This isn't a new version of "stealth commerce," but it is an important evolution. For example, can you "see" EDI working? Not really, but it does the job.

The information structure of Web sites must be able to be "picked up" by the several agents and other intermediaries that will be constantly crawling the Web, looking for bargains or matching needs. The XML standard (an evolution from HTML) will allow a certain standardization in the taxonomy of information, so that certain key information elements become accurately identifiable by outsiders, without a prior knowledge of the information structure.

Well before the Web, every organization had a wealth of information and services in its existing information systems. These hidden treasures must be made available to customers in the form of new value. The Web in this case is the ideal delivery platform, so it needs to become a direct extension of your current IT systems. Marshall Industries would not introduce any major feature to its Web site if the process or the information weren't linked to its inside systems. Most organizations develop the Web site as an island, and then later begin to think about how to link it to the inside. If the linkage was done the other way around, it would be much easier. So, instead of developing a new Web order-taking capability, think about extending your current order entry systems to the outside. In this manner, you would connect the rest of your order management subsystems at the same time, and provide much more to your customers.

### Desired Outcome of Step 6

- Make your Web site functionality a back end, in addition to a façade.

- Extend and link internal systems to the Web as an intended goal, not as an afterthought.

- Find internal applications that can be Web-enabled to get a quick bang.

## STEP 7: TRACK NEW COMPETITORS AND MARKET SHARES IN THE NEW DIGITAL MARKETSPACE

It used to be clear how to determine who your competition is. In the Internet marketplace, this picture is not as clear any more. Because of the volatility of old value chains, new services can be introduced by totally unexpected parties that become your competition. The Internet levels the competitive playing field by allowing these unexpected competitors to enter new or traditional markets. Once you begin to get a clearer picture as to who your competitors really are in the new digital markets, you will need to begin to track them accordingly. Future market shares will be measured in the Internet marketplace, independently from the physical marketplace.

First, you can predict who these competitors are on the basis of the likely markets that are at risk. Second, you must be able to assess the intensity of their competition in the electronic marketplace. Unfortunately, there isn't enough history to be able to base a competitive assessment solely on the activity and results in the on-line marketplace. Most electronic ventures are still being supported by the other traditional methods of commerce and trade, so the lines are not always clearly delineated.

More and more, market shares are beginning to be compared in the electronic world, separately from the physical world. Do we know who sells more personal computers or digital cameras on the Internet? Who has the largest market share among the on-line brokerage firms: e*Trade, eSchwab, eBroker, or Waterhouse? Some data are beginning to become available, even though in certain cases the Internet business is part of an existing business and can't be broken down separately.

Not only market shares are being measured in the marketplace, but also ratings for quality and usefulness of various services offered. For example, Microsoft's Investor Relations section on its Web site was rated in 1997 as the most user-friendly among large corporate organizations. There are so many other first-time surveys that probably can place your organization at an advantage—if you find the right niche to excel in, and exploit it accordingly by forcing a comparison with your competitors that will catch them off-guard.

Begin a new list immediately that includes your current competitors and their Internet strategy, other possible organizations that may enter your marketplace in the marketspace, and how you may react to it.

### Desired Outcome of Step 7

- List new entrants, the ones you haven't thought about before.
- Develop competitive strategies on the basis of the dynamics of digital markets.
- Reevaluate your business model in relation to your competition's.

## STEP 8: DEVELOP A WEB-CENTRIC MARKETING STRATEGY

Even if your current marketing strategy has taken the Web into account, you must develop a marketing strategy that clearly targets the Web as a primary marketing channel and medium to support the Internet commerce activities. This includes using the Internet as a primary medium for all marketing communications activities, such as press relations, investor relations, and advertising. A new breed of advertising and marketing agencies are repositioning their offerings to include what they call "digital marketing" or "interactive marketing." The following list of real Internet jobs indicates what is happening in this area: Internet marketing manager, business development manager/new media partners, on-line channel marketing manager, Internet product manager, Internet sales and marketing agent, Internet sales account manager, Internet business marketer.

What is the life cycle of an Internet product? Probably a lot shorter than that in the physical world. The new types of products or services designed for and marketed on the Web are different and more volatile. Strategically and tactically, Web-savvy marketing will be important for success in the digital markets.

Digital branding is also becoming an important requirement. As more and more businesses get established on the Internet, especially for consumers, promoting and raising the awareness of the digital brand becomes a priority. For each segment, the Coke, Pepsi, and 7-Up distinctions are still being defined. The URL address plays a key role with its association to the digital brand, but it doesn't have to be the only anchor to the digital universe.

### Desired Outcome of Step 8

- Develop a 100 percent Web-centric marketing program that relies on the Web as the marketing channel, taking into account the electronic distribution segmentation outlined in Chapter 5.

- After building your value with customers, work on your digital brand process.


### STEP 9: PARTICIPATE IN THE CREATION AND DEVELOPMENT OF VIRTUAL MARKETPLACES AND INTERMEDIARIES, NOW

Beyond pushing your own distribution channels in the electronic markets that you are targeting, you have to think about creating your own virtual marketplaces. You can lead the creation of new marketplace communities that later become transaction and trading communities for your products and services.

Also, by practicing early with your partners, suppliers, and distribution channels throughout the supply chain, you can learn substantial lessons that will determine how you proceed with further investments, including the differences between your business customers and consumers. By practicing in small doses, you minimize the price of learning, and your organization's readiness will get higher in time. Follow the new motto "When they come, keep building it quicker."

In the Internet marketplace, new intermediaries can change the rules of competition in totally unexpected ways. From a strategic perspective, you will need to uncover, predict, and assess the impact of new and current intermediaries on your marketplace and customers. These intermediaries could be your next competition. They may not be confined to your industry, and they could be coming from an international territory. I have provided a list of these emerging segments in Chapter 7. New intermediaries can threaten existing intermediaries or they can threaten other businesses.

By using a "next-squared" analogy, identify and target a new market that is a juxtaposition of an existing one you currently compete in. Start small, nurture the market, and watch it grow at least at the rate of growth of the Internet. Sometimes you may have to begin to cannibalize some of your own markets by being a new electronic intermediary for your products. It is better that you do it to yourself, rather than have somebody else do it to you.

If you can't become an intermediary, at least make sure that you are continuously adding digital value to your current value propositions, in order to protect them from unwanted hijacking from emerging intermediaries.

## Desired Outcome of Step 9

- Identify five new types of intermediary businesses that threaten your current model.
- Identify two new types of intermediary businesses you may be able to enter.
- Strengthen your intermediary-to-intermediary relationships.
- List three potential Internet businesses you would like to acquire and approach them to investigate it further.

- Find new partners to strengthen your new-found virtual value chain. You will begin to depend on them in the same way that you depend today on your current partners.

- Stop and review what you have learned over the last year in all your Web-related activities. Have an independent third party give you an assessment, and reassess your current objectives on the basis of your findings.

- Find a model Web-based business or organization that you admire, and learn from it.

- If your partners and suppliers seem to be more advanced than you are in implementing Web-based processes, consult with them.

The following are some examples of new market entrants that changed the rules of competition.

*Is Security First Network Bank a Bank or a Software Company?*

Security First Network Bank, the world's first Internet bank, allows customers to access checking accounts, money market accounts, and certificates of deposit, and to transfer money between accounts in real time. While most other banks are now offering Internet banking as a value-added service, SFNB holds Internet banking as a primary focus. SFNB enables anyone with Internet access to be a potential customer.

SFNB's solution provides a seamless integration between technology and banking. So is it a bank or a software technology company? The software technology underlying SFNB's business is definitely a core proprietary strength. As it competes with traditional banks in on-line services, SFNB is really competing on the strength of its software capabilities. This is an important risk factor to existing banks, which usually don't have the same business model as a nimble upstart software company. In the long term, if the user interface and interactive capabilities are the differentiating factors, a software company may have an edge over a bank. This means that banks may have to partner more closely with software companies to compete favorably in the future.

*Amazon.com versus Barnes and Noble*

As of June 1996, after about a year and a half of operation, Amazon.com claimed $3.5 million in sales. In the 12 months following, it had $56.5 million in sales. In 1996, Barnes and Noble had sales of $2.51 billion, with approximately 1000 stores. This meant an average of $2.5 million per store, slightly less than Amazon's total sales before June 1996. So, Amazon.com probably wasn't even on Barnes and Noble's radar screen. It was only in 1997 that Barnes and Noble started to take Amazon seriously. At the current sales rate, Amazon might very well be a $100 million corporation by 1998, or the equivalent of about 40 Barnes and Noble stores. Amazon's SEC's filing says that "Amazon.com intends to use technology to deliver an outstanding service offering and to achieve the significant economies inherent in the on-line store model. The company's strategy is to build strong brand recognition, customer loyalty, and supplier relationships, while creating an economic model that is superior to that of the capital and real estate intensive traditional book retailing business." Obviously, the above statement indicates radical changes in the way a business is run. Amazon has clearly based its entire business model on the Internet, whereas Barnes and Noble and other traditional bookstores venturing in the Internet have to continuously struggle with both models.

## STEP 10: INSTILL ELECTRONIC MARKETS MANAGEMENT STYLE

It is essential to move decision making from the physical to the electronic space. The Internet is a marketplace with distinct characteristics, some of which are similar to the traditional physical marketplace, and some different. Treat your decisions accordingly as you evaluate your actions for the electronic marketplace. Think of it as an entirely new territory, and give it new parameters of success and measurements. However, while doing that, do not forget about sound business management practices that generally would still apply.

Most organizations now must compete in two marketplaces: a physical (traditional) one, and the emerging electronic one, mediated by the Internet. Unless your business is entirely devoted to the Web, you will have to manage in both spaces. This poses a dilemma, since management thinking is different for each. In reality, the lines are blurring regarding how the two marketplaces interrelate.

**Desired Outcome of Step 10.** Treat decisions separately depending on the following suggested classification:

- Decisions for electronic markets that do not affect anything else (e.g., regarding the status of a given service)
- Decisions for electronic markets that affect your traditional marketplace (e.g., channel conflict)
- Decisions for traditional markets that affect electronic markets (e.g., the process for customer support delivery)
- Decisions for traditional markets that do not affect electronic markets (e.g., old products that won't make it in the electronic marketplace)

# UNCOVERING NEW OPPORTUNITIES

*...The real move to electronic commerce will demand several layers of intermediaries to form new communities to support new rules. Electronic commerce requires those changes, which will also provide companies with the greatest opportunity for profit. In cyberspace, the real power will lie with those who make the rules.*

DEBORA SPAR AND JEFFREY BUSSGANG
HBR, *May–June 1996*

In all my consulting engagements, one of the most popular questions clients ask me to work on is: "What is the right opportunity for us?" If I could answer this question for them in just a few minutes, not only would I be putting myself out of a job, but I would also be misleading them. One of the key aspects of electronic commerce is to understand how buyers and sellers interact in the new digital markets, without being influenced by preconceived notions of the physical world. After a thorough understanding of these dynamics, you can begin to map opportunities that match your current competencies and markets.

There are a number of ways to approach learning how to benefit from Internet commerce. In this chapter, we analyze and classify intermediary opportunities in several ways. The objective is an important one. It is to instill within you "inter-mediary think" and "intermediary flair," which will allow you to uncover real opportunities for your own organization.

# THE NEW INTERMEDIARIES

What is a new intermediary? In its simplest form, a new intermediary is an Internet business or a function that replaces another one carried out in the physical world. A new intermediary could also consist of a new set of services that form the basis of trade between two trading partners: a buyer and a seller. Going further, several intermediaries could be chained together, one leading to another who then leads to a buyer. Furthermore, a virtual marketplace could include several intermediaries linked together.

Deciding in which segment to find your opportunity is an important step. Please refer to the "New Internet-driven value chain" model described in Chapter 5. Also, after you go through the steps suggested as "actions to take in preparing for electronic commerce" (Chapter 6), a number of business opportunities will emerge. These will be different for each industry.

# THEORY AND BEHAVIOR OF VIRTUAL MARKETPLACES

One of the most exciting elements of participating in electronic commerce is the actual creation of virtual marketplaces as viable businesses. I have studied the behavior and characteristics of several electronic marketplace examples and have concluded with the following observations on their theory and behavior. Somehow paradoxical, somehow logical, electronic markets exhibit special characteristics. Understanding them allows you to better design your strategy for potential entry in virtual marketplaces. Let's call them principles.

## PRINCIPLE 1: ORGANIZATION OF INFORMATION LEADS TO NEW MARKET POWER

There are three entities that can be organized: buyers, sellers, and the marketplace between them. This isn't a new theory, since history serves to prove it, but it is amplified with the Internet. In business-to-business markets, for example, the procurement function consists of well-organized buyers that have purchasing power over sellers. Organized buying is also known to have worked for the U.S. government, which holds much power with its suppliers. Organized labor is known to have worked for workers, as their rights and demands are often acted on thanks to their collective bargaining power. The Nasdaq is an effective marketplace that has organized buyers, sellers, and processes that govern the relationship between all of them. On the Internet, we are awaiting organized markets that give equal powers to buyers and equal opportunities to sellers.

Mark Gross, director of new media strategies at Cowles Media Company, is in charge of leading his company to take advantage of emerging digital markets. Says Gross:

> To compete in the new economy, we can play on the seller/supply side, create market makers, or play on the buyer side. Supply-oriented players add value by organizing inventory, informing sellers, reducing their risk, etc. Demand-oriented players organize buyers, empower them with information, and reduce their risk. Market makers are neutral facilitators that provide infrastructure and rules for efficient transactions. At issue is the fight for power. In today's consumer markets, sellers often have more power. The real barrier to consumer power is organization. New intermediaries will create value by shifting power, as value sellers and their agents square off against informed buyers and their agents.

The above illustrates the choices a company must make. Let us investigate further how to organize the three different choices.

**Organizing Sellers.**    Organized sellers are what we are mostly seeing today. First-generation Internet malls did a poor job at organizing sellers, but only a good one at linking them. Second-generation malls are organizing sellers or sellers' products and services in ways that really facilitate buyers' tasks. Examples include CUC International's NetMarket and U.Vision's Computer ESP. Both have a very large virtual inventory of products and services which are easily found by buyers. They have done a great job at organizing sellers and their inventories.

**Organizing Buyers.**    It can be argued that agents will organize buyers. This is what the early models indicate. Large virtual retailers such as Computer ESP and Amazon.com offer a personal agent capability which returns value to buyers. Computer ESP allows you to specify a price target for a given product, and Amazon notifies you of new publications in your areas of interest. Both examples are closed organization models, but they are valid, because of the vast array of choices they offer to buyers. In another, more open agent model, the agent looks at various Web sites regardless of a prearranged organization. Examples of companies that are providing these emerging capabilities include NetBot (Jango product), Identify, and Agentics.

**Organizing the Market.**    In market organizing, the business consists of taking full ownership for running and operating a market-maker type of marketplace, where sellers and organized, buyers are organized, and the way they interact with each other is also organized. This is like the stock market model. The system is so tight that it is not possible to really circumvent it if you'd like to buy or sell. This approach offers benefits for the buyers (savings in time and money, reduction in risk) and for the sellers (qualified buyers, incremental business), as well as providing new linkages in services not possible before. You can think of them as features you would need in a market-maker marketplace.

**Anatomy of a Market-Maker Factory.**    Just as a factory is in charge of production, the market maker's primary function is to create digital value, a production task. This is somehow an invisible task, but the resulting output is the visible part. What goes in is information about buyers and their needs, preferences, criteria, and profile, in addition to information about sellers and their inventories, products, services, terms, and conditions (Figure 7-1). What comes out are various matching tickets, and new aggregate services for buyers and sellers. This makes for an efficient market operation. The following are examples of market-maker functions that could be performed by the marketplace manager:

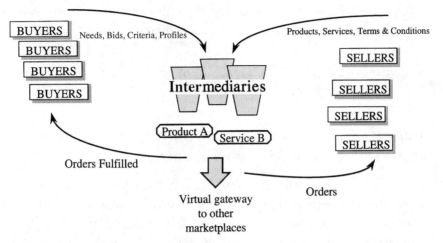

**FIGURE 7-1.** The dynamics of a virtual marketplace and its various players. (*CYBERManagement Inc.*)

- *Match making.*  Matches buyers' needs with products and services from sellers, without a priori knowledge of either one.

- *Aggregation of services.*  Combines several existing services to create a new service or category that didn't exist before.

- *Aggregation of needs.*  Combines several existing needs into a new category of needs that didn't exist before.

- *Bid/ask engine.*  Creates a demand/supply floating pricing system in which buyers and sellers bid and or ask for prices, like a Nasdaq trading system.

- *Hidden inventory.*  Takes orders for a nonexistent category of services. Sources the services after enough demand is created for it.

- *Notification service.*  Tells you when the service becomes available, or when it becomes cheaper, or when it goes on sale in your neighborhood.

- *Smart needs adviser.*  "If you want it at this price, you have to wait until September, or if you want this service, you may want to consider also this other one."

- *Negotiation.*  Price, quantity, or features are negotiated according to a set of parameters.

- *Upsell.*   Suggests an additional product or service, so that if you buy both, you get a combined discount or an additional benefit.
- *Consultative adviser.*   "Here's a tip on this new service you're about to purchase."

## PRINCIPLE 2: THE UNCERTAINTY OF A TRANSACTION JOURNEY LEADS TO MARKET EFFICIENCY

In the physical world, the path taken by a product or service from the moment it leaves the seller until it reaches the buyer is usually well known. For example, wholesaler A will distribute to distributor B who then goes to retailer C, and this is where buyers go. In a virtual marketplace configuration, the presence of intermediaries between buyers and sellers has the effect of dynamically configuring a transaction journey, depending on specific parameters or criteria at the time of the transaction. When a buying request is initiated by an agent, the agent will match the seller with the right set of intermediaries that are suitable for the buyer. This all happens in the background, efficiently and invisibly in most cases. The buyer makes the final decision regarding whom to buy from. The uncertainty of the transaction journey means that intermediaries have to tune their strategies to the most favorable market requirements that may be imposed on them, in order to maximize buyer's traffic, and the chances of them being chosen (Figure 7-2).

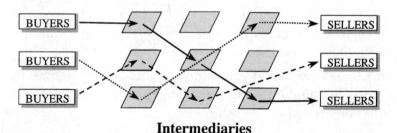

**Intermediaries**

FIGURE 7-2.   The unpredictable journey of a transaction in the new value chain. (*CYBERManagement Inc.*)

At Computer ESP, for example, a given query returns a choice of available retailers where a product can be bought. Similarly, a Jango query will likely return a choice of places where a book can be purchased. These two examples illustrate a case where there is only one type of intermediary to choose from (the retailer), but the action was initiated by another intermediary (Computer ESP or a Jango query). In the future, you can expect that several layers of intermediaries could be placed in the middle, appearing only when they are needed.

## Principle 3: The Order-of-Magnitude Factor Is the Paradigm Shifter

Anybody interacting with the Web to conduct business or buy something has to have a compelling and sustainable reason for doing it. A common trigger factor that entices the first-time electronic user to try the service is the order-of-magnitude factor. Here are some examples.

On day 1 of Amazon.com's opening in 1995, it had 1 million titles in its virtual inventory. Given that the largest physical inventory of a retail bookstore was 175,000 titles at the most, Amazon had already captured our attention with the order-of-magnitude factor.

ConsumersEdge's bicycle section allows a user to sift through 2500 various models on the basis of a variety of parameters, such as type, price, manufacturer, and characteristics. Within two or three minutes, anybody will arrive at just a handful of available choices that match the needs criteria. Compare this with an actual process where you would have to go through several magazines or Web sites or telephone calls to stores, before being able to reasonably narrow down your range of possibilities.

## Principle 4: Markets Will Do Business with Other Markets

Given that virtual markets are developing on top of existing markets, a provision has to be made for market services to be available to each other. This market-to-market connection can be multiplied almost to the *n*th degree, to culminate with the seamless creation of a multitude of open markets that expand the digital universe. The following illustrates a market-to-market cooperative alliance between two existing businesses. In the future, markets will communicate with other markets, interactively and spontaneously by utilizing various filter techniques.

### e-XPENSE Meets e-Travel

Travel and expenses: two words that go hand in hand. One leads to another. e-XPENSE and e-Travel are two businesses that are combining their services to leverage the integration level that is so appealing to their customers. e-XPENSE (a service of ADP) is an automated expense-report-processing administration system that includes expense report creation and submission, approval, auditing, reimbursement, financial systems posting, and receipt auditing and archiving. e-Travel is a multitiered application that allows business travelers or administrators to plan, authorize, and book their own airline, hotel and rental car reservations from their network PCs or remote laptops in a real-time travel booking environment. The system is designed to administer a corporation's travel policy, including vendor preferences, negotiated fare discounts, and pre-trip authorizations. It is available with both Windows and Internet browser traveler reservations modules and is compatible with all three major U.S. reservations systems—Apollo, Sabre, and Worldspan. The e-XPENSE and e-Travel agreement will provide an integrated and completely automated travel and expense management system that is not directly tied to a particular travel reservations system.

### Greeting Card Looking for Photo

Add-a-Photo™ is a new service that integrates American Greetings' electronic e-mail cards service with PhotoNet's photo uploading capabilities. The service allows users to seamlessly append a photo that was just developed to personalize a greeting card. This example shows how a part from one intermediary business complements another part from a second intermediary business to form a new service.

## A SAMPLE LIST OF INTERMEDIARIES

Table 7-1 illustrates some categories in which intermediary classes are beginning to emerge. For some of them, the raison

TABLE 7-1. A Sample of New versus Old Intermediaries

| TYPE OF NEW INTERMEDIARY | PRIME EXAMPLES | OLD INTERMEDIARY IT IS REPLACING |
|---|---|---|
| Electronic auctions | ONSALE<br>Internet Liquidators<br>First Auction | Catalogs, in-person auctions |
| On-line software delivery | CyberSource<br>Megasoft<br>Portland Software<br>Software.net<br>Release Software Corp. | Retail stores, software duplication services |
| On-line support and service | TuneUp.com<br>Connected Corp.<br>CyberMedia | In-person support |
| Outsourced professional services | The Employease Network<br>e-XPENSE | In-house departments |
| Multimedia content delivery | PhotoDisc, Inc.<br>SonicNet<br>PhotoNet<br>Build-a-Card<br>ENEN<br>American Greetings | Specialized stores and catalogs, TV, theater, video stores |
| Financial transaction brokers | WIT Capital, E*Trade<br>e.Schwab online<br>DirectIPO<br>DCT-On-line | Financial brokers and underwriters, in-person outlets or banks |
| Marketplace directories | Gamelan Direct<br>InfoSpace<br>BigYellow<br>Inquiry.com | Paper catalogs and directories |

*(Continued)*

TABLE 7-1. A Sample of New versus Old Intermediaries (*Continued*)

| TYPE OF NEW INTERMEDIARY | PRIME EXAMPLES | OLD INTERMEDIARY IT IS REPLACING |
|---|---|---|
| Products and services brokers | PartsNet, FastParts<br>Travelocity, PCTravel<br>CouponNet<br>CompareNet<br>ConsumersEdge | Catalogs, in-person shopping, travel agents |
| Fulfillment and logistics support | FedEx, UPS<br>Skyway<br>PackageNet<br>Milestone | Phone-in for the information, traditional logistics |
| VAN-less EDI and procurement services | GE TradeWeb<br>WWShipNet<br>Chase/Shamrock<br>B. of America/L.<br>Livermore National Labs | VANs, EDI services |
| Virtual trading communities | GE's InterBusiness Partner<br>Australia's TRADE'ex<br>Unibex<br>WOMEX<br>AIMSNet<br>InterTrade | EDI, trade shows, catalogs, years of being in the business |
| Marketplace aggregators | ComputerESP<br>netMarket | Individual stores, catalogs |

TABLE 7-1. A Sample of New versus Old Intermediaries
(*Continued*)

| TYPE OF NEW INTERMEDIARY | PRIME EXAMPLES | OLD INTERMEDIARY IT IS REPLACING |
|---|---|---|
| Digital rights management authorities | NetDox<br>SOFTBANK Net Solutions<br>Certco | No direct equivalent |
| Customer profiles | CyberGold<br>Firefly<br>NetStakes | Direct marketing profiles |

SOURCE: CYBERManagement Inc.

d'être is clear, but for others, the lines of delineation may appear to be blurring. This is normal. The classification described here may have been the overriding entry point for the chosen business. This list will help spark your imagination regarding where you may see opportunities for your organization. Try to extrapolate into the future, and ask yourself what would happen if entire industries and models were based on these early cases.

## CHECKLIST FOR NEW INTERMEDIARIES

The following 10 criteria can serve as a checklist for assessing the strength of the intermediary venture you may be thinking about. You can rate your strategy against each one of them to assess the strength of your idea. The more items you comply with, the better positioned you may be.

1. There is a high concentration of information not available elsewhere. Information is organized in ways not available before, with quick and efficient access to it.

2. The Internet is the delivery vehicle, in addition to the market medium.

3. The intermediary has the ability to complete the transaction, not just start it.

4. A critical mass or captive audience is key to their success.

5. There is no apparent immediate competition. If there is competition, it is from another new Internet business. Old competition from the physical world doesn't count.

6. Three types of information are offered to brokers:

   - Competitive (across competing products or companies)
   - Complementary (this is a noncompetitive case, where the seller provides choices within its own products)
   - Decision-support based (the information provided is used to make decisions, not to buy)

7. A person-to-person interaction is eliminated.

8. Entering other new markets by juxtaposition of services becomes easy.

9. Success depends on several virtual partnerships. The intermediary ties them together and goes to market.

10. Costs could be an order of magnitude lower than those of the traditional method, with added convenience.

## A CASE OF A "MULTIBROKER"

What is both an information broker and an electronic clearinghouse, competes with nobody, attracts its competitors as customers, empowers the consumer, has the potential to capture a transaction fee from an annual market worth approximately $600 billion per year, and has an upsell market of billions of dollars? The following case answers these questions.

*Online Mortgage Explorer: The Perfect Intermediary?*

The Online Mortgage Explorer (OME), exclusively operated and marketed in North America by Cebra Inc., allows consumers to shop, qualify, and apply for a mortgage from a choice of financial institutions. From a single point of entry, users work with a qualification form (on their PC). This process tells them which financial institutions will accept their application. Once they decide which ones to pursue, the mortgage application is sent directly to the lending institutions who follow up directly with the borrowers. This scenario is attractive to them, as it resembles a giant lead referral vehicle. The lending institutions find qualified borrowers and save on the costs associated with a rejected application.

What seems so simple on the outside has enormous strategic implications for the changing roles and value of almost every player in the old value chain. Here are the multiple features of this type of service.

- *Information broker.* Up-to-date information on the various rates and terms are available during the prequalification stage.

- *Clearinghouse.* A multitude of choices is presented to consumers. The OME directs them to the lending institution.

- *No competition.* There is no perceived competition of its kind, yet.

- *Attracting competition as customers.* This approach is friendly to all lending institutions, since they have nothing to lose. Actually, Cebra Inc. (a wholly owned subsidiary of Bank of Montreal) has been able to enlist other competing Canadian financial institutions, such as CIBC and The Mutual Group.

- *Empowering the consumer.* Consumers can perform comparison shopping and review options presented by financial institutions. Consumers are empowered almost to "bid out" their requests, and come forward only when they are comfortable or ready to do so.

- *Enormous potential market.* The first-time residential mortgage market in North America has been estimated at more than $600 billion. If OME captures a fraction of it, with a 0.2 percent transaction fee, revenues can be enormous.

- *Upsell potential.* Lending institutions could potentially cross-sell other services, such car loans and retirement plans, using the same qualifying and personal data, but at the consumer's choice.

# NEW INTERMEDIARIES EXAMPLES

## ELECTRONIC AUCTIONS

ONSALE re-creates in electronic form bidding at an auction, where prices and availability change in response to customers' actions. By focusing on a limited quantity of goods, and offering them in a series of fast-action sales formats where prices and availability vary instantly in response to demand, ONSALE creates an entertaining retail experience. ONSALE searches out bargains on refurbished and closeout goods, and brings these deals to the on-line community. Orders placed through ONSALE are transmitted to the participating merchants, who process the orders and collect the payments. On average, ONSALE offers about 500 different items at any given time, selling from one to several hundred of each item with prices that generally range from $25 to $1500 each. Customers can bid 24 hours a day, 7 days a week.

Internet Liquidators is a "Dutch" auction version. It offers an auction format in which the price actually goes down. In a limited-time reverse auction you have the freedom to make your bid at the lowest price you wish. On-screen counters keep you informed as to declining price.

## ON-LINE SOFTWARE DELIVERY

The on-line software delivery industry is expected to grow exponentially, and account for a large percentage of the $150 billion worldwide software market by the year 2000. The intermediary business in charge of the software distribution becomes like a worldwide distribution channel for software publishers. Thanks to development in secure electronic packaging of software, users receive instantaneous gratification when they order products over the Internet. This industry's process consists of companies specializing in the electronic packaging/encryption of the software, and of the software distribution itself.

Software.net is delivering electronically over the Internet $50 million worth of Microsoft software products to key U.S.

defense agencies. As a result, the federal government is able to avoid over $30 million in packaging, shipping, installation, and maintenance costs.

Release Software Corporation's SalesAgent technology creates time-restricted (e.g., 15 days) or feature-restricted (e.g., no print capability) try-before-you-buy software. It is becoming a popular first step for several users.

## ON-LINE SUPPORT AND SERVICE

Remote on-line support seems to be a natural for the millions of worldwide PC users. From software upgrades or backups to virus checkups, vendors can increase customer satisfaction over distance, and at the same time decrease the long-term support costs for users.

TuneUp.com offers a complete computer service center via the Internet. It automatically provides updates to PC and peripherals users, a preventive maintenance service, parts upgrades, and a data backup service to store critical information files securely.

Connected Corporation has a suite of automated on-line PC support services which include data backups, disaster recovery, virus protection, and device driver or applications updating.

CyberMedia supplies automated service and support technology for PC users. It specializes in a new category of self-help software, including automatic delivery of fixes and updates, that allows users to solve software and hardware problems.

## OUTSOURCED PROFESSIONAL SERVICES

The Employease Network was one of the first companies to bring employee benefits administration to the employer's desktop, via the Internet. It addresses the costs involved with most human resource software packages through its Benefits Management Network (BMN), which simplifies core administrative functions. BMN's Web-based technologies provide electronic connections to insurance carriers and to employees that further streamline record keeping, billing, enrollment, and eligibility checking. It also provides employers with an intuitive and customized application for administering employee and benefits plan information. The BMN connects all members of the benefits commerce cycle (employees, employers, brokers, and insurance carriers).

## MULTIMEDIA CONTENT DELIVERY

PhotoDisc publishes high-quality images both on-line and on CD-ROM for graphic designers, advertising agencies, desktop publishers, and other communications professionals and enthusiasts—all royalty free. Now it is allowing users to search for and download images on-line.

SonicNet produces live concerts and full-length albums presented live on the Internet. PhotoNet automatically transfers photos developed at your retail store to the Internet. Build-a-Card and American Greetings allow you to design and send e-mail personalized greeting cards. ENEN broadcasts NetSeminars™ focused on the education, entertainment, and news markets.

## FINANCIAL TRANSACTION BROKERS

Offering on-line direct trading capabilities over the Internet is an area of services that has had an early start. This market segment therefore includes a multitude of players—E*Trade, e.Schwab, Waterhouse, and E-Broker, just to name a few. New financial services being added include investment banking and Internet venture capital raising (WIT Capital, DirectIPO). Another innovation involves the direct selling and buying of securities between companies and their shareholders, bypassing the stock exchange system.

The DCT-On-Line Trading System allows investors worldwide to buy or sell securities among themselves in participating companies directly on the Internet—commission free. The DCT-On-Line Trading System automatically matches orders and sends automated e-mail confirmations to the buyer, seller, and transfer agent.

WitCapital Corporation is an investment bank dedicated to arranging the public offering of securities through the Web. In each public offering arranged by the company, the issuer's shares are sold directly to the public through the posting on the company's Web site of a prospectus as well as additional audio and video promotional material. By eliminating layers of intermediaries as well as by printing and distributing prospectuses by post and courier, WitCapital expects to offer issuers access to capital at a lower cost, without having to use traditional brokers or pay commissions.

## MARKETPLACE CONCENTRATORS

Gamelan Direct is an on-line marketplace for the Java community. Gamelan Direct's mission is to provide an open marketplace where both large and small developers can buy and sell Java software and other related products safely on-line. Gamelan Direct is pioneering the sale of applets over the Net with a number of new business models including leads referral, on-line delivery, complete transactions, software authentication, locking, and rights management technologies. The majority of content in Gamelan is created by its users, and this model has been very successful. Gamelan is the largest archive of reviewed links to Java information and Java examples in the world. This means that users (mostly developers) have instant access to almost everything they need related to Java and applets. Users are also able to announce their own programs to other developers via the site. Advertisers have also benefited from having a focused venue for reaching the Java developer market. Merchants benefit from being able to do on-line transactions via the site without having to set up and manage their own transaction systems.

## PRODUCTS AND SERVICES BROKERS

PartsNet is an Internet-based parts information service that allows engineers and designers to search parts suppliers' product information databases for electronic, electromechanical, and mechanical parts using any combination of user-supplied parts names, parts numbers, or technical specifications. The parts data come directly from the suppliers' databases, ensuring that the user sees only the most accurate and up-to-date parts information. In addition to the technical specifications and pricing information displayed by PartsNet in response to a query, the user may retrieve product data sheets on selected parts in various electronic formats. The PartsNet product family is a network information broker (NIB) system that provides "information about information." This creates a virtual information network from many dissimilar databases across many different companies.

The FastParts Trading Exchange is like the Nasdaq of parts. It provide the electronics industry with a market-driven trading exchange for fast and anonymous buying and selling of brand-new semiconductors and other electronic components. FastParts is a neutral transaction facilitator. It provides a trading venue in which buyers and sellers of electronic components can directly negotiate and trade in a secure, real-time on-line environment. FastParts provides the trading facility and coordinates all trade fulfillment activities, from collecting funds to shipping parts to ensuring buyer and seller anonymity, but never takes a position in any trade. Its revenues come from a small percentage of each completed transaction shared between the buyer and the seller. FastParts is solely a "match maker" between subscribers to form trade transactions. While FastParts is directly involved in physically transferring component parts, it never stocks, owns, or takes title to any parts. It is a facility to the electronics industry as Nasdaq is a facility to the securities industry.

## VAN-LESS EDI

The Chase Manhattan Bank is exchanging EDI payment instructions with Diamond Shamrock, a $4 billion petroleum products retailer, over the Internet. Chase and Diamond Shamrock were able to exploit their existing EDI application configuration, including all the integration to business applications by using Premenos's Templar to launch Internet EDI. No additional investment or reconfiguration was required to migrate the transmissions to the Internet. Chase plans to roll out Internet EDI to its cash management client base as part of its Treasury management services. It is also developing Internet versions of letters of credit, remittance advices, and international payments systems. As a result of this implementation, Diamond Shamrock estimates that Internet EDI could eventually cut costs in the company's accounts payable department up to 75 percent. Using Internet EDI enabled by Templar software, Chase and Diamond Shamrock disintermediate the value-added networks that typically facilitate these electronic transfers.

## VIRTUAL TRADING COMMUNITIES

GE's Trading Process Network Post (TPNPost) is a secure on-line commerce network linking suppliers and buyers, an electronic channel for distributing information around the world, and a suite of tools for conducting interactive negotiations. TPNPost employs a private-offer negotiation style, which is similar to a sealed-bid process. With TPNPost, organizations can locate and bid on major business opportunities worldwide in a private Internet environment.

TRADE'ex Electronic Commerce Systems, Inc. (TRADE'ex) creates on-line marketplaces via the Internet by offering a wide variety of software products that enable businesses to organize multiple buyers and sellers in industry-specific markets. The TRADE'ex Market Maker™ connects an unlimited number of buyers with multiple sellers of any given product in the live marketplace. Multiple buyers and sellers trade and negotiate interactively in their marketplace. They can quickly find a product, compare the price and availability among several, and then place an order on-line. This participative business model and associated information services allow companies, associations, and governments to have access to trade and market services and to obtain commercial efficiency. A partnership with the Australian Chamber of Manufacturers brought 1500 firms from various industries to roll out "live" buying and selling via the TRADE'ex Market Maker and the Internet.

WOMEX has implemented a new on-line global trading service that essentially is an on-line community linking buyers and sellers of general merchandise on an Intranet. The system includes a Product Database, a state-of-the-art Communications Network, a Commerce Information Database, and a focused, comprehensive News Section. Subscribers include many of the top chain drugstores in the world and the largest retailers in the United States, Europe, and South Africa, such as Kmart, Toys 'R' Us, IKEA, Dollar General, Eckerd, and Long's Drugs. WOMEX's services make it possible for exporters to market and importers to source on a global basis, and to communicate directly with each other, with no third-party intermediary. Retailers can compare products in more than 135 countries and discuss needs with manufacturers 24 hours a day. Time, distance, location, and communication are no longer hurdles to doing business.

Unibex is a secure, business-to-business electronic commerce service, designed for businesses of all sizes, giving them the ability to research new markets, locate and qualify trading partners, manage their own interactive home pages, and establish secure, virtual private Intranets linking suppliers, distributors, and customers. The service is accessible primarily through the Internet's World Wide Web but can also be reached through private networks or electronic mail, permitting unlimited availability to virtually every business in the world.

## DIGITAL RIGHTS INTERMEDIARIES

NetDox is exploiting the lack of certificate authorities' standards in interoperability. With the existence of multiple CAs, there is a risk of the multiplicity of handling information between incompatible CAs. The NetDox service is a general-purpose Internet messaging solution that offers secure, global, end-to-end document delivery with comprehensive verification and authentication services provided by a commercially trusted third party. Messages go through a central hub which authenticates, records, and "digitally notarizes" every message sent, without compromising the privacy of those messages, using a pay-per-use system similar to existing overnight delivery services. NetDox also acts as a clearinghouse for digital certificates, or digital IDs. This allows holders of digital certificates issued by different certification authorities, public or private, to exchange secure documents without holding the "root keys" from each certificate authority—thereby enabling ubiquitous, secure, and easy-to-use message delivery.

## CUSTOMER INFORMATION INTERMEDIARIES

CyberGold, Inc. offers cash rewards to people who respond to Web ads and promotions. The rewards are paid in "CyberGold" tokens that can be transferred to a member's real-money checking account, donated to nonprofits, or even spent on-line. CyberGold advertisers offer incentives ranging from 50 cents to several dollars for such activities as visiting Web sites, taking surveys, filling out application and registration forms, downloading software, and making purchases. Anticipating a user's mind, CyberGold also matches ads and other on-line information to people's personal interests and demographics. A trial posted on Time Warner's Pathfinder Network indicated that a CyberGold paying banner outperformed others for the same product fourfold.

# BEYOND INTERMEDIARIES: REAL VIRTUAL MARKETPLACES

Virtual marketplaces rely on an array of intermediary services to organize buyers, sellers, or entire marketplaces. They rely on their suppliers' relationships to manage a large virtual inventory, and depend on the Web to communicate and update their products and services to clients faster than their competition can. They could also rely on other subintermediaries in the process of delivering an end-to-end service to their customers. These include large virtual superstores, such as Amazon.com, NetMarket, and Computer ESP, and "virtually" integrated organizations, such as Monorail and Milestone.

## INTERMEDIARIES ON TOP OF OTHER INTERMEDIARIES

Disintermediating other electronic intermediaries is one way to gain the upper hand in developing a new virtual marketplace. Because of the fragmentation of the digital value chain into a series of several components, it is possible for intermediaries to seize one of these components and insert themselves between buyers and sellers. They may overlay new services on top of existing ones or aggregate existing services to create a metaservice that is of greater value than ones it replaced.

Let's take the fulfillment industry. Today, if you want to send a package or track one, you have to go to the respective shipping company's Web site individually and use its own proprietary software technology. But why should it be like that? Why not a fictitious universal intermediary that would interface on your behalf with the shipping company being used? If you wish to track a package, for example, a standard interface would route the request directly to the appropriate tracking system. If you want to ship a package, it would "bid" on your behalf and give you the best possible choice to meet your requirements. This service may not be particularly appealing to large organizations, which usually have a single carrier of choice that gives them a deep enough discount on the basis of their volume. Thus they need not shop around for better prices, since they are really locked in. However, for small to medium-size companies that do not have the luxury of obtaining deep discounts, this service seems to offer an ideal fit. By dealing with one entity instead of several shipping companies, small to medium-size enterprises could pool their purchasing power and therefore obtain better discounts and a variety of new service options. Figure 7-3 illustrates this fictitious scenario.

*Milestone Systems: Beware of the Aggregator!*

Milestone Systems, Inc. is targeting the express delivery market segment by developing a new category of services that depend on a clever aggregation of heterogeneous shipping options, in addition to adding unique features not available before. The Click & Send™ service allows organizations to submit their shipping orders to Milestone's Web site. Click & Send does the rest. By avoiding multiple phone calls to "shop

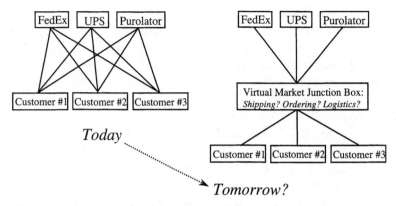

**FIGURE 7-3.** A fictitious scenario for building a new business on top of existing services. (*CYBERManagement Inc.*)

around," users save valuable time. And by ensuring a thorough search of all possibilities, users can save money. Click & Send will present a variety of options for delivery times, costs, and route choices from several couriers, including DHL, U.S. Postal Service, and Airborne. Says Chris Reynolds, president and CEO of Milestone Systems, Inc.: "When we tested our service with clients, we found out that they seldom select the least expensive vendor. Rather, they look at all other variables combined, such as convenience, value added, traceability, shipping options, etc. These benefits outweigh price only."

Milestone has even added a number of services not possible before. For example, it will print plain-paper airbills on a laser printer, integrate with existing address book or contact manager software to avoid retyping addresses, include up-to-date details on carrier rates, zip codes, and customs regulations, and present an on-line detailed transaction history for all shipping activity. The system even memorizes delivery transactions you make regularly by letting you preset the package type and delivery method for specific recipients. So, Milestone is more than just a service. It almost allows a company to outsource its shipping function, with any employee in the company able to invoke the service.

## VIRTUAL EVERYTHING, INC.: FOUR EXAMPLES

This section highlights four examples of virtual corporations that depend on the Internet to develop and maintain virtual relationships, partnerships, and chains of services.

*"Have Boat and Catalog, Will Take Your Order"*

Eric Levert, owner-manager of Sport Warehouse in Montreal, Canada, told me the following, with a grin on his face: "In a perfect world, I would live on a 54-foot catamaran going from port to port, gathering pictures, descriptions, and prices of sports products, which I would place on the Internet as a catalog. I would allow anybody to browse the complete catalog for free; however, if people wished to see our low prices, I would charge them $5. If they wished to see our wholesale prices, I would charge them $100, and that would give them a feel for the suggested retail prices in their own regions. Then I would take credit card orders over the Internet, and fulfill them by asking suppliers to ship directly to customers." Eric's vision is simplistic in some ways, but may become practical with the Internet. Sport Warehouse operates large warehouse-style retail stores, specializing in new and used ski, snowboard, and bike equipment, with over 12,000 articles in stock. The business also consists of keeping an inventory of hard-to-find sports accessories. One of its key strength lies in the relationships it has built with the right suppliers and manufacturers. Therefore Eric's idea of spinning off the business entirely to the virtual space, and leveraging the linkages it has in sourcing the right product for a given customer.

*"You Order It, You'll Touch It First"*

Monorail specializes in the space-saving, easy-to-use, $1000-to-$1500 PCs. It relies on FedEx's logistics, ordering, and distribution systems to operate a virtual manufacturing-to-order operation. Distributors and resellers place their orders directly with FedEx, and automatically see their inventory updated in record time. Orders are electronically relayed to Monorail, which then relays them to one of several contract manufacturers where the product is assembled, tested, packed, and shipped via FedEx. In most cases this process, from initial order to the reseller's door, can be completed in two business days. A reseller ordering Monorail products may never "touch" the product. Monorail and FedEx are allowing this process to take place over the Internet, from order placement to order tracking and receipt confirmation. Monorail has even partnered with a call service center to handle all product information, product support, and product upgrade telephone calls. Finally, SunTrust Bank acts as Monorail's credit department, collections department, and accounts receivable department. Almost all these outsourced functions are billed to Monorail on a per-unit cost, so it can scale its business to ultrahigh volumes in a very short period of time.

### "Sitting Pretty" on Top of 1 Million Prices

U.vision's Computer ESP is a mega virtual store grouping over 1 million prices from major computer cyberstores in the United States and Canada, with an average of over 100,000 price updates a day. It has linked up electronically to hundreds of electronic storefronts, and allows users to bargain-hunt from 80,000 computer products. By seamlessly indexing and cross-linking prices, products, vendors, and cyberstores, Computer ESP allows shoppers to find the best up-to-date prices available from a choice of electronic stores. So, it really is an aggregator of information, sitting on top of existing cyberstores, but adding considerable value by virtue of the integration process. Other interesting features of Computer ESP include a price alert that sends you a friendly e-mail when the product has reached your specified price trigger, a product description agent that automatically searches 84 databases for computer product and lowest pricing information, and multiparameter simultaneous searching and comparison shopping.

### Microsoft: Superintermediary?

If its competitors are on-line intermediaries, why wouldn't Microsoft be? To get a feel for Microsoft's direction into intermediary services, we need to look at the organization of the Microsoft Network (MSN). MSN's home page features some prominent choices which are really divided into two categories: communities of interest and communities of transaction. While communities of interest bring in advertising fees, the communities of transaction bring advertising, subscription fees, transaction fees, and advertising revenue. Table 7-2 summarizes the situation.

Each of the Web businesses in Table 7-2 has its own brand identity in addition to being symbiotically linked through MSN's high-traffic area. Marshall Industries runs 11 different Web sites from its main Web roof, but each site could also stand on its own with its own brand identity. The lesson here is that if you run a medium-size to large organization, it is OK to split the various business segments you are competing in, and focus them with their own identities toward the targeted community you are aiming at. You can always link them in ways that leverage your corporate identity, but you will probably bring in more traffic from each of the different businesses on their own.

## Table 7-2. Microsoft's Superintermediary Strategy

| Business | Type of Community | Revenues | Competition |
|---|---|---|---|
| Cinemania | | | MovieLink |
| | | | Cinema Sites |
| Internet Gaming Zone | | | The Software Zone |
| | | | Ultima Online |
| Encarta | • Free communities of interest | • Advertising | Britannica CD |
| | | | World Book |
| | | | Compton's |
| | | | Grolier's |
| Computing on MSN | | | ZD-Net |
| | | | Cnet |
| Sidewalk | | | The CityNet |
| | | | City.net |
| Expedia | | | Travelocity |
| | | | Preview |
| | | | Internet Travel Network |
| CarPoint | | • Transaction fee | Auto By Tel |
| | | | AutoMall USA |
| Microsoft Investor | • Communities of transaction | • Sale of goods and services | E*Trade |
| | | | e.Schwab |
| Music Central | | • Monthly fee | CD Now |
| Microsoft Plaza | | • Advertising | NetMarket |
| | | | The Internet Mall |
| Boardwalk (code name for Real Estate Venture) | | | Realtor.com |
| | | | HomeShark |
| | | | E.Loan |

source: CYBERManagement Inc.

# THE WIRED CONSUMER

*One of the profound consequences of the ongoing information revolution is its influence on how economic value is created and extracted.*

J. F. RAYPORT AND J. J. SVIOKLA

HBR, *November–December 1994*

If consumers are to use the Internet pervasively, it must be simple for them. New features and capabilities, especially secure functionality, should be made as transparent and easy to use as possible. For example, most consumers do not understand anything about cryptography and never will. However, in reality, a certain amount of education has to take place, since there will be a new way of transacting electronically.

Today a consumer user or business user needs to convert a standard PC to an Internet-enabled device in order to begin the journey into the Internet. Most PC manufacturers are now including browsers and Internet accounts as part of a bundled service. However, in the future, more will be required. Interaction will happen with a variety of new Internet-ready devices. Imagine the next wave of commerce-enabled PCs coming with an electronic wallet, a smart card interface, a cable or high-speed modem, a supercharged browser including all available plug-ins and channels, and VRML front-end and smart agent software. In addition, all PC applications and documents will become activated with hot links to the Internet. The future PC will literally come "alive" and "transaction-ready," out of the box. Or it may be a simple networked PC or an Internet appliance.

# WHY FIRST-GENERATION CONSUMER MALLS FAILED

Hindsight is powerful. And history repeats itself. Imagine yourself in a real mall, trying to find out where to buy a certain item. After scratching your head for a few seconds, you decide to face the mall's directory display. Since the listings are usually categorized by store name, you have to take a shot at guessing which store might carry the item you are looking for. If you are lucky, you find it in a few seconds, and you then figure out where you are in relation to the map, and where the store is. You head there, after getting lost once, and you find the store you were looking for. But when you ask the salesperson about the product, it is no longer in stock. This time, you decide to head to the information booth to talk to a real person. When you get there, there is no attendant. You decide to go back to the directory display, and choose three other possible stores, each turning out to be in a separate direction. You plot the best route to take, which you end up deviating from anyway. Finally, at the third store you find what you were looking for. The whole process excluding driving time took you half an hour to an hour, depending on how much you got distracted between stores. Nonetheless, this is part of a typical Saturday shopping experience of many North American consumers.

First-generation Internet malls that have failed forced a similar experience on users, including the inability to communicate "live" with somebody when they needed to. Most of these early models hosted several independent stores, as silos, without integration. The mall creators thought that if stores were juxtaposed, consumers would go and shop there. The same analogy holds for somebody who decides to get into the mail-order catalog business by assembling separate catalog pages from different suppliers, each having its own rules for shipping and payments options. Luckily for electronic consumers, the way out from the mall was easy—only a mouse click away.

A very serious flaw with most of these early malls was that they were operated by companies not in the retail business: telephone companies, banks, and computer companies. Any

Internet mall not operated by an organization that has retailing and merchandising experience is destined to fail again.

Second-generation malls look more like organized market-places, having several of the characteristics necessary for success in electronic consumer shopping. Some of the emerging examples include CUC's NetMarket, U.Vision's Computer ESP, ConsumersEdge, Cnet's BuyDirect, and Ziff-Davis's NetBuyer. To understand the critical success factors for business-to-consumer Internet commerce, let's look at the required key needs. We will then revisit the concept of second-generation Internet malls.

# EVOLUTION OF THE WIRED CONSUMER

The "wired consumer" needs to fully take advantage of the world of Internet commerce in ways that are efficient, effective, and secure. Consumers are, however, dependent on the vehicle they use and the capabilities available to them. The vehicle they use will have different phases of evolution and functionality requirements that depend on the required capabilities of the consumer. The richness and availability of services will also be an evolutionary factor toward the ideal pervasive state. Figure 8-1 shows the suggested evolution.

## EARLY AND CURIOUS ADOPTERS

The minimum requirements for most early adopters consisted of a PC with a browser, a modem, and an Internet service provider (ISP) account. This gave them a limited experience, absent a number of enhancements that came later. A few of these users purchased items on-line by entering their credit cards in a secure or nonsecure manner directly from their PCs. We all remember those days.

## ADVANTAGE-DRIVEN USERS

In early 1996, corporations and concerned professionals became aware that the Internet would be a source of personal

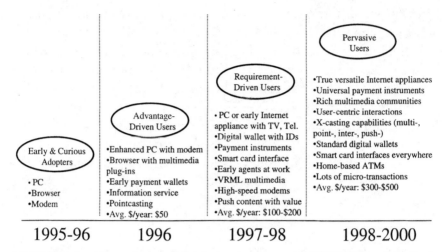

**FIGURE 8-1.** The evolution of the electronic consumer. (*CYBERManagement Inc.*)

or business competitive advantage. It became evident that several enhancements and accessories were needed to make the PC a more useful shopping device, and a more able device to complete a secure transaction. To start with, a browser enhancement with a multitude of Java and Shockwaved plug-ins became common. They provided a welcome evolution from static Web pages. Early (and proprietary) payment wallets, such as CyberCash, First Virtual, and DigiCash, provided users with some sense of added security as they placed their orders. Secure credit card screens became popular. A typical user probably had a subscription service that provided some form of customized news. More users bought something on the Internet, perhaps at an average value of $50 per year.

## REQUIREMENT-DRIVEN USERS

In 1997 and 1998, the much-touted Internet appliances and networked PCs made their way in early forms. The Internet was getting married to other devices such as the telephone and the TV. Digital IDs, digital wallets, universal payment instruments, and keyboard smart card interfaces were facilitating secure and authenticated user-initiated transactions. Early agents were able to efficiently retrieve and filter required information on their own. A new level of user experience was born with virtual reality enhancements to shopping experiences or remote services. The average consumer began to spend upward of $200 per year, perhaps even booking a travel ticket on the Internet for the first time.

## PERVASIVE USERS

Finally, toward 1998 and beyond, we will begin to feel the effect of the Internet on a more pervasive basis, in the same way that the telephone or fax has tinted our lives. We will buy from personal or domestic information appliances, televisions, and telephones connected to the Internet. Using digital or electronic currency will be as common as opening our wallet, which will turn completely digital. We will definitely be able to visit three-dimensional communities, rich enough in multimedia so that they can give us the effect of "being there." The consumer will gain full control of the buying process, with real user-centric interactions and "bidding out" on the Internet for given needs. Multicasting and Net casting will become widespread to allow instantaneous human-to-human interactions as well as live video broadcasts from a variety of sources and locations. Finally, smart cards will carry token values redeemable for actual products and services. They will be used pervasively in the home, restaurant, parking lot, gas station, airport, or bank. Smart cards will also allow user authentication of electronic transactions and credentials. The average wired consumer will conduct a handful of microtransactions daily, and spend between $300 and $500 per year on the Internet in products and services.

# KEY NEEDS FOR CONSUMER INTERNET COMMERCE

There are nine key needs required for successful implementation of Internet commerce for consumers. As of this writing, no single Web site or business includes all of them at the same time.

## NEED 1: CUSTOMER SELF-SERVICE

Customer self-service is a trend that is gaining momentum through Internet-mediated interactions. While offering customers new choices, added convenience, and control, companies are saving costs by offloading some duties of customer interactions to the customers themselves, therefore freeing up human resources internally. However, this should be done only when it makes sense. Added convenience is according to the customer, not the organization. The challenge is to find the areas that save the company money, save the customers time, and give them more than they asked for. Usually, these functions can replace a telephone call to a call center where every time a live operator answers, it costs the company from $8 to $20.

A typical example of self-service includes entering a waybill number to track the shipment of a package. Any order-related queries, also referred to as "wismo" calls ("Where *is* my order?"), are ideally suited for customer self-service. Several financial institutions that already have a large number of electronic banking customers are beginning to experience reductions in the call rate to their call centers from customers asking the same question: "Could you please tell me what this charge was for?"

Even if a company is able to reroute only a percentage of all these calls to a self-service mode, the resulting outcome is a direct cost saving. This answers the following question, which has become a proverbial one: "How do you make money on the Internet?" Answer: "If you can't make money, as a start, try to save money!"

*Amazon.com's Suppliers Rely on Self-Service*

In order to manage the growth and dynamic information environment of its huge virtual inventory (2.5 million titles), Amazon.com publishes detailed "processes" for publishers and authors to follow. The following activities are self-submitted to Amazon.com in a format that is automatically "read" and "reviewed" electronically: new books listings (including publisher contact, book availability, pricing, excerpts, author biographies, and cover art), author and publisher reviews, user reviews, author interviews, and corrections to material submitted and to catalog entries. This gives Amazon the capability to dynamically and almost instantaneously update the contents of its Web site with minimal effort.

## NEED 2: EFFICIENT INFORMATION ACCESS

As the amount and complexity of information and services increase, so does the requirement for efficient and more sophisticated user interface techniques and search methods. The user interface must think like the user. The navigation and interactivity experiences can leave memorable effects on any consumer. The bottom line is always to have the user leave the site satisfied, wanting and remembering to come back for more (Figure 8-2).

Through a clever linkage of information, while you are looking for a particular book, Amazon.com will suggest to you books that were purchased by other readers. This is done so subtly that it is seen as an instructive suggestion. No salesperson

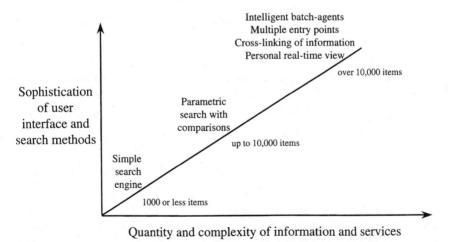

**FIGURE 8-2.** The relationship between the quantity and complexity of information and services and the user interface requirements. (*CYBERManagement Inc.*)

would ever dream of suggesting the same to a potential customer who is browsing a particular aisle or flipping the pages of a given book in a bookstore!

Two aspects are important to help ease the user experience: intelligent agents and personalized interactive catalogs.

**Intelligent Agents at Your Service.**    Even though the concept of intelligent agents has been around for a number of years, there is probably no common definition, given the infancy of their practical applications. Variously referred to as intelligent agents, software agents, or just agents, they are software programs that can assist people in finding or filtering information. At the discretion of their sender, agents can be delegated to initiate requests or make decisions over various computer networks such as the Internet. Usually, they act independently of their user, learn and adapt from actions or the environment, and are highly mobile and autonomous in their actions. A business definition of an agent may be "something that does what you wish it to," whereas a technical definition may be more intriguing as "a software object that thinks." The analogy to real life is that an agent could be the equivalent of a secretary, real estate agent, or assistant—namely, somebody who acts on your instructions and doesn't tie up your time while doing it.

A simple example of an agent is "Eyes," the automated personal notification service from Amazon.com books. Eyes functions as an agent, tracking every newly released book for you according to your area of interest. You, as the user, decide which criteria to base your interest on, whether it is only to track a particular author, subject matter, or general field of interest (e.g., fly fishing in Australia), or whether you are interested in the paperback version of a specific title. Depending on how frequently new information becomes available, Eyes sends you an e-mail informing you of the latest arrivals. So, the agent does the work for you, while you are not even thinking about it. This feature is free of charge to the user, and doesn't hold the user to any purchase obligation. So, if you follow the previous example, you could remain extremely informed about your areas of interest without even having to bother going to a given Web site to find the information. This is why, in the future, agents will contribute to making many Web sites increasingly "invisible." Agents hold a promise to do a lot of the work for us, according to specific criteria or tasks we assign. They will come in different flavors, and they will place the buyer in control, ready to face the toughest sellers.

There will be an evolution in the availability of agents according to the sophistication and added value they offer. The following examples describe various degrees of evolution by outlining what agents will do in each case:

- *Locating information or products with search engines or directory searching.* You may think of this approach as using primitive agents. However, it represents the norm today for most users. Some examples are Infoseek, AltaVista, Yahoo!, HotBot, and Lycos. However, there is an emerging choice, which is to use a "metasearch" engine capability that will search all other engines for you while you do something else, and return the results to your PC for later viewing. One example is EchoSearch from Iconovex. EchoSearch uses multiple search engines simultaneously, in about the same time it would take you to use only one engine, to build a complete hit list. Then it simultaneously downloads and analyzes those documents and presents you with a list of concepts related to your query.

- *Receiving personalized information on the basis of a predetermined profile.* These types of agents are mostly used as a personalized news service, but they represent a growing area. Some examples are ZD-Net's Personal View, PointCast Network, NewsPage, and Amazon's Eyes. Two other newcomers (WiseWire and NetAngels) learn from user ratings of each page read, and adapt the information on the next visit.

- *Intelligent agents that return comparative information on the basis of user needs.* Two popular examples that have been introduced for experimental purposes are Agents Inc.'s Firefly Network and Andersen Consulting's BargainFinder. Firefly allows sites to register and recognize users, in order to immediately personalize the end-user experience in real time without any customized programming. As a personal agent, Firefly intelligently navigates and learns through the Firefly community space to discover information and people who would be of most interest to the initiator.

**Interactive Personalized "Smart Catalogs."**   One example that illustrates the agent concept is the experimental work that was developed by Stanford University, Hewlett-Packard, and CommerceNet. The goal was to demonstrate the efficiencies and added capabilities afforded by making catalogs accessible on the Web, in a form that allows potential customers to locate products according to descriptions of their specifications, and for data in the catalogs to include descriptions of function as well as structure. The setup lets users quickly focus on their area of need, and obtain a "personalized" view of it. By linking information about a product and its attributes throughout the entire distribution chain, buyers can view "virtual" catalogs in real time, as new products become available. Consumers need truly interactive personalized smart catalogs to enhance the shopping experience. Future advances in personalized interactive catalogs will make it easier to locate products and their attributes throughout the value chain.

To get a glimpse of the future direction of agents and their impact on bringing us personalized information, look at Junglee's Canopy, AgentSoft's LiveAgent, Tesserea's Unifind, NetBot's Jango, and Agentics' CatalogExpert. If we extrapolate the role of these agents into a future where they are widespread, some unresolved issues will surface, such as:

- *Agent bargaining power.*   Would retailers turn down certain agents' buying power?
- *Privacy issues in collecting data.*   Will agents have to divulge the sources of their information?
- *Agent decision power.*   When will we let agents make decisions for us (on the basis of what they know about our preferences)?

- *Loyalty shift.* Will intelligent agents cause a shift in customer loyalty?

- *Agent autonomy.* What happens when consumers are at the mercy of what agents find for them?

## NEED 3: USER-CENTRIC QUERIES ALLOWING BIDDING

How many times have you been trapped in a given Web site, wishing you had never entered it because you didn't find what you wanted? How many times have you stared at the results of a keyword search, trying to guess which one of the responses might be closest to your needs, and finally deciding to take a pick at one of the entries without a real assurance of where it would lead you?

Both examples, unfortunately, are an accurate reflection of where we are with Internet comparative shopping. There are two models for Internet commerce: the Web-centric model and the user-centric model. Today, we still live in a Web-centric world, but one that promises a healthier evolution toward a user-centric world (Figure 8-3).

In a Web-centric model, the seller is in control. The goal is to generate traffic to the seller's Web site. Sellers want not only to get you there but to keep you there until you find what you are looking for. Naturally, they won't usually allow you to make

1) Seller-driven / Web-centric

Many users ⟷ One Web location

2) Buyer-driven / User-centric

One user ⟷ Many Web locations

**FIGURE 8-3.**   Web-centric versus user-centric models. (*CYBERManagement Inc.*)

comparisons with other products available elsewhere, unless you purposely go to another site to do so. This model is dead, or soon to be.

In a user-centric model, the customer is in control. A customer with a given need decides to evaluate what is available by doing a comparison, as the first step, before going to one particular seller's site. Combining agent technology with the concepts of interactive catalogs and interactive bidding is a powerful concept which will contribute increasingly to empower consumers to gain control of the buying process. Sellers will have to respond to consumer bids and hope to attract buyers accordingly.

Here are some examples of the types of queries that consumers will be able to submit to agents, which in turn will deliver them to the appropriate sellers:

- *When will a specific model of a laser printer go on sale in my neighborhood?* In this case, the buyer's bid will "sit" in the pool of requests until the sale event triggers the agent to inform its owner.

- *When will a color digital camera become available under $50?* In this case, the buyer has put a bid on a future scenario that isn't available at all today. Most color digital cameras are $200 and up. But it is not inconceivable that in the near future prices will drop to the under-$50 level.

The same technology that gave sellers instant access to a multitude of customers is allowing those same customers to seek out and choose sellers on their own. As more value is shifting closer to the buyer, buyers will be able to bid out their requests to the Web, almost like requests for proposals. Suppliers will respond to them. This is similar to the bid/ask system that the stock market has been operating on for years, but it is applied in reverse to favor the consumer.

The Electronic Travel Auction (ETA) allows business and consumers to bid for airline seats, cruise packages, hotel rooms, vacation packages, and other travel-related products over the Web. ETA benefits the traveler, the travel supplier, and the travel distributor by offering an open marketplace where demand determines pricing. ETA auctions are classified in several categories, such as condominium rentals and cruises, to allow travelers to search ETA's database and generate a list of auctions relevant to their vacation plans.

This system has benefits to both buyers and sellers. Buyers receive information that is timely to their buying decision. Sellers know exactly what the potential demand for future products is. For example, sellers can apply this concept to get rid of excess or unused inventory capacity. If a seller allows customers to bid out their requests, the seller has better control of the supply side. If a certain product is not moving fast enough, and enough customers are bidding on it at a lower price, a seller automatically knows the effects of lowering the price accordingly. Wouldn't it be nice to know for sure that if you lowered the price by 25 percent, you would immediately get 50 more orders?

If you would like to give your customers a taste of agents to make their interactions with your Web site more pleasant and effective, you should start by adding simple agent capabilities. For example, you can install an automated personal notification service to inform customers and prospects of your recent arrivals or offerings. Next, you can give them the capability to bid their requests via your company Web site, and in this manner you begin to get insights into "prospective" demand for your products and services. Finally, you can give customers the capabilities to bid their fantasies, then use the information either for market research or for leverage with a given supplier, or even to target your next source of products.

## NEED 4: INFORMATION APPLIANCES

It has been said that between the years 2000 and 2005, the Internet will probably reach 1 billion people. During roughly the same period, close to 25 percent of all devices connected to the Internet will not be personal computers. This means that a multitude of new non-PC information appliances will get connected to the Internet. These include the TV, the telephone, the automated banking machine, a stereo, a car, a watch, a kitchen appliance, and a kiosk. All these devices want to get married to the Internet.

There are two major types of information appliances: personal and domestic.

1. Personal information appliances are mostly aimed at increasing personal or business productivity. Examples: the Internet PC, a PC wallet, the Web-Telephone, and other not-yet-determined appliances that serve a specific purpose tied to Internet connectivity.

2. Domestic information appliances promise to simplify our lives in the future. Think about when a car will be able to send a message to the service department with the appropriate maintenance information. Or when your other domestic appliances such as the refrigerator, microwave, and dishwasher become connected to the Internet and are able to send messages to you or to the manufacturer about their status. This is not farfetched, considering that, by the end of 1997, over 25 million computers were connected to the Internet. Future versions of the Internet Protocol (IP) standard are being designed to be able to support 1000 billion computer connections to the Internet by the year 2020. Given that the world's population will be 8 billion in 2020, this will produce a ratio of 125 computers per human!

Why are these information appliances important to electronic commerce? Simply, because they are the next point-of-sale (POS) devices for initiating the sales transactions. The PC as we know is a poor POS device, but it has been nonetheless predominantly used so far by most consumers. Future Internet-POS devices will be designed to facilitate seamless transactions initiated by consumers and will contain a plethora of mobile agents and applets.

## NEED 5: VIRTUAL REALITY EXPERIENCE

Consumers want to be entertained. A virtual reality environment on the Web makes a Web experience more engaging and entertaining. VRML (Virtual Reality Modeling Language), also pronounced "vermel," is an industry-standard description language for 3-D scenes, or worlds, on the Internet. With VRML and certain software tools, sellers are creating interactive 3-D worlds that are rich with text, images, animation, sound, music, and even video.

3-D offers the possibilities of creating entirely new on-line communities that re-create reality and transport users to a new level of experience. The impact of Internet commerce is directly related to enhancing interaction with the sellers, therefore attracting and retaining customers accordingly. In the near future, we can expect to be able to "manipulate" the products being purchased, or interact with multiple users in real time, to collaborate, play games, or gamble.

**The Role of Avatars.**   In the on-line world, an avatar is the graphical representation of a human in cyberspace for the purpose of facilitating remote communications with others. Even though they usually have a humanoid appearance, avatars could be whatever you want—a cat, a fish, a cartoon, or any other graphical form—as long as the linkage is made that the avatar represents who you are. In other words, avatars are "digital actors," that represent you, while hiding your real identity. They can move around, handle, and manipulate objects, engage in conversations as a group or privately with one another, or emulate sounds and motion, each under the specific control of an individual person.

A consumer can choose to enter different Web sites disguised as different avatars, each carrying its own physical attributes, belongings, mood, behaviors, and preferences within one universally recognized format. This allows virtual reality super-stores to market to those avatars according to their buying patterns or characteristics.

## NEED 6: ON-LINE CUSTOMER SERVICE AND TRANSACTION HISTORY

It is important to treat customer service as a top priority, and to build the interface requirement to allow customers to receive instantaneous and efficient support on-line. This area is poised to become a customer's paradise. The real test will be when we read surveys indicating that on-line customer satisfaction exceeds personal, telephone, or other types of customer support. Once users are used to the new on-line connection with their suppliers, they will begin to expect more transaction history and instantaneous support to occur on the Internet. Organizations building a new user channel over the Internet must take into account this capability.

It is advisable to augment a virtual reality experience with a live video or audio link to a customer support representative. Users thus come full circle back to real human interaction. Several telecommunications companies are experimenting with call management functions by allowing users to initiate an Internet phone conversation with the customer support representative. IBM has a section on its Web site to help users solve usage problems with their printers. A step-by-step process walks the user interactively through the troubleshooting steps required to solve the problem. Imagine if IBM augmented this process with a live link to a real person if the user still wanted to speak to a representative. Marshall Industries is using a live chat capability with real people at the other end. Actually, when a call is initiated via the Web, a telephone-like ring sounds at the other end to prompt the customer representative on duty to answer the chat request. Nothing prevents Marshall from augmenting this interaction with a live multimedia link.

An evolution to the customer service concept could include:

1. Responses to frequently asked questions
2. Use of e-mail for support
3. Product updates and software available on line
4. Instantaneous on-line chat possible with a customer representative
5. Click option for a live connection to a customer support representative
6. Automated, personalized "push" of information and services

On-line transaction history will also be essential to complete the electronic nature of the relationship with consumers. The added convenience of not having to call a customer representative is a cost saving related to self-service. This area is expected to be part of new electronic services such as on-line banking, trading, and purchasing, but it is also emerging for other types of services. Adding on-line transaction history can bring an uplifting effect to an old service and help you differentiate yourself from the competition.

Manitoba Telecom Services (MTS) allows customers to access their telephone bill statement over the Internet. This free service is available to customers who voluntarily preregister. The new service is available to residential customers and small to medium-size business customers with phone bills that have fewer than 20 pages. Initially, the phone bill information will include customer name, account number, billing number, amount due, and a calculation of long-distance savings. In addition, customers will be able to download the information to spreadsheets and other budget management programs to manage the data on the bill the same way they do other electronically based information. Future plans include the automatic option of paying the bill directly via the Internet, saving time and completely eliminating the paper transaction.

Conductor, the technology-driven financial services arm of Block Financial Corporation, offers The WebCard, exclusively created for Internet users. In addition to having all the features of a standard credit card, The WebCard lets you view your most current transactions or as far back as 12 months, 24 hours a day, every single day of the year, directly from the Web.

## NEED 7: UNIVERSAL PAYMENT INSTRUMENTS, DIGITAL WALLETS, AND SMART CARDS

Today a multitude of new electronic payment instruments are emerging. We are sure to end up with a variety similar to the physical instruments we are used to today. However, it will be important for these payment instruments to be accepted in as many places as possible so that we don't have to carry all of them, all the time, and so we don't run into the Diner's Club syndrome: "Sorry, we don't accept Diner's Club."

**Smart Cards: The Trump Card.**   If Internet electronic commerce is waiting for security, and security is waiting for a trusted infrastructure to authenticate users, the arrival of personal smart cards will definitely break a deadlock on widespread initiation of electronic transactions over the Internet.

In September 1996, an international group of leading PC and smart card companies finally came together to develop open standards that integrate smart cards with personal computers. The new technology will allow application developers to take advantage of the smart card's portability and hardware-based security, which are critical to enabling new smart-card-based PC applications for health care, banking, corporate security, and electronic commerce.

The PC/SC Workgroup will ensure interoperability among smart cards, smart card readers, and computers made by different manufacturers. This means that finally we will see the arrival of smart card ID to allow the storage of digital cash or authenticate and validate users over the Internet. Smart cards will become pervasive in personal computers and other electronic commerce entry devices.

Smart cards are the "trump card" for electronic payments and electronic commerce. Consider this fact: Credit is 300 times more expensive than cash. This is a result of the complexity and multiplicity of credit transactions with authorizing parties, as well as the reporting activities required. Therefore, it is likely that cash-value smart cards will prosper as financial institutions' new incentive to lower the costs of processing credit. From Mondex to Visa Cash to other forms of electronic currency, North Americans are destined to embrace smart cards in the same way that Europe has over the last decade.

> Sweden Post is renting multipurpose smart ID cards to citizens for a fee. After the cards are returned, they can be reprogrammed and reused, just like magnetic hotel keys.

There will be two versions of wallets: a "soft" one that will reside in your PC, and a "hard" one that will be in your pocket. With all the various types of electronic currencies, digital tokens, digital signatures, digital certificates, private keys, and other electronic cash schemes, you will need a "digital wallet" to keep track of all your digital values.

Today most digital wallets are proprietary. They accept only currency or tokens minted or specified by the originators of the wallet. This is like buying a wallet that accepts bills only from the country that sold it to you.

A true universal digital wallet should:

- Include international currencies
- Accept universal payment instruments (credit card, debit card, smart cash card, electronic checks)
- Be versatile (work the same from home, office, bank, shopping center, parking lot, gas station)
- Store digital signatures, digital certificates, and private keys
- Accept multiple types of smart cards

Some wallets that are leading the race with demonstrated versions of these features are:

- VeriFone's vWallet
- Imagine Card (Informix/HP/Gemplus venture)
- CAFÉ initiative, which is a pan-European project

Watch for Microsoft and Netscape's entry in this arena, as they hold the most promise for popularizing and mass-marketing digital wallets, as part of the browser. Also, CyberCash is beginning to look more and more like a universal wallet. It has integrated the Mondex smart card technology into the CyberCash wallet, along with other payment brands. Furthermore, it recently added a micropayment capability called CyberCoin.

Another important development to notice is smart card readers and interfaces that connect to telephones, personal computers, or other information appliances. Combined with smart card applications, they can bring ATM convenience right to the office or home. A recent development in this area is

VeriFone's Personal ATM, as part of its VeriSmart System architecture.

CAFÉ (an acronym for Conditional Access for Europe) is a European multicountry initiative with an intent is to develop and deploy an electronic payment system that works as a digital wallet and cash card, with multiple simultaneous currencies. It is supposed to work the same way at a bank machine, parking lot, store, restaurant, or home. The digital wallet is filled up during an infrared wireless session in front of the bank machine, or from home, via the Internet. CAFÉ is a pan-European project, carried out by a consortium of companies active in electronic payments together with other research organizations. It is also supported financially by the European Commission.

## NEED 8: MICROTRANSACTIONS

In a world where more and more of our intellectual capital resides in the hard drive of our personal computers, there is an increasing need to protect it, sell it, or buy it. However, how can we efficiently conduct transactions that may be worth only a few dollars or just a few cents? If the cost of a transaction exceeds the value transacted, the economic model has failed. Hence the increasing role of microtransactions, especially with consumers.

Microtransactions represent a new scheme that allows micropayments to be handled efficiently between buyers and sellers. Their widespread availability will unleash an unlimited number of possibilities. Daniel Lynch, founder and chairman of CyberCash, claims that microtransactions are the energy pill for a new world order. Furthermore, he maintains that micro-transactions are destined to affect the soft-goods world radically, in the same way that bar coding has changed retail and manufacturing (in the hard-goods world). Lynch further says: "Microtransactions is bar coding at the financial level." You can start to imagine applications such as a Mega Lottery: For as low as 25 cents perhaps, millions of people around the world could participate. You could have draws every hour.

PLUS Lotto is a charitable Internet lottery that conducts hourly, daily, and weekly lotto draws for as low as 1 Swiss franc. Suppose you are playing one of your child's video games, like Super Mario. The intent is to get through a dangerous maze, overcome obstacles, fight dragons, and arrive at the hidden treasure. What if, while you are trapped or facing the enemy for a few seconds, a dialog box appears that says: "Would you like to rent a gun for 5 cents, or would you like a grenade for 25 cents?" You can imagine the rest...

The future of microtransactions will include (1) the ability to transact efficiently down to the 10-cent level, (2) peer-to-peer transactions settled without a financial intermediary, and (3) tying microtransactions and microcredentials to generate microcommerce.

## NEED 9: CASTING TECHNOLOGIES

The "cast" of new characters refers to the emerging casting technologies, all far from traditional broad "casting." Even though these will affect businesses as well as consumers, I have chosen to include them in a chapter on consumer requirements.

For businesses, new casting technologies allow real-time collaboration and distance learning to achieve business objectives. For consumers, they allow new dimensions for entertainment, information access, and communications.

The new "casting" technologies that affect Internet commerce are:

1. *Intercasting.*  Combining Web content and TV content to a PC.

2. *Web casting.*  Broadcasting sound and/or video over the Internet to a PC equipped with audio/video capabilities.

3. *Point casting.*  Receiving narrowly defined (but highly valued) channels of information to a PC.

4. *Web multicasting.*  Combining Web casting with traditional video conference multicasting to create simultaneous, multipoint interactions over the Internet.

**5.** *Push casting.*   By far the most rapidly emerging area, push technology has taken the Web by storm since early 1997. "Push" refers to the ability to send information automatically to your desktop according to a preestablished schedule or set of needs. So, instead of browsing to pull information, you can wait until it is pushed to you. Only a percentage of information is suitable to this format, so it is critical to know what to push and what not to push. One potential growth area is in pushing information related to the customer support aspects of your business.

The Intercast medium is a new technology being promoted by Intel and the Intercast Industry Group. It combines the Internet with traditional casting. Intercasting makes it possible for your home PC to receive HTML-formatted Web pages and video streaming information along with your regular television programming. So, the idea is that while you are watching your favorite show, you can also get in-depth articles and links to related sites. Or, for a more divergent viewpoint, you could be working on a spreadsheet while you're watching the Super Bowl!

According to Intel, research indicates that people are excited about the Internet, but few know what to do when they get there. Recognizing that the most popular sites on the Web are related to television, Intel decided to use the fun and familiar context of television to feed people into a more interactive experience. Out of this research, Intercast technology was born. So, it was the desire for instantaneous results that led Intel to develop Intercast technology in the first place. Intercasting epitomizes the marriage of the television and the Internet.

Members of the Intercast Group include leading television networks, program providers, cable operators, broadband communications equipment suppliers, computer manufacturers, and computer hardware and software vendors.

Following Intercast programming's public debut in 1995, popular crime dramas like *Homicide*, news programs like NBC's *Dateline*, and educational series like *NOVA* all began broadcasting Intercast-technology-enhanced signals. The selection of programming content continues to grow. Other major corporations like CNN, QVC, and WGBH-Boston are broadcasting Intercast programming 24 hours a day, 7 days a week.*

During the 1997 NBA All-Star Game, NBC broadcast Intercast content containing a "virtual locker room," a three-dimensional area that simulated an actual NBA team locker room. It was filled with "hot buttons" that, when clicked, gave statistics on players and an animated coaches' chalkboard with play diagrams. Other interactive areas included an animated quiz on referee hand signals and a sports fan sound effect button that cheered.

# IDEAL VIRTUAL SHOPPING STORE ON THE INTERNET

PersonaLogic Inc. is a software company that specializes in helping other Web sites provide more knowledge to their buyers during the buying decision process. It has designed ConsumersEdge as a free "showroom" for the PersonaLogic™ process. The specialty of the software is that it guides consumers' choices along with parallel advice, anticipating questions that typical buyers might have on the features and benefits of the product they are looking for. For example, if you are looking for a bicycle, you can narrow down your choice to under a dozen possibilities in less than 2 minutes, by drilling down on your list of needs and criteria from a database of 2500 models.

netMarket is CUC International's entry into electronic retailing. By leveraging the buying power of CUC's more than 68 million members, netMarket is able to offer significant savings on a broad array of products and services in the travel, shopping, auto, dining, time-share exchange, and financial segments. Operating with a virtual inventory of over 250,000 products and services descriptions, CUC leverages its relationships and distribution agreements with suppliers that ship directly to members' homes upon ordering. CUC is casting its retailing and merchandising expertise on the Net to its 350,000 on-line members.

---

*Source: The Intercast Group Web Site, www.intercast.org.

The result is an impressive array of service features offered on CUC's Web site that rivals the most sophisticated retailers operating today. These features include a gift finder for those running short on gift ideas, a date reminder which sends you an e-mail about a special occasion worth buying something for, a live and silent auction, a choice of searching by brand or type of product, a flea market for closeout items, a bargain finder, a lowest-price guarantee, a 30-day money back guarantee, prize giveaways, frequent buyer points and discounts for members, a multitude of other discount coupons for car and travel services, extended warranty options, a sign-up gift, a classifieds section, and, to top it off, a three-month trial for only $1.

Welcome to the future of megaretailing on the Internet!

## ANATOMY OF AN IDEAL SUPER VIRTUAL RETAIL STORE

Here is a comprehensive list of the required features (from a user's perspective) of the ideal super virtual store. You can expect many of them to appear gradually in Internet consumer electronic-oriented markets.

- Side-by-side products and services comparison
- Multiple options for purchasing
- Top sellers list, new arrivals list, today's specials
- Easy payment options, including microtransactions
- On-line transaction history
- Personalized view of products and services
- Multiparameter notification service by e-mail and/or push channel
- Extensive linkages to other related information and services for cross-selling purposes
- Order tracking and shipment status by account number
- Proactive advice while shopping

- Advanced search techniques such as parametric search or agent-based search
- On-line auction capability
- Virtual reality handling of products
- Live chat with a real person for customer service
- Ability to download a personal catalog for off-line viewing
- Extremely efficient interfaces that rival the most user-friendly information kiosks

# IT STRATEGIES FOR ELECTRONIC COMMERCE

*You cannot plan the future by the past.*

EDWARD BURKE
*1729–1797*

This chapter addresses the various approaches and issues in implementing Internet commerce capabilities from an information technology (IT) perspective. Internet commerce applications are being built in quantities and in different flavors. This chapter intentionally stays at the strategic level, highlighting the major elements that do not fluctuate on a weekly basis. Given the rapidity of innovations in this field, it is essential to stay abreast of developments almost on a daily basis.

## TECHNICAL STRATEGY STARTING POINTS

Even though Internet commerce is much more than just a technology issue, we are still being influenced by the major technology vendors regarding what viewpoints to take. Each vendor will view the opportunity from a different angle, and each will suggest a different approach to electronic commerce for your organization. These different approaches are perhaps all valid. The best ones will depend on where you are coming from and exactly what area of your organization you plan on transforming with electronic commerce.

For example, build-versus-buy is a classic decision, even more important with Internet-emerging technologies. In most cases, there may not be enough mature applications, and those that claim to have the most comprehensive offerings demand a price premium, as they target Fortune 1000 or Global 1000 types of organizations which they later flaunt as trophies.

Each approach has its own merits and pitfalls. In other words, *"Where you stand depends on where you sit."* Discussing the efficacy applicability of each one of these approaches is beyond the realm of this book, and really depends on your situation. Reviewing the following list is a good checkpoint for evaluating what you have done so far.

1. *The Web server* approach assumes that you can start by developing content on a "commerce server" that may or may not be tied to the rest of your information systems. This Web server becomes your electronic storefront and you can evolve it accordingly.

2. *The transaction engine* approach relies on a back-end transaction platform that supports front-end merchant services and content management services.

3. *The electronic sales and marketing* approach focuses on exploiting the Internet as an interactive sales and marketing medium with one-to-one relationship marketing and selling.

4. *The universal payment switch/gateway* approach allows merchants to guarantee the universality and interoperability of various payment instruments. A secure payment interface takes care of the financial institutions.

5. *The systems integration* approach focuses on the perceived complexities in putting heterogeneous pieces together.

6. *The database application* approach assumes that you already have existing business applications that need to be "Web-lifted," or commerce-enabled. By extending your current applications on the Web, you can enable transactions to happen on your content.

7. *The client/server computing* approach is the closest thing to Internet computing. So, by extending and enhancing

client/server applications with new tools and technologies, you can reach Internet users outside your corporation.

8. *The enterprisewide legacy data* approach helps you extend your current mainframe or legacy data and applications to your customers in order to offer self-service functions or new on-line services.

## STRATEGIES FOR CIOs AND CORPORATE WEB EXECUTIVES

For any medium-size to large organization, gone are the days when the organization's Web strategy rested on the shoulders of its first Webmaster. Embracing electronic commerce as a way of doing business demands serious corporate commitments to investments and strategy formulation. The following eight corporate issues need to be addressed. They can also serve as guiding principles.

### Issue 1: The Internet Redefines the Term *Legacy*

Just as we were getting over the client/server computing wave, here comes Internet computing. While we used to think of anything pre-client/server as legacy, now anything pre-Internet is legacy. Several first-generation Web sites are also probably close to being legacy. Especially for large organizations wishing to engage in world-class electronic commerce, it is unlikely that any software application installed in 1995 or 1996 will get past 1997 in terms of what the market is demanding.

### Issue 2: The Internet Is a Strategic IT Platform

As mentioned in Chapter 1, on the many faces of the Internet, one of the pillars of the Internet is that it is now a major software development platform. The Internet is therefore becoming more and more strategic to IT. However, is it IT, is it more powerful than IT, or is it an expected evolution of IT? The answers are all yes. The Internet is a gateway for an organization's future; therefore the Internet has to amplify IT's capabilities. The more strategic and effective IT has been to your organization, the more likely that the Internet will follow IT's footsteps. By combining your IT infrastructure with the Internet and allowing it to meld into it, you will be able to truly maximize the potential of electronic commerce for your organization.

## ISSUE 3: TAKE CARE OF THE INTERNETWORKING PLATFORM QUICKLY

An IT executive from a large Fortune 100 company lamented to me that his business management didn't comprehend why he had to spend $10 million just on the networking and desktop infrastructure environment, even before the company would see any Internet benefits. The TCP/IP* platform is a required and necessary platform upon which the Internet relies. For several organizations, this is a given now, and they are reaping the benefits of open interconnectivity. This is why others are focusing on getting their Intranets developed, in order to possess the minimum requirements in terms of a standard and universal networking platform.

## ISSUE 4: IT NEEDS WEBMASTER, WEBMASTER NEEDS IT, MANAGEMENT NEEDS BOTH

In some large organizations, the Webmaster has now evolved to become a corporate Webmaster. On the one hand, the Webmaster is used to speed up implementation, and on the other, the CIO is usually more cautious and wants to use proven processes for developing and rolling out applications. In reality, both approaches are needed. Whereas client/server allowed applications to be developed much faster than old monolithic applications, Web component and object technologies are even accelerating this trend. The CIO needs the corporate Webmaster for his or her better knowledge of the Internet. The

---

*TCP/IP is the standard communications protocol for the Internet.

Webmaster needs the CIO for his or her ability and discipline to deliver high-end mission-critical applications for the organization. Management needs to ensure that both leverage each other's strength and contribute to advancing the company's capabilities in Web commerce.

## ISSUE 5: YOU WANT IT DONE IN THREE MONTHS?

A classic situation arises when a business unit decides to enter an Internet commerce venture and presents it to IT, which doesn't have the capabilities to deliver. One way to break the deadlock is for IT to focus on developing a core set of capabilities that are leverageable across departments and projects. Specific to Web-based initiatives, the following areas are somehow generic to any electronic commerce project: (1) Internet security, (2) payment methods and choices, (3) end-to-end financial transaction fulfillment, (4) customer information management/data mining, and (5) integration with legacy or existing systems. All these functional subsystems are needed regardless of the nature of the Internet business being entered. By developing expertise in these areas, the IT function can smoothly complement new Web initiatives with its core competencies. In a world where competitive advantage can be achieved in just a few months, speed of implementation becomes a very critical factor in pursuing the business opportunities identified.

## ISSUE 6: BUILD VERSUS INTEGRATE

Given the fragmented and immature nature of several Web software applications, the issue of integration is at the forefront of any decision. No "turnkey" application will work without integration. The Web is about integration with the organization and with partners, suppliers, and customers, and so will your Web applications be from day 1. The classic build-versus-buy decision gets more confusing, since you still have to build more integration, even if you buy off-the-shelf applications. This leads us to the next area of interest: outsourcing.

## ISSUE 7: OUTSOURCING VERSUS BOT

For years, the BOT (build, operate, transfer) philosophy has been applied by governments to large construction and infrastructure projects around the world. Governments that do not have the expertise to fully manage the complete undertaking of a project such as a highway, dam, bridge, or airport, will contract it to a company that builds it, operates it for a few years, and then transfers it back to the original owners. Large Internet commerce projects can benefit from a BOT approach. Companies must ensure that the BOT contractor effectively handles the knowledge transfer required during the transition of operations. Here is an overview of the BOT concept.

1. *Build.*   A technology company builds the prototype and fully operational model, according to your strict specifications. It has a prototype ready within three months, and a working model three to nine months later.

2. *Operate.*   The technology company rolls out the full Web site as if it were operating it, with a goal to minimize the technology stress on your company. This allows you to concentrate on the business launch, business partnerships, selling to customers and suppliers, and other necessary success factors.

3. *Transfer.*   Upon reaching a cruising stage where the technology is stable, and the business predictions are working to a satisfactory level, the technology company is responsible for transferring the management of the application and associated technologies to you, while ensuring that the proper knowledge transfer takes place. The technology company could still be retained for updates and enhancements vital for the evolution of the software application (Figure 9-1).

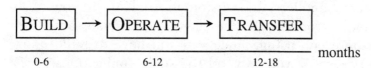

FIGURE 9-1.   The BOT (build, operate, transfer) principle applies very well to Internet development. (*CYBERManagement Inc.*)

## Issue 8: Get to Know the New Electronic Commerce Standards

Another major IT contribution is to stay informed about the development of standards and to develop expertise in implementing the most important ones. There are a number of important emerging standards to the deployment of electronic commerce on the Internet, and the bar keeps getting raised regarding what is considered a minimum requirement for keeping up with the marketplace. For example, while Secure Electronic Transaction (SET) compliance is important to accept universal payments on the Internet, now organizations have to also think about compliance with the Open Buying on the Internet (OBI) for purchasing , the Open Trading Protocol (OTP) for trading, EDI-INT for Internet EDI, the Open Financial Exchange (OFX) for bill presentment, and so on. In addition, it is important to monitor standards development spearheaded by the following key organizations: Cross Industry Working Team (XIWT), World Wide Web Consortium (W3C), Internet Engineering Task Force (IETF), CommerceNet, and the Financial Services Technology Consortium (FSTC). These leading organizations are the precursors of technologies that will be adopted later. Here is an overview of some of the standards.

**Open Financial Exchange (OFX).** Led by Microsoft, CheckFree, and Intuit, the OFX is a unified specification for the electronic exchange of financial data between financial institutions, businesses, and consumers via the Internet. It supports a wide range of financial activities including consumer and small business banking; consumer and small business bill payment; and bill presentment and investments, including stocks, bonds, and mutual funds. Other financial services, including financial planning and insurance, will be added in the future and will be incorporated into the specification.

**Open Buying on the Internet (OBI).** With a promising future, the OBI standard is an open, flexible design for business-to-business purchasing over the Internet. It is intended for the high-volume, low-dollar transactions that account for the majority (80 percent) of most organizations' purchasing activities. As more and more organizations become OBI-compliant, it will become easier to establish a trading relationship with other OBI-compliant organizations, and therefore a more open environment for virtual trading will actually develop.

**Open Trading Protocol (OTP).**   The OTP is a global standard for all forms of trade on the Internet. It enables a consistent framework for multiple forms of Internet electronic commerce, heralding an easy-to-use and consistent consumer purchasing experience regardless of the payment instrument or software and hardware product used. The OTP specifies how Internet trading transactions can occur easily, safely, and efficiently for all parties, independent of the method of payment—very similar to the trading environment in the physical world. It complements but does not replace existing protocols such as SET. The OTP covers the following areas: offers for sale; agreements to purchase, payment (by using existing payment protocols, such as SET), transfer of goods and services, delivery, receipts for purchases, and multiple methods of payment and support for problem resolution. In addition, it will allow consumers to have records of purchases which can be used for filing taxes, making expense claims, feeding into financial management software, or sending a claim back to a merchant to solve a problem.

## ARCHITECTURAL APPROACHES TO INTERNET COMMERCE

The following section highlights functional approaches to an electronic commerce architecture, from three different angles: (1) Web to legacy, (2) Web-enabled applications, and (3) end-to-end Internet commerce.

1. *Web to legacy.*   An internal Web server acts as a secure gateway to provide access to your legacy data to customers and partners. This may be one of the early steps to give access to your company data that is valued by customers. Example: Federal Express' waybill tracking application.

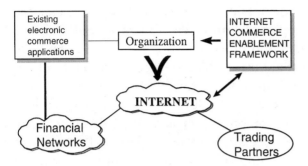

**FIGURE 9-2.** End-to-end Internet commerce framework. (*CYBERManagement Inc.*)

2. *Web-enabled applications.* Existing applications are extended to the Internet via a Web server that replicates or works with the existing application. The current application could reside on an Intranet.

3. *End-to-end Internet commerce.* A new "Internet enablement framework" brings the Internet capabilities described later in this chapter. This framework allows your company to mix existing electronic commerce applications and reaches more than one function of your business applications. End-to-end Internet commerce requires more complex implementation and a careful choice of technology and technology partners (Figure 9-2).

## SYSTEMS ARCHITECTURE FRAMEWORK

Once you have decided to get into Internet commerce, how do you put together the various pieces necessary to support your activities from a technical perspective? The task at hand may appear like assembling a large puzzle. Actually, if Internet commerce were an airplane, it might look like 1000 parts flying in close formation. One way to simplify this undertaking is by thinking of Internet commerce as an extension of your current systems. Your current systems are critical to supporting your customers, so by extending them to the outside you are extending these capabilities to attract and support electronic customers as well.

To allow customers and prospects to tap into your electronic universe requires that you enable an "electronic back office" environment for handling orders, transactions, payments, and so on. This back-office environment needs to be supported by a commerce server. A commerce server is a Web server or a collection of servers that specializes in managing and supporting the electronic buying/selling process for a company. Some of the desirable features in a commerce server include security, compatibility with various types of payment transactions and instruments, and a certificate management capability. The commerce server must be able to accept your "digital content" from other servers as long as standard formats and procedures are followed. Finally, technical and business process integration become key to making the electronic commerce environment a part of your extended enterprise.

A suggested "generic" functional framework for building an electronic commerce environment might include the following elements (Figure 9-3):

1. *Content and services in digital format.* Digital content must be created to form the inventory you have. It has been said that "digital content is the inventory" of the Internet. This digital inventory can be information about hard-goods products or soft-goods products that can be automatically downloaded by your customers. Most content today takes the form of multimedia, since multimedia provide more engaging features.

2. *Merchant services.* As you get into electronic commerce, you become an electronic merchant, with an electronic (or digital) storefront. This capability brings features required for a digital storefront, the ones similar to a regular physical storefront. Some of these are a shopping cart, a cash register, and product display/layout choices.

3. *Transactions management.* This includes processing digital offers and receipts with the required authentication, order management, and record keeping.

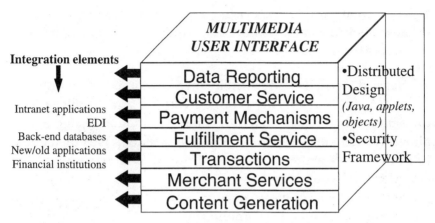

**FIGURE 9-3.** The new electronic commerce framework architecture. (*CYBERManagement Inc.*)

4. *Payment mechanisms.* From credit card processing to other types of payment methods, you need to have the capability to receive universal payment options, and to interface with the required financial institutions and/or your own accounting systems.

5. *Order fulfillment.* The product fulfillment strategy should cover four types of products: soft (software, information), hard (shirt, book), interactive services (access to processed information), and digital token (ticketless ticket) products. Depending on the types of products being delivered, either you need to connect the ordering process to a transportation logistics system or you need to deliver the products yourself.

6. *Customer service and support.* It is important to treat the customer service area as a critical one to enhance your ability to retain electronic customers. Electronic customers like to receive instantaneous and efficient customer support online, including statements about their own transaction history and efficient responses to their on-line queries.

7. *Data reporting and analysis.* This includes internal controls and data reporting on customer and Web site activity. Measurements vary from hits distribution to accurate cus-

tomer behavior analysis. The electronic marketplace requires new decision making, and new kinds of data are needed to support it.

Several vendors offer their own versions of commerce servers. Some versions are bundled with features similar to the ones mentioned above, and others have a modular design which allows for new features to be added as needed. As your maturity evolves within the world of Internet commerce, so will the complexity of your commerce servers.

Several other components are essential to the success of an electronic commerce implementation.

*Multimedia user interface.*   More and more, an engaging user experience will become a differentiating factor in attracting and retaining customers. This includes all aspects of ease of navigation, efficiency of information access, interactivity factors, and entertaining aspects (for consumers). Think of 3-D virtual reality to enhance the user experience.

*Distributed design requirements.*   All the buzzwords you have heard are true. You need Java, ActiveX, lots of applets, and object-oriented programming for maximum reusability.

*Security framework.*   Security is about implementing a comprehensive framework that goes well beyond firewalls, routers, passwords, and encryption. Security is pervasive.

*Integration elements.*   To truly integrate an electronic commerce application within your organization and with the rest of the world, you have to implement appropriate elements into your Intranet applications, EDI transactions, back-end databases, new and old applications, and existing links to financial institutions.

## COSTS OF IMPLEMENTATION

The cost question is becoming very difficult to answer with the complexity, depth, and breadth that Web sites can have. Initially, a company's Web site consisted of a well-defined set of technical resources. At the most basic level, it might have included a single Web server, its connection to the Internet, basic Web server software to publish Web pages, and a Webmaster. Today, a Web site supporting electronic commerce for even a medium-size company may consist of a much more intricate set of servers and services not physically in the same location. Several more people, from both the technical and business side, may be involved in it. Furthermore, Web sites will certainly be interfaced to several other existing IT systems and databases, internally and externally. So, the lines that used to define what constitutes a Web site are blurring and melding very rapidly with the rest of the organization. This means that the costs incurred in rolling out Web site capabilities are also being mixed with other costs, and therefore are more difficult to track on their own.

In addition, a given Web site for a large organization might consist of actually 30 different physical sites, mirrored across the universe. *Mirroring* a Web site consists of duplicating and replicating certain (or all) functional parts of the site into various geographical locations. Mirroring is common for Web sites with heavy traffic or sites running complex transaction-based applications. When the bandwidth requirements are spread closer to users, and/or the functional components of an application are separated, efficiency and speed of access are greatly increased.

Overall, costs can be spread into five categories:

1. *Platform:* hardware, systems software, Web software and tools, peripherals, networking and infrastructure, security, and Internet connection costs

2. *Content:* digital content creation, design and enhancements, digital catalogs, Internet applications development, software customization, applets, and other Internet software tools and utilities

3. *Integration:* database integration, legacy systems integration, data mining interfaces, applications to applications integration, Internet applications to other existing IT systems integration, business process integration, and workflow enhancements

4. *Human resources:*   various human costs in technical and business responsibilities

5. *Promotion and marketing:*   both on-line and off-line, the costs of launching the business, educating customers, advertising, public relations, links to other sites, direct-mail activities, and other print media

## SECURITY ARCHITECTURE

Security is required at several levels and in various and specific models. The following pieces of security must be addressed and tied together in the context of an overall framework: firewalls, authentication, authorization, nonrepudiation, data integrity, secure transactions, private/public key management, encryption, digital signatures, certification process, tunneling, privacy issues, digital certificates, access security, certification management process, antivirus software, secure payments, secure content distribution, secure EDI, security middleware management, intrusion detection software, ethical hacking, security procedures, and trusted operating systems.

According to Bruce Schneier in *E-Mail Security* (John Wiley, 1995), "Security is really like a chain which is as good as its weakest link." From an implementation perspective, you should look at the following five functional areas of security:

- User access (for physical and remote user authentication and authorization)
- Data, application, and database security (for data storage and retrieval and during software-to-software interactions)
- Transaction and payment security (during payment transactions and other Web transactions)
- Network and systems security (for the operating system and the network environment)
- Security maintenance and management (for security management and monitoring, ethical hacking, preemptive monitoring, disaster recovery)

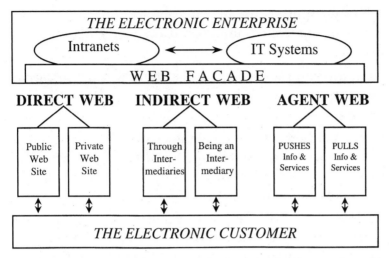

**FIGURE 9-4.** Supporting the multiple electronic distribution channels. (*CYBERManagement Inc.*)

# WEB DELIVERY ARCHITECTURE

IT needs to support the various electronic distribution channels that organizations are setting up (see Chapter 5). Ideally, support is given through a common Web façade that bridges content and applications between IT systems and Intranets into the outside world (Figure 9-4).

# INTERNET COMPUTING GOES LIVE

Since 1995, a new wave of computing has emerged, sparked by the advent of business's exploitation of the Internet. This new wave has been labeled *Internet computing.* Internet computing is coming at us with a new set of emerging technologies, tools, and philosophies about how to develop and roll out information technology across organizations. It has old flavors of previous computing generations mixed with a smarter implementation perspective. For example, Internet computing contains:

- Mainframe computing, for allowing applications to stay away from users but be called on demand (networked computing applications)

- Minicomputers, for allowing the distribution and replication of servers geographically between users and larger servers (Web servers)

- PCs, as the platform of choice for accessing any applications from a common and absolutely universal interface called the browser (PC browsers, networked PCs, and other appliances as entry points to the Internet)

- Client/server and LANs, for favoring a distributed computing architecture that mixes the old with the new and makes the whole look like a homogeneous environment (e.g., Netscape's Open Network Environment architecture and Oracle's Network Computing Architecture)

In migrating to Internet computing, organizations need to think about extending their internal information systems and applications to the outside world in order to reach their trading partners and customers. The objective is to integrate PCs, existing client/server applications, and legacy data and applications, while combining them with new Internet technology. But the emerging Internet technology presents a dilemma. Realistically, companies cannot throw out the old applications and rewrite new ones right away. What they really need is a clever mix of the new with the old in order to gain the best of both worlds: the strength of client/server architecture with the flexibility and speed of deployment of Web technologies.

Most technology vendors aiming to enable enterprise use of the World Wide Web have recognized that the standard Hypertext Transport Protocol (HTTP) and Common Gateway Interface (CGI) path, although effective for distributing multimedia information, are insufficient for supporting enterprise business applications. Most have augmented the HTTP mechanism with an alternative middleware link connecting a Web-triggered client to enterprise applications. Internet computing takes advantage of these new "middleware services" that are the glue between Web clients and software applications.

So, Internet computing is a new style of writing and deploying software where new Internet technologies are being used, from software tools to standards. Internet computing is best seen as a natural evolution or extension of the client/server computing model. Internet computing is also given the "network-centric" label, since it allows software applications to depend on the network, and not the specific operating systems or hardware platform. The concept of applets, popularized by Sun Microsystems and its Java strategy, is ideal for the Internet. Another important trend is the convergence of client/server, Web, and object technology, which is giving rise to new internetworked capabilities for software applications.

The following are general characteristics of Internet computing:

- Rapid development of Web-based applications
- The Internet or Intranet as the deployment platform
- Applications that communicate with other applications via the Internet, in an Intranet-to-Intranet model
- Heavy reliance on component software technology to facilitate migration and updates, as well as integration with other applications
- Using new industry standard software tools and technologies, such as JavaScript, Internet-Inter Object Request Brokers Protocol (IIOP), applets, ActiveX, and Netscape's ONE model
- Lower cost of deployment and maintenance

## DISTRIBUTED DESIGN REQUIREMENTS AND PLUG-AND-GO SOFTWARE

We are seeing the rise of reusable "component" software that extends the reach of existing applications into the Internet.

They enable rapid development to take place, and they include business and technical objects.

The Web is a perfect platform for component software to flourish. The benefits of this approach are direct savings resulting from speed of development (because of the reuse aspect), speed of integration (because of the previous experience gained), and overall cost of deployment (a part of the costs have been shared by others). Finally, the Web provides a higher quality of software given that components can be tested separately to make troubleshooting much more efficient. Several object-oriented applications are being tried on the Web, including complete software development environments, interconnection technologies, and ActiveX software.

However, organizations cannot necessarily throw away an estimated $10 billion of client/server software developed over the last three years and rewrite older applications using Java, ActiveX, and other new and hot Internet technologies. The business challenge lies in taking advantage of these new Internet technologies, protecting investments in current software, integrating the old with the new quickly and smoothly, and avoiding the cost of making the wrong choices. Ideally, a standard framework that enables multiple computing models to be deployed through a unified component architecture is needed.

The following are samples of solutions that address these concerns.

## NETSCAPE'S ONE MODEL

An example of the capabilities behind Internet computing is the Netscape environment called ONE (Open Network Environment). The proof was in the delivery in September 1996 of a collection of "live" business applications (under the AppFoundry banner) that were developed independently by other developers. All of them run in a plug-and-go fashion with minimal programming involved.

The ONE model of computing, which relies on a new breed of software technologies based on HTML, object architectures, Javaware, and Netscape followers, threatens the traditional computing model, where software applications are designed to run and depend on a given platform only. We will see more and more new electronic commerce software components that fit within this model, which will help accelerate the deployment of Internet commerce applications.

## Oracle's Network Computing Architecture™

Oracle's Network Computing Architecture is a common set of technologies that allows PCs, Network Computers,™ and other client devices to work with all Web servers, database servers, and applications servers over any network. It is a cross-platform infrastructure for developing and deploying object-based, network-centric applications. It facilitates the incorporation of newly developed applications and legacy mainframe systems, as well as existing client/server applications. This is an example of an open architecture that bridges the old with the new, supports the emerging style of distributed-objects Internet computing, and integrates with new standards such as IIOP, Java, ActiveX, and CORBA (Common Object Request Broker Architecture).

In addition, Oracle has developed comprehensive end-to-end applications software solutions that support the business-to-business and business-to-consumer elements of electronic commerce.

## Java Electronic Commerce Framework

The Java Electronic Commerce Framework (JECF) is an emerging virtual point-of-sale device implemented in software. It is a framework that offers "pluggable" modules to facilitate specific functions within Java-enabled environments. This advanced model includes functions such as payment methods (SET, smart cards, electronic checks, tokens), security services, personal database records, and financial and administrative reporting.

# THE FUTURE OF THE BROWSER

Several technical developments will continue at a rapid pace. Some of them will create temporary unanswered questions. For example: If Microsoft makes Windows and Internet Explorer so intricately tied together, will it obsolete the need for Netscape's Navigator? Or will the availability of thousands of Netscape ONE-compatible applications make Windows obsolete, and give rise to the "Nettop" or "Netstation," as a replacement to the desktop? The so-called browser war of the summer of 1996 may appear as just a skirmish, compared with the bigger battle that is looming at the horizon. The real battle of the future is how Internet applications are going to be rapidly developed and deployed to enable new capabilities, not possible before.

## INTERNET/INTRANET INTEGRATION ISSUES

In developing an Internet commerce platform, organizations must think about the role of Intranets. The richness of Intranet corporate applications will positively affect electronic commerce capabilities. Intranets are the "stamina" of Internet commerce. Extending Intranet applications into the Internet permits an organization to provide more value to customers in several ways:

- Real-time access to information
- Ability to perform business transactions
- Developing new relationships

A certain evolution and maturity of Intranet development might include the following areas:

1. Gathering, sharing, locating, processing, and publishing information. This includes applications such as knowledge sharing, full-text retrieval, directories, on-line catalogs, and audio-visual broadcasting.
2. Collaboration, communication, and education with people, computers, and entities. This includes e-mail, discussion forums, and calendaring or scheduling.

3. Internal mission-critical applications development and deployment. This includes customer support and other administrative applications, such as accounting, HR, and purchasing.

4. Information and services exchange with external partners. This includes order tracking applications, shipping logistics, and product and marketing information.

5. Electronic commerce with suppliers and customers. This includes procurement services, all aspects of buying and selling, certificate management services, payments processing, and delivery of information-based products and services.

The seamless integration of Intranets with the Internet is a phenomenon which represents an advanced, but required evolution of an Intranet strategy. This Intranet-to-Intranet evolution could be referred to as an Extranet:

My Intranet + Your Intranet = An Extranet

The communication of extranet applications becomes a necessity for engaging trading partners in electronic commerce. A suggested evolution of an Intranet strategy is depicted in Figure 9-5, and the steps are explained as follows.

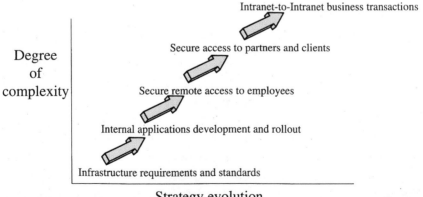

**FIGURE 9-5.** The evolution of Intranets leads to integration with business transactions. (*CYBERManagement Inc.*)

1. *Infrastructure requirements and standards.*   Organizations that have a TCP/IP-based infrastructure take it for granted, but it really is the basis for applications deployment. Furthermore, the required technical and policy standards have to be in place to ensure effective centralized management of decentralized development.

2. *Internal applications development rollout.*   Once the hardware and software platform infrastructures are in place, you are ready to support the multiplicity of Intranet applications throughout the organization. Innovation takes place here.

3. *Secure remote access to employees.*   After content maturing takes place for Intranet applications, traveling and at-home employees will want access to the same applications which they are accustomed to in the office. This is where you can apply your Internet security skills.

4. *Secure access to partners and clients.*   In this stage, your partners and clients have heard of your Intranet applications, and they begin to expect you to give them access to specific information that supports their working relationship with you.

5. *Intranet-to-Intranet business transactions.*   The ultimate stage of maturity involves the integration of key internal workflow requirements by allowing the supporting business applications to interact with each other from your Intranet to another company's Intranet, via the Internet.

Inter-Intranet development is not only tied to integrating the technology; it relates to linking and integrating business-to-business applications, such as placing and processing orders, coordinating shipping logistics, funds transfers, bidding, brokering, and other procurement services. Therefore, it is important that organizations treat their Intranet and Internet developments as one unit rather than as two unrelated initiatives. Integration can be addressed only by implementing both the Internet and the Intranet as if they were one seamless process. In this manner, the business process can travel inside the Intranet, outside onto the Internet, and then

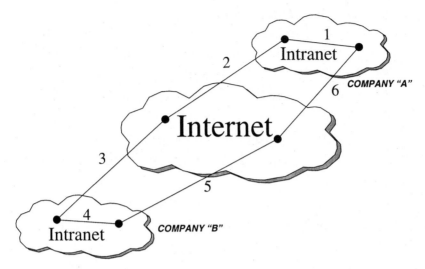

**FIGURE 9-6.**   Intranet-to-Intranet business process integration between two companies. (*CYBERManagement Inc.*)

back into another Intranet (Figure 9-6). The following are two examples.

### Example 1: Health Claim Processing Steps

1. An employee fills out a health benefit form from the company's Intranet.
2. When the form is submitted, it travels through the company's Intranet via the Internet to the health insurance company.
3. An Intranet application captures the request.
4. The request is processed by an employee of the insurance company.
5. Upon processing or approval, the request is resent via the Internet to its originator. The reply could be a confirmation of the claim, or the refund itself, through one of several acceptable Internet payment mechanisms.
6. The Internet routes the request back to its originator with the appropriate action that resulted from the original request.

### Example 2: Sales Order Processing Steps

1. Through the Intranet, an authorized employee accesses a "corporate procurement" application.
2. The employee places the order for a specific product from an approved vendor.
3. The vendor receives the request via the Internet.
4. The order is automatically integrated into the vendor's order entry system.
5. The order is acknowledged via the Internet.
6. Order acknowledgment is received by the initiating customer.

The above example could continue with a similar process that includes a shipping notification and then a payment authorization through the Internet.

Traditional EDI-based applications are likely to move toward this Intranet-to-Intranet architecture. In the past, the network and security services were provided by the EDI VANs. Now the Internet can provide a similar functionality at a lower cost. These services will include forms-to-forms systems for funds transfer, electronic product catalogs, bidding systems, procurement services, and order management systems. After all, business-to-business electronic commerce may end up being driven by Intranet-to-Intranet applications integration.

## DON'T INTEGRATE, AUTOMATE!

A new category of software technology that is turning conventional Web application development wisdom on its head is known as *Web automation*. The premise is that instead of making applications available to the Web, why not make the Web available to applications, instead? The leader and creator of this methodology is webMethods, Inc. Says Keith Ellis, vice president for webMethods: "Most of the business-to-business side of electronic commerce is automated. But when you introduce the World Wide Web into the mix, you create a bottleneck: a human being sitting in front of a browser." Now webMethods, Inc., has developed software to allow programmatic access to the Web from within business applications. This new technology provides an API to the World Wide Web which allows any business application to exchange data with any Web site automatically, without human intervention.

The consequences for electronic commerce are profound. Organizations can use the webMethods API to automate secure transactions with customers, business partners, financial institutions, and suppliers—all via the Web—without having to resort to the expense or complexity of leased lines, VANs, or EDI. For example, companies with a business-to-business electronic catalog can use this technology to insert their catalog into the automated purchasing applications of their customers and thus become the default choice for purchases. Developers can also treat the Web as a vast source of data for their automated business applications.

The browser is dead. Long live the Web!

## EVOLUTION OF BUSINESS-TO-BUSINESS APPLICATIONS

The following procurement service applications have to begin to migrate toward the Internet (away from EDI only). This can be done in two ways: (1) via Internet gateways or (2) by replacing older "private network" communities with the public Internet. These services include:

*Basic procurement services:*   global/specialized directories, on-line catalogs/ordering, banking services, credit reporting/ approval, vendor qualification/certification, quality assurance, and transportation

*Advanced procurement services:*   competitive bidding, broker-ing, auction service, parts locating/buying, production costing, order aggregation, scheduling/coordination, logistic support, on-line catalogs, product data exchange, and collaborative engineering/design

*InfoTest International: From Proprietary Systems to Internet-Based Commerce*

InfoTest International, an alliance of high-tech companies and organizations, has joined forces with the U.S. government to develop an experimental information system that uses the Internet to enable manufacturers to work together on-line and respond to customers' needs anywhere in the world. The initiative—enhanced product realization (EPR)—is believed to be the world's largest Internet-based manufacturing technology trial. EPR is the first to integrate the Internet with other technologies to enable collaborative manufacturing and electronic commerce computing applications, such as computer-assisted design and manufacturing, product data management, electronic data interchange, and multipoint desktop videoconferencing. While these applications are in use today, they typically work only with proprietary systems. Thus it is tough to link the entire product supply chain—manufacturers, suppliers, dealers, offsite contractors, and customers—since different computers and networks don't talk to each other. With the Internet, virtual product design and supply chain management will give North American manufacturers an enormous competitive advantage.

# IN PURSUIT OF VIRTUAL VALUE-ADDED DISTRIBUTION

## Marshall Industries' Experience

*You have to decisively say: Good-bye industrial age.*

Robert Rodin

*President and CEO*
*Marshall Industries*

The following case study was developed as a result of cooperation and approval from Robert Edelman, vice president of Marshall Industries, Inc. I have chosen Marshall Industries because its story supports several theories and beliefs covered in this book. Marshall's actions exemplify how the Internet can positively transform a company. Furthermore, it has sustained the rate of innovation and development of its electronic commerce capabilities, pushing one limit after another.

## COMPANY BACKGROUND

Marshall Industries is the world's fourth largest distributor (in sales volume) of industrial electronic components and production supplies and was the first to distribute via the Internet. Combined with its European counterpart (S.E.I.), it achieved total sales of more than $2 billion a year, with approximately 2500 employees worldwide. The company services over 400 suppliers, 50,000 customers, and 150,000 parts, 24 hours a day, 7 days a week, in 25 countries. Marshall Industries went on line in the United States in July 1994 and globally in November 1994.

Marshall's customers are mainly original equipment manufacturers in the major industries of computer mainframes and peripherals, capital and office equipment, communications, control and medical equipment and instrumentation, and aerospace. General product areas include semiconductor products, connectors, passive components, computer systems and peripherals, production supplies, toolkits, instrumentation and workstations. Value-added services range from component testing and assembly to sophisticated computer interface services such as electronic data interchange (EDI). Its suppliers include Texas Instruments, Toshiba, Hitachi, AMD, Siemens, Tektronix, Fujitsu, U.S. Robotics, Sony, and NEC (Figure 10-1).

## THE BIRTH OF A VISION

In 1990, well before the Internet's rise as a valid business tool, Marshall Industries initiated electronic commerce as an executive management directive, not as an isolated project. This vision was driven by the need to support customers and suppliers that wanted to do business any time, anywhere, and by any method. An enterprise framework of people and technology was

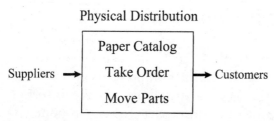

FIGURE 10-1.   Marshall's old business model was focused on physical distribution.
(*CYBERManagement Inc.*)

created called Virtual Distribution. Marshall created a strategy that aligned Marshall's organization through a common compensation structure. Marshall Virtual Distribution was enabled.

This structure enabled people and technology to collaborate in a global virtual distribution environment. Today Marshall has a number of IT initiatives that affect electronic commerce, including inter-Intranets, Extranets, Lotus Notes/Domino, Internet Broadcasting (through ENEN subsidiary), and other Internet business applications. It has developed a rapid deployment philosophy in the sense that no organizational barriers stand in the way of new initiatives. Trained and fit for rapid organizational changes, Marshall was able to thrive when the Internet challenge came knocking.

For Marshall, the total number of Internet users and the real size of the market were irrelevant factors. It wanted to participate in a big way, knowing the Internet was going to be important. Early in 1994, president and CEO Robert Rodin recognized that the Internet was going to become an agent of change that would affect how Marshall competes and how its customers buy, and that it would radically change the definition of value in the eyes of customers and suppliers. The essence of this vision described the Internet as a catalyst poised to fundamentally change Marshall's business model, a change that was necessary to embrace fully, creatively, and decisively. In the words of Rodin, "You have to decisively say: Good-bye industrial age."

## READYING THE ORGANIZATION BY SENSING THE CHANGING ENVIRONMENT

A number of potential organizational barriers had to be removed in order to pave the way for rapid change deployment. Marshall spent close to a year training its senior managers, before embarking on making the changes happen. It linked employee compensation to overall company success, in order to speed up the buy-in process for corporate decisions. By providing similar benefits to all employees, Marshall removed any conflict of interest on the impact of decisions. It implemented cross-functional teams for electronic commerce, including marketing, IT, and operations. It stopped focusing on opening new physical locations in 1991, because it recognized that the physical distribution model was changing to an electronic distribution model, and that electronic commerce was beginning to evolve through EDI channels and direct customer connections to mainframes.

Marshall began to sense the changing environment from its customer's point of view, and began to take actions on the changing requirements. All these actions were directed at the electronic marketplace, and later at Internet commerce. The following are some of the key business drivers that affected Marshall's Internet strategy:

- *The move away from mass marketing.*   Marshall used to think that it was acceptable to market the same thing to all its customers. In reality, every project that a customer is working on is different, so Marshall began to profile customers at every single level, down to the project level. The profiling started six years ago, on paper, then moved to a PC client/server, and now it is on the Internet, so that anybody in the organization can look at it.

- *Customer retention versus acquisition.*   Marshall recognized that it wasn't good enough to just acquire new customers. Retaining them and doing more business with them became more important. The Internet is helping Marshall enhance its customer intimacy, therefore increasing revenues per customer.

- *Low-cost production.*   In 1991, the industry average for selling, general, and administrative (SGA) costs was 18 percent. Now it is moving into single digits. Marshall had to be able to mass-customize services to its customers in order to lower the SGA.

- *Quality of service.*   The issue of quality of service to the customer becomes more significant on the Internet. Improving the service becomes tied to delivering predictable information over the Internet.

- *Time-to-volume issue.*   According to Robert Rodin, "Time is the currency of the 1990s." With the Internet, delivering products faster to the marketplace becomes possible, and customers value the time saved.

## INTRODUCING "VIRTUAL DISTRIBUTION"

In the old value chain, moving parts was key to the business. Today Marshall Industries is actually transforming itself by evolving beyond just being an electronics parts distributor. It looks at its business as a virtual junction box connecting suppliers and customers, with virtual entities actually making up the value chain. Because of the heavy reliance on information technology to help achieve its goal, Marshall started to look at itself as a technology organization (not only a physical distribution organization).

Marshall embraced the concept of virtual distribution—that is, getting anything, anywhere, any time, in any method. This radical change was taking the company away from the physical plane, into the virtual plane. The virtual distribution channel gets layered on the physical distribution channel, and becomes the value added (Figure 10-2).

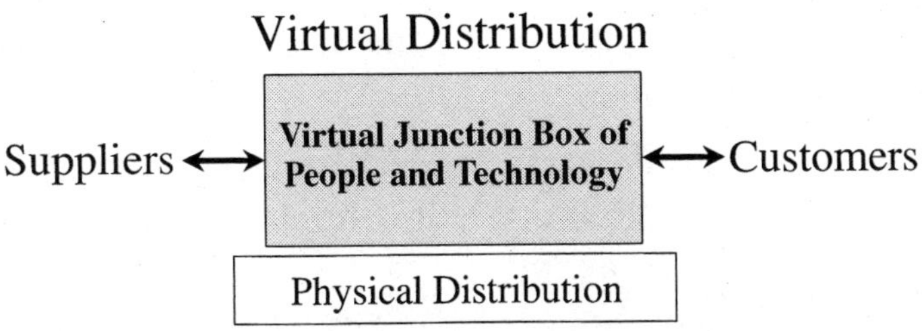

Virtual Distribution

Suppliers ⟷ **Virtual Junction Box of People and Technology** ⟷ Customers

Physical Distribution

**FIGURE 10-2.**   Marshall's virtual distribution channel gets layered on the physical distribution. (*CYBERManagement Inc.*)

# EVOLUTION OF THE WEB TO ENHANCE THE BUSINESS

Marshall Industries believed that getting into a Web site development project should be done strictly for basic business reasons. Once you embark on it, and let it change your business processes, it can become very complex to manage.

Marshall Industries launched its Web site in July 1994, but at that time it did not predict everything that would happen. At first, engineers began to use the site, because they liked the contents (product specifications). Then, Marshall launched an ordering system. In May 1995 it conducted the first audio NetSeminar™, which was later spun off as a separate business.

Here are some ideas that supported Marshall's ability to introduce the new system.

**Directed Content.**  Directed content means that content location is directed and controlled by Marshall, so that customers never really leave Marshall's site, even when they are looking at information that doesn't originate from the main Web site. Thus content is never hyperlinked such that users have a chance to leave the Marshall site. The setup requires a backdoor entry to the Web sites of Marshall's partners, which include AMP and United Parcel Service (UPS).

**Integrated Business System.**  Marshall treats its Web site as an integrated business system that is an extension of its existing corporate order systems or marketing follow-up systems. The Web is not an island, but rather the front end to the business. According to Robert Edelman, "We were not building a Web site; we were building an Internet business, connected to legacy systems and customers."

**Simplicity Hides Complexity.**  Marshall realized that there had to be a short distance to everything. Simplicity is important on the front end, so the company placed the complexity behind it. For example, Marshall wanted users to be able to request and view customized information that was tied to their changing requirements. To do so, it adopted the concept of dynamic information access for most of the site's content. Marshall recognized early that static information is of less value to its customers (e.g., in Marshall's business prices and lead time change almost as quickly as the stock market).

**Not Falling in Love with the Technology.**    Marshall learned not to be in love with the technology. Technology had to find its purpose in a business application. For example, when Marshall used audio, it did so for a business application, which was to do NetSeminars for business-to-business training purposes.

## WEB SITE FEATURES THAT PRODUCE RESULTS

The following are features that are implemented in Marshall's Web site, and the associated results that are being derived from this approach (Figure 10-3).

**Billboards.**    Billboards have generated thousands of sales leads and new customers. This feature has become one of the most important sources for developing new customers and new opportunities. Marshall now has several advertising sponsors on its Web site, with a waiting list for its home page. It uses both rotating billboards and keyword-linked advertisement banners. Marshall stopped measuring hits a long time ago, because they

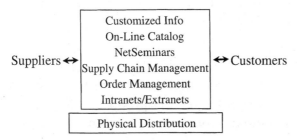

**FIGURE 10-3.**    Marshall's virtual distribution includes a number of digital value services. (*CYBERManagement Inc.*)

are irrelevant. "Measuring success is done by seeing if we are reaching the right audience," says Edelman. "We are interested in targeting a specific audience—think of it as 20,000 unique visitors per month. We now do business with 70 nations a month, as a result of countries coming on line from various parts of the world."

**Customized Information.** Marshall recognized early that customers would spend time giving personal information only in exchange for higher-value information. So, instead of initiating a user registration process, Marshall has developed a personal knowledge assistant process, called Plugged-IN™. By specifying the product categories they are interested in, customers receive only information specific to their interest. This is like a self-service function, which provides Marshall with significant savings. Previously, a data sheet request would cost anywhere from $6 to $10 to get fulfilled. Marshall has over 300,000 data sheets on-line.

**NetSeminars™.** At first sight, it may appear that NetSeminars really has nothing to do with Marshall's business. However, Marshall is creating more demand and customer intimacy by using this technology through their newly formed subsidiary ENEN. NetSeminars is a service that allows its suppliers to do business training anywhere in the world. Companies such as Toshiba, Texas Instruments, and AMD are now broadcasting interactive seminars and training programs for their customers, via the Marshall Web site. These are large companies that do not usually have a problem in reaching their customers. However, they really see the value of Marshall as a powerful intermediary, having the undivided attention of 50,000 customers!

**NetInterview™.** Marshall also developed NetInterview, which allows it to broadcast live interviews from trade shows. By interviewing people about specific product information, Marshall creates more demand for customers to come to its site for more value.

**Headline News.** Marshall has introduced a daily radio-style industry news service about the semiconductor business. The service can be accessed directly from the home page or the timecast network, or it can be delivered daily as an e-mail, depending on customer preference.

**Virtual Search Engine.**   A virtual search engine allows simple or complex selection by part number, description, cross-referencing, or manufacturer. This can lead customers to simple or multitier ordering, multitier pricing, sample requests, getting a data sheet, and so on. All information is dynamically created, on demand, so if there isn't a single data sheet on a given product, it can be dynamically re-created.

**Order Tracking.**   Marshall has worked with UPS on a tunneling technique (secure back-door entry) so that customers can track their orders without leaving the Marshall site.

**Extranets (or Inter-Intranets).**   By extending the reach of Intranet applications to its known business or trading partners, Marshall allows them access to even more specialized information. Through MarshallNet, suppliers access very narrowly requested information, via a secure and private method. For example, a Hitachi representative based in Dallas can review real-time customer activity and sales performance in his or her territory, without access to any other confidential information.

## REDEFINING SUPPLY CHAIN MANAGEMENT

Marshall recognized that streamlining the supply chain was a definitive source of competitive advantage. It seemed that the Internet was a natural for facilitating the hidden powers of supply chain efficiencies. A good supply chain means direct cost savings, an agile capacity for business expansion, and close relationships with partners, customers, and suppliers. With MacroLink, Marshall's service mark for supply chain management, Marshall even helps customers manage their bills of materials. The following are additional elements that Marshall introduced.

**Order Management.**   In addition to price and quantity verification, the placement of a customer order automatically initiates real-time credit authorization and subinstant approval. Marshall calls this capability OrderAgent$^{SM}$. As soon as the order is approved, an automated request is sent to the warehouse for scheduling. Soon after, an order acknowledgment is initiated directly to the customer, with the relevant shipping and logistics information from UPS. Order status messages are automatically pushed to the customer. The arrangement provides for a real integration of the order-to-shipment process.

**XPressOrder.**   XPressOrder is a fast way to order parts on-line. If you know the parts numbers, even randomly, you're almost finished.

**Live Help.**   For 24 hours a day, 7 days a week, customers around the world initiate an on-line chat session with a real Marshall technical support engineer available to answer questions and provide technical assistance. Actually, when a customer initiates the on-line chat call, a telephonelike "ring" sounds at the Marshall's technical support desk to prompt the next available customer support representative to respond. This is a unique feature in the industry.

**Electronic Design Center.**   A free and real virtual electronic design center allows Marshall customers to test and run their designs over the Internet. With this on-line laboratory, engineers benchmark their designs without the need to own the necessary development tools. Then, they submit these designs to be burned on programmable chips to be delivered by Marshall within two days of order. Previously, it would take up to seven days for customers to receive their orders.

## FROM DIGITAL VALUE TO DIGITAL SERVICE TO DIGITAL BUSINESS

Marshall's NetSeminar™ service, which started as another value-added item for customers, is now a business on its own. Following the Marshall tradition of spinning off successful segments of the businesses, (such as Marshall Consulting, which specializes in

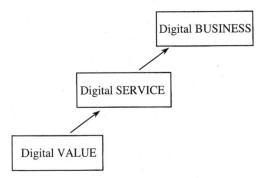

**FIGURE 10-4.** The digital value creation process can lead to a digital business. (*CYBERManagement Inc.*)

supply chain management), NetSeminar is now part of a separate venture called ENEN (Education, News, and Entertainment Network) since December 1996. ENEN has added to its portfolio of services NetPresentation™, NetInterview™, NetIndustry Headline News™, and NetEvent™. The key lesson here is that introducing a well-thought-out digital value service can go a long way to becoming a viable business by itself (Figure 10-4).

ENEN is betting its future on the emerging market for continuing distance education, virtual presentations, and professional training over the Internet, all part of the highest area of growth on the Internet over the next two years, according to a mid-1997 survey of the American Management Association (predicted growth of 272 percent). In addition to its traditional electronics industry customers, such as Xilinx, Texas Instruments, and AMD, ENEN has added new-found customers in other industries such as health care groups, professional speaking associations, financial analysts, celebrities, and book authors. In late 1997 it even introduced a pay-per-view capability.

## A LOOK AHEAD

Given its track record, Marshall will continue to evolve its rich Web site with additional functionality. It is looking at some of the following areas, which are of general interest to the Internet industry as well:

- Private certificates and digital IDs, to conduct authenticated transactions
- Real-time on-line collaboration, so that people can work with white boards, share applications, and interact with audio and multimedia capabilities
- Seamless instantaneous transactions capabilities, to increase value added and enhance the customer interaction Web experience

## 10 LESSONS LEARNED

The following excerpt from Robert Edelman, vice president of Marshall Industries, explains 10 lessons the company has learned from its Internet venture:

1. You can build a Web site for a few thousand dollars, but to become an Internet provider of business services takes thousands or millions of dollars (that is the hard reality). It is a challenge to allow users to come to a site where all information is dynamically created and updated constantly.

2. Keep focused on the business benefits, such as selling products, improving quality, reducing costs, expanding your marketplace, and increasing the number of customers.

3. Work on enhancing your company's brand on the Internet. Customers are beginning to identify more and more with business brands on the Internet. As you establish your brand on the Internet, you strengthen your linkages with suppliers and customers, and gain a competitive advantage that is very hard for your competition to emulate.

4. Accept and embrace new workflows that are being created as a result of your customers' interacting with the Web. You have to recognize that what represented high value last week or last year may no longer be valued. For example, if

coming in with the data sheet was part of the value that sales representatives had, what happens now that all data sheets are available instantaneously on the Web?

5. Use patience and stepwise development to allow for growth to happen. If the Web doesn't make you anxious, you may not be realizing the full potential of the Internet on your business. Actually, the velocity of change in Internet technology is more rapid than a human being can digest.

6. You can be paralyzed, you can lead, or you can follow, depending on your desired market position. To lead calls for resources, commitment, and a vision.

7. If you try nothing, you'll get nothing. If you try a lot, you'll get a lot. If you make mistakes, you will learn from them.

8. There is no cookbook. You still have to apply the basic management principles and executive management tools that exist in the physical world.

9. The Web has to integrate directly into your traditional business model. It has to effect the changes within your current business model; otherwise, it is not going to benefit you.

10. There are never enough resources for all ideas, so prioritization is key. Ignore initial negative responses you may get from your information systems department. If the technology can't do it today, the future is very near, and possibly two or three months can make a difference.

## CONCLUSION

Marshall Industries has evolved beyond just being an electronics parts distributor. It was blessed by having already been successful at implementing IT-driven organizational change. For Marshall, the Internet was another form of IT, or another catalyst for change. Its top-down management vision and executive commitments were essential. The Internet was too important for Marshall to treat it as an isolated project.

Marshall truly believed that its current value chain, based on the industrial model, had changed radically in favor of an information age value chain model driven by Virtual Distribution™. Furthermore, it was able to identify exactly how the chain had changed, and where new value needed to be injected. Accordingly, Marshall embraced the Internet as an extension of its electronic business vision, and began to reap the rewards while watching its customer intimacy grow. Marshall also enabled its customers and suppliers to collaborate by using information and capabilities directly from its Web site.

In retrospect, Marshall is getting the luxury and rewards of early experience in doing business on the Internet, where the Internet is a critical part of its business. This luxury is tied to the fact that its customers (most of them in the electronics industry) were themselves Internet early adopters, so the critical-mass problem was resolved. Marshall already had the audience, and already had captivated it.

Finally, in addition to having seen its sales and earnings significantly improve as a result of these implementations, Marshall Industries and its president, Robert Rodin, started to collect recognized industry awards for their achievements and leadership in Internet commerce.

Another way to learn from Marshall's strategy is to recap its actions with a series of questions. The value of this exercise is to draw possible analogies to your business, which might allow you to give fuel to your case for action.

- Did Marshall's old business look like a low-value commodity business?
- Did it initiate a top-down direction and vision?
- Did it go through an evolutionary educational process?
- Did it take a cross-functional focus?
- Did it follow up by changing internal measurements criteria?
- Did it say: "Good-bye industrial age"?
- Did it recognize and identify the changing nature of its business?
- Did it recognize how value was changing in the "eyes of the customer"?

- Did it have a "captive" audience?
- Did it integrate the Web with its back-end processes from day 1?
- Did it introduce new capabilities beyond "copying the physical world"?
- Did it take advantage of the strengths of its Intranets and internal IT systems?
- Is Marshall allowing transactions to happen?
- Is it becoming a 7X24 (7 days, 24 hours a day) virtual machine?
- Has it derived business value and profits from the Internet?
- Does it continue to push the limits with new capabilities?
- If the Internet ceased to exist, would it negatively affect Marshall's business? (This is a scary question, but since it is unlikely to happen, Marshall's upside is now tremendous.)

# MANAGING SUCCESSFUL INTERNET COMMERCE

*For many businesses, the Internet is still a technology in search of strategy.*

MARY CRONIN

*Internet Author and Professor of Management, Boston College*

In May 1997, as I was getting ready to deliver a two-hour overview to 15 banking executives about effective management strategies for Internet commerce, the executive who hired me for the job told me: "We have all recently read about Nets Inc.'s bankruptcy last weekend, and some of us are now skeptical about the Internet as a whole, so we'd like you to give us your opinion on it." Nice damper as a starting point! After being startled for a few seconds, I scratched my head and, with some quick research, came up with the following analysis that provides valuable lessons.

One way to interpret the reason behind Nets Inc.'s failure is to think that this is no different from other failures in other businesses in the real world. Would the failure of a retail store next to yours entice you to get out of the retail business, if you were doing well? Did the failure of Eastern Airlines in 1994 signal the end of the airline industry or cause other carriers to rethink the business they were in? No. In each case, the failure was discreetly welcomed by the competition, which quickly moved in on the loser's territory and took away its customers. That was the best way for me to explain the Nets Inc. situation.

Having said that, I still consider it useful to analyze other related points in order to learn from this failure. Nets Inc. had built up too-high expectations, being touted so often as the most successful model for business-to-business commerce on the Internet. In reality, Nets Inc. did not move as fast as the Internet demanded. Its model remained stagnant. It did not introduce transactional capabilities or organize its sellers and buyers in more sophisticated ways. It appeared to have stayed pat as a glorified bulletin board, a loose community of information, good for finding anything from anybody, from a pencil eraser in Kansas City to a bulldozer in Denver. On the technical side, Nets Inc. was also criticized for attempting too much software development on its own, and this was perhaps another factor to its detriment. By July 1997, Nets Inc.'s failure stopped making headlines, and that was the end of it.

This chapter introduces the concepts of benchmarking, measuring business value, the burning-platform case for action, scenario planning, and chaos and complexity theory. Even though they are all current management principles, the difference is that they are now applied for managing and measuring Internet commerce opportunities.

## TOP 10 REASONS FOR NOT EMBRACING INTERNET COMMERCE

With tongue in cheek, I have attempted to re-create a "David Letterman Top 10 Reasons" in order to highlight some of the perceptions that exist in the marketplace. I confess to having heard all of them at one time or another. I have also added appropriate responses to address these concerns, but with a business sarcasm that arguably is deserved to be heard by those who made the objection (Table 11-1).

## POSITIONING THE CASE FOR ACTION

Is electronic commerce giving you anxiety? I think it should. If it isn't, you may not be doing enough. As Bob Edelman, vice

## Table 11-1. Top 10 Reasons and Responses for Not Doing Internet Commerce

| Reason for Not Embracing Internet Commerce | Response |
|---|---|
| 10. We are doing EDI. | It's not enough. Please reread Chapter 1 to understand the differences between EDI and Internet commerce. |
| 9. The Internet is a fad. We're waiting for it to go away. | If you wait long enough, you are the one who is likely to go away, because the Internet is here to stay. |
| 8. It smells like reengineering. | So, why are you afraid of change? If you can't allow change to happen in your organization, you have a problem. |
| 7. The Internet is not fast enough. | Internet commerce is not about surfing the Internet at T1 speed. Many Internet commerce applications do not require heavy bandwidth. |
| 6. There is no security. | Security is multifaceted and must be understood. Please hire somebody who doesn't think it is a problem. |
| 5. Our customers don't want it. | Ask them again. Your competition may be doing it. |
| 4. Who's going to pay for it? | Initially, there is an investment price to pay. You can begin immediately to cut costs, then later generate revenue. |
| 3. We're looking at it. | If that is all you have to say about it, you are only involved, not committed. |
| 2. MIS is in charge of it. | Yes, but MIS needs to be led and given direction to help you meet your business objectives. |
| 1. We already have a Web site. | Good for you, and so do 1.5 million other organizations, so how are you planning on differentiating your company? |

SOURCE: CYBERManagement Inc.

president of Marshall Industries, points out: "If the Internet is not giving you anxiety, you may not be realizing its full potential." The kind of anxiety being talked about here is not necessarily the personal anxiety that keeps you awake at night. It is rather corporate anxiety that is at stake. Given the profound changes that a full deployment of Internet commerce imposes on an organization, the resulting impact may measure fairly high on the corporate anxiety scale alongside other major and usually unwanted or uncontrolled corporate crisis events (Figure 11-1).

It is the executive's responsibility to reduce this anxiety by depicting the benefits to be reached for the organization. A sense of urgency based on a burning-platform scenario may be necessary to move the organization forward. To paraphrase the wise man who was asked "What are you afraid of?" Answer: "The unknown."

To reduce the corporate anxiety, make a concerted effort to answer the following questions:

- Could our entire business get disintermediated by other intermediaries we have never heard about before?

- Are we competing (without knowing it) with a new type of organization that is constantly reinventing itself every six months?

- Do we know how much market share we are susceptible to losing, not in the physical marketplace, but in the new electronic marketplace?

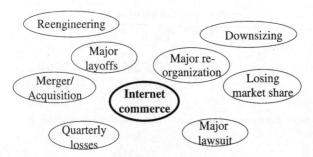

**FIGURE 11-1.** Internet commerce ranks with other high corporate anxiety events. (*CYBERManagement Inc.*)

## Guiding Principles

The difficulty in justifying a companywide awareness of electronic commerce is directly proportional to the size and complexity of your organization. Furthermore, what you see on the Web by surfing it doesn't tell you what is really going on or how your competitors are benefiting from their Web strategies. The following observations are worth evaluating for your enterprise. They are meant to stimulate your thinking and direct you into specific actions. As a mental exercise, ask yourself if you agree with the following statements:

- Leapfrogging what reengineering promised, the Internet has to permeate the internal business processes and customer interface points for it to create a sustainable competitive advantage.

- Internet commerce represents a once-in-a-lifetime opportunity for CEOs to restructure their organizations to take advantage of the fundamental change imposed on them for conducting business with partners, suppliers, and customers.

- Executive education concerning the Internet should be taken seriously. Better-informed managers will make better decisions affecting the Internet strategy for their companies.

- Organizations must evolve an Internet strategy beyond a Web presence to introduce new services that integrate business processes and enable the organization to be ready for the new digital economy.

- Intranet applications must be integrated via the Internet to your trading partners' and customers' Intranets in order to conduct business-to-business electronic commerce.

- Business managers must look at the Internet as a multifaceted catalyst, and take full advantage of each facet. The Internet is simultaneously a network, a market, a medium, a transaction platform, and a development platform.

- Deriving measurable business value from the Internet is required for a sustainable investment strategy. Business value is derived from: reducing costs, simplifying a process, improving customer service, generating new revenue, making better decisions, or impacting corporate knowledge.

## BUSINESS VALUE OF ELECTRONIC COMMERCE

Regardless of the level of commitment that you have embarked on, if you are not able to measure the results of your objectives, it will be difficult to proceed further with higher levels of funding and executive approvals. Various types of key measurements could be estimated prior to getting approval for a full implementation. Alternatively, the same measures can be documented after an implementation in order to judge the degree of success achieved. The old adage "If you can't measure it, you can't manage it" applies. Here are some key measures that allow you to assess business value.

- *Reducing costs.*   Basic cost reductions might start with publishing costs, which include the cost of producing, printing, and distributing information for customers or employees. Another area involves looking at the buying/selling model and measuring cost reductions associated with each step of the process, such as general marketing, selling, and support costs.
- *Simplifying a process.*   Instead of using paper for an approval process, use the Web to simplify it and speed it up. You can think of many other types of processes that are simplified or eliminated with the introduction of their Internet equivalent. The end result could be a productivity gain that can be measured.
- *Improving customer service.*   By giving your customers self-access to their accounts, transactions, orders, and so on, you are providing them with valuable information in a more timely and accurate manner. The level of satisfaction for those customers interacting electronically with you will undoubtedly rise. In many cases, customers will decrease their calling rate when looking for information.

- *Generating new revenue.*   The new Internet electronic marketplace allows you to generate new revenue by (1) selling new products and services specifically designed for the electronic marketplace or (2) using the incremental channel-of-distribution power of the Internet to sell existing products and services.

- *Making better (and faster) decisions.*   The Web facilitates access to competitive and marketplace information. For example, if you receive information about your competition through an Intranet information retrieval database, you are able to develop a competitive strategy faster. This is not to imply that decisions are not made quickly without the Internet. However, the Internet accelerates information dissemination and its quality, which then leads to better decisions.

- *Cost of not doing.*   No action could be a hidden cost initially. If it doesn't appear that you are able to measure any of the above elements, then you can start with a reverse scenario, and estimate the costs incurred to your company if the given Internet commerce initiatives are not undertaken.

- *Impact on corporate knowledge.*   How is the Internet contributing to your corporate IQ? This may be a more difficult objective to measure, but Japanese companies are used to it. They treat the concept of knowledge as a key element for sustainable competitive advantage.

## BENCHMARKING YOUR EVOLUTION

*Fool you are to say you learn by your experience! I prefer to profit by others' mistakes, and avoid the price of my own.*

PRINCE OTTO VON BISMARCK

*Keep on the lookout for novel and interesting ideas that others have used successfully. Your idea has to be original only in its adaptation to the problem you're currently working on.*

THOMAS EDISON

The Internet may be a new paradigm, but business is still business. Established management practices can well apply to the Internet. The "benchmarking" concept is highlighted here only as an example to encourage managers to apply other proven management principles to manage the Internet commerce strategy.

Benchmarking assumes that you can learn by adapting existing knowledge and experience from the recognized best, and use it to fit your own needs. It is an essential concept that is used routinely by the world's largest and best organizations.

With the Internet, history and experience are both new, so it seems that benchmarking is a more difficult issue to tackle. Nonetheless, by remembering some basic principles about benchmarking, organizations can benefit from the advantages it offers. It is likely that this exercise will be more useful for organizations that already have had some experience on the Internet, even though it could also be applied in smaller doses to test an idea that hasn't been introduced yet.

How does this exercise apply to the Internet? To answer the question, you must first recognize that there are three types of benchmarking. Then think about how each can be applied to your situation. Table 11-2 summarizes the areas addressed by each, and how they apply to the Internet.

## SCENARIO PLANNING

A recent conference on scenario planning touted the following headlines in its promotional material: "Optimizing decision making through scenario planning." "Achieving real growth in uncertain times and unpredictable markets." How appropriate for the Internet! Since Internet commerce carries several uncertainties about an unpredictable future, one way to better prepare for it is by developing scenario-planning techniques.

At the heart of scenario planning is the ability provided for accurately predicting change that affects you. Scenario planning attempts to compensate for two common errors in decision making—underprediction (tunnel vision) and overprediction (over-

## TABLE 11-2. Benchmarking Principles Applied to the Internet

| TYPE OF BENCHMARKING | BUSINESS FOCUS | INTERNET ANALOGY |
|---|---|---|
| Process benchmarking | • Look at operating practices that perform similar work functions: discrete work processes such as customer complaint process, billing process, order and fulfillment process.<br><br>• Short-term benefits.<br><br>• Increased productivity, lower costs, improved sales. | • How do we increase productivity and lower costs in digital content generation, overall Web design, exposure with targeted users, rapid Web implementation of new ideas, attracting new electronic customers? |
| Performance benchmarking | • Product and service comparison. Elements of price, technical quality, features, speed, reliability. Use reverse engineering. | • How can we improve content quality and variety?<br><br>• Can we add or go beyond new features and services that our competition has? |
| Strategic benchmarking | • Examine how companies compete, and how they have become successful in their marketplaces.<br><br>• Long-term benefits. | • How successful have we been in creating and exploiting new marketplaces from the Internet?<br><br>• Have we successfully entered markets not available to us before? |

SOURCE: Adapted from Christopher Bogan and Michael English, *Benchmarking for Best Practices* (McGraw-Hill, 1994).

confidence) of change. The process is a disciplined one that involves imagining possibilities against a wide array of issues.

Looking ahead and understanding likely and unlikely scenarios enables you to act with more confidence. *The Long View,* written by Peter Schwartz, contains excellent step-by-step guidelines for scenario planning. These can very well apply to Internet commerce. Here are some of the likely scenarios that should be investigated.

- What if we bypassed our distribution channels?
- What if we were bypassed by other new intermediaries?
- What if 100 percent of our customers expected electronic distribution of products and services two years from now?
- What if our current customer value added is perceived to be worth nothing any more?
- What if 50 percent of our revenues now originated from Internet-mediated marketplaces?
- What is the impact of us competing more vigorously now in the electronic marketplace as opposed to the traditional markets we are in today?

## APPLY CHAOS AND COMPLEXITY THEORY

Just as in scenario planning, chaos and complexity theory seems to be ideally suited to Internet commerce strategy planning. Chaos refers to a situation where patterns cannot be easily made and where details are poorly understood. Complexity refers to one of the following two situations:

1. Patterns cannot be made but details, parts, and subsystems can be understood.
2. Details cannot be understood but the whole (or general result) can be understood by the ability to make patterns.

To take better control of this apparent complexity, it appears that the discovery of patterns and rules is key to improving management decision making and to developing effective predictions. Given the dynamic nature of the Internet as an industry on steroids, how can the relevant patterns be discerned? This isn't about predicting the future, but rather about enabling a short-term forecasting that is useful. In 1997 Peter Drucker was asked in a *Forbes* interview about his abilities to predict the future, judging by his track record of writing insightful management books for the last 50 years. His response was: "I never predict. I just look out the window and see what's visible—but not yet seen."

Seeing what is visible, but not yet seen is really about discerning patterns and making sense of them. The successful Internet businesses of today—Amazon, Marshall, and others—did not go to great lengths to try to validate the Internet patterns they had discerned in 1994 and 1995. They had seen them, and acted accordingly. During that time, it wasn't obvious, but today it may seem to be. Unfortunately for others, what is obvious is obvious after it becomes obvious!

## FROM DIGITAL VALUE TO DIGITAL MARKETS

What do Marshall Industries, Fruit of the Loom, and AMP have in common? All three were successful companies that relied for years on a certain set of core values they were used to delivering to their customers. But today, as they shift more to Internet-based commerce, they are beginning to rely on entirely new types of values: the digital ones. These digital values, in the form of a product or service, are what will ensure their future success. Current (old) value is no longer a prerequisite for their success.

By offering a strong set of digital value services, these companies are forcing their customers and suppliers to migrate to them. Electronic buyers will migrate to where digital value is, thereby creating new "virtually" integrated digital markets.

Three characteristics are common to this set of digital values (Figure 11-2).

1. *It is information-based.*   For speed of delivery and pace of innovation purposes.
2. *Its ownership is questionable.*   Digital value could be owned by you or by other intermediaries
3. *It surrounds current value.*   Digital value surrounds, complements, and sometimes obsoletes old value.

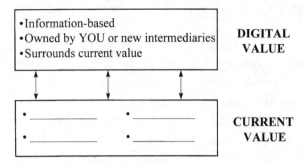

**FIGURE 11-2.** Applying digital value on top of existing value. (*CYBERManagement Inc.*)

# THE RISE OF DIGITAL MARKETS

When all is said and done, more will be accomplished by those who know that the choices made today will make a big difference in the future. The rise of digital value is leading to the creation of digital markets (Figure 11-3).

Traditional physical markets are becoming a shrinking part of the worldwide available trade markets. Digital markets (or iMarkets) are capturing an increasing share of these available markets. So, if you don't start playing in the new digital markets, there won't be too many markets left for you to play in.

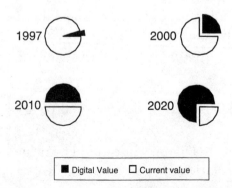

**FIGURE 11-3.** The rise of digital value is an unstoppable trend. (*CYBERManagement Inc.*)

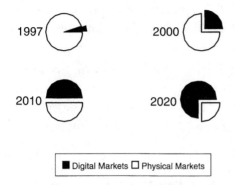

FIGURE 11-4. The shrinking physical markets mean fewer markets to compete in.
(*CYBERManagement Inc.*)

Figure 11-4 dramatizes what might happen to your current markets if you don't act today. The year 2000 may appear to be a turning point, as digital markets begin to account for very significant revenues and profits for most organizations. After all, few organizations want to have another major problem at the turn of the century besides the Year2000 IT challenge!

To prove the rise of "virtually" integrated commerce and the opening of digital markets, consider the following facts:

- In the first quarter of 1997, less than two years after it started its on-line auction business, ONSALE Inc. was grossing $6 million per month in Internet auction sales.

- In 1996, Cisco saved $350 million on an expense base of $1.5 billion, thanks to the Internet. In 1997, Cisco was doing over $5 million in sales per day from the Internet with its distribution partners.

- By mid-1997, Microsoft's Expedia announced it was booking over $2 million in travel tickets per week, and barely keeping up with the demand.

- In October 1997, a year after the launch of its on-line store on the Internet, Dell Computers was selling over $3 million per day.

- In the first nine months of 1997, Amazon.com posted sales of $81.7 million, versus $7.2 million for the same period in 1996.

- On April 18, 1997, the Red Cross/Red Crescent Societies launched PLUS Lotto, an Internet sweepstakes. On July 4, 1997 (11 weeks later), the first Internet millionaire won 1.25 million Swiss francs, the single largest lump-sum payout as of that date on the Internet.

- Signaling the debut of large-scale business-to-business procurement on the Internet, in October 1997, MIT signed for an estimated $125 million, five-year commitment to buy all its computers over the Internet from reseller NECX, Inc.

- By the end of its third quarter (June 1997), E*Trade, the on-line securities brokerage business, had 182,000 active accounts worth $5.5 billion in assets. It posted $94.3 million in revenues and was already profitable.

After looking at the above facts, we quickly realize that this shift has taken on an exponential momentum. Undoubtedly, small companies are getting bigger, but large companies are also prospering with electronic commerce on the Internet.

To seize this opportunity is to seize an opportunity of a lifetime.

# EPILOGUE

One of the main challenges I have had in writing this book was actually to stop writing! Given the rapid technological developments in the Internet electronic commerce marketplace, there was no shortage of lessons or implementations worth commenting on. I really had to stop reading the news and talking to people in the last few days of writing in order to get the publication out on time!

This book was meant to enlighten managers and senior executives about digital market possibilities with Internet commerce. *Internet commerce is not a one-time event, nor is it a walk in the park.* It requires a solid corporate commitment, with a case for action that is firmly endorsed by senior management. To move the organization forward with the required synergy and resources, executives are encouraged to instill a burning-platform case for action.

The digital organization of the future will be "virtually" integrated and will depend on the dynamics, behaviors, and paradoxes of digital markets. Virtual partnerships that get configured on the fly, at a moment's notice, will be part of the new value chain, between you and your customers. Make sure that you are ready for it so you can benefit from the renewal of power, profits, and commerce on the Internet.

Every organization will have to be successful at exploiting the Internet for electronic commerce purposes. The earlier you start, the better you will be at doing it. Success in Internet commerce doesn't depend solely on your Web site; more important, it will depend on how you strategically position your products and services vis à vis other Internet-based electronic communities and intermediaries, as well as on how you facilitate your interactions with customers, suppliers, and partners.

Internet commerce is not an extension of EDI. So, it might be self-limiting to rely on your EDI strategy or resources to get you there. You have to break new ground in Internet territory in order to capture emerging digital markets or global iMarkets.

My hope is that, by reading this book, you can decisively declare that for your organization the Internet electronic commerce march is on.

Only the future will show that the cost of inaction may be far greater than the cost of taking action.

# DIGITAL PAYMENT OPTIONS

When you pay for something in the real world, the following options are available: cash, checks, credit cards, traveler's cheques, prepaid cards, debit cards, physical tokens, bank notes, secure wire transfers, money orders, and letters of credit. However, none of these mechanisms is directly transferable in an unmodified form to the Internet, mainly because each one assumes a physical presence or because a delay is incurred in the processing of funds so that fraud can be detected.

## GENERIC FLAVORS OF INTERNET PAYMENT INSTRUMENTS

When you look at the various options for payment instruments, it is important to keep the following classification in mind. Given the multitude on new options that are emerging, it becomes easy to confuse them (Table A-1). The following are generic flavors of the new Internet payment instruments.

### DIGITAL CASH

Also referred to as electronic cash, digital cash is a software-based currency which translates into equivalent real currency units that are guaranteed by a bank. Usually, there is a trusted authority that allows the user to conduct and pay for transactions of this nature after a predetermined relationship has been established (e.g., DigiCash). There are no interoperability standards for digital cash, yet.

TABLE A-1. Type, Protocol, and Brand of Payment Instrument

| TYPE OF PAYMENT | PAYMENT PROTOCOL | BRANDING |
|---|---|---|
| Credit card | SET | Visa Cash |
| Digital currency | OTP | Mondex |
| Smart card | JEPI | CyberCash |
| Internet check | GlobeID | DigiCash |
| Debit card | C-SET (SET on a chip) | First Virtual |
| | | KLELine |
| | | Proton |

## SMART CARDS

Smart cards can be used with or without a stored value. These can also be "smart" extensions of debit cards. Usually, the user is able to pay with them without having to connect to a remote system. If they have a stored value which contains "real digital cash," they are known as *cash cards* because they replace carrying cash (e.g., Mondex). The cardholder can use the Internet or other electronic connections to replenish the card with new money from remote locations. If the card doesn't store a currency value, it may contain a private encryption key, a digital signature, or an electronic token that can be used to initiate an authentication process during a payment transaction.

A next generation of smart cards is referred to as *relationship cards*. These cards store a lot more information and are linked to a database for updates. They enable multipurpose applications, such as the ImagineCard alliance (Hewlett-Packard, Informix, and Gemplus). A single card accommodates the following functions: electronic purse, conference evaluation, logical and physical access, and registration with full customer accessibility and card-owner-controlled authentication.

Figure A-1 summarizes the various types of emerging smart cards and their usage. Please note that reusable smart cards could be single function or multipurpose.

| Consumable | Reusable |
|---|---|
| (Use once, throw away) | (Use, reload, reuse) |

| | |
|---|---|
| •Vending machines | •Identification |
| •Telephone calls | •Electronic access |
| •Retailer specific | •Device control |
| | •Physical access |
| | •Ticketing |
| | •Loyalty programs |
| | •Health records |
| | •Cash value |

**FIGURE A-1.** There are two types of smart cards: consumable and reusable. (*CYBERManagement Inc.*)

## ENCRYPTED CREDIT CARDS

There are varying degrees of encryption implementations of credit cards over the Internet, with Secure Electronic Transaction (SET) holding the most promise. Usually, confidentiality of information, payment integrity, and authenticity of both the merchant and cardholder are requirements. Digital signatures may augment the transaction as a way to ensure non-repudiation of the transaction and the authenticity of the originator (e.g., CyberCash).

## ELECTRONIC CHECKS

Electronic checks are the Internet equivalent of paper-based checks. They are initiated during an on-screen dialog which results in the payment transaction. Authentication and verification are usually performed instantaneously by using digital signatures and time-stamping controls during the transaction (e.g., CheckFree).

## INTERNET FINANCIAL EDI

Internet financial EDI will be used by businesses that were already doing financial EDI with VANs. One of the first large organizations that demonstrated the validity of this method and later fully embraced it was the Lawrence Livermore National Laboratories, in cooperation with Bank of America. Livermore reportedly processed $300 million through this method in 1996. Also, Chase Manhattan Bank and Diamond Shamrock have engaged in large financial EDI transactions over the Internet (see case story in Chapter 7).

All of the above choices (except financial EDI) dictate several systems and implementation methods not universally backed. Each one is trying to secure a beachhead or carve its own niche without regard for interoperability with other instruments. Several of these systems have their own proprietary applications program interfaces to allow integration with the merchant and banking systems.

Acknowledging that this new era of electronic payments needs some order, the U.S. Treasury Secretary recently formed a task force to study and guide the government in supporting and regulating the electronic money revolution. This task force is also seeking participation from other industrialized nations, since these changes affect the financial industry across borders.

## CRITERIA FOR CHOOSING INTERNET INSTRUMENTS

Organizations need to view the payments issue as an architectural module of electronic commerce, and they must offer several alternatives to their customers. It is almost useless to analyze the inner workings of each one of the existing payment instruments today. What is important is to understand the implementation requirements, as well as the cost implications if you decide to integrate a given payment mechanism within your "electronic storefront" or "electronic back office."

I recommend that you investigate one or several of the above payment options, depending on your understanding of how your needs fit their specific implementation. The following questions may help you choose an appropriate method:

1. Do you want the system to handle microtransactions?

2. Do you want a real-time cash, debit, or credit type option?

3. Do you need a peer-to-peer on-line payment system? In this case, interoperability is still an issue.

4. Do you want to process the financial charges yourself, or are you willing to pay a fee to a third party?

5. Do you favor a smart card stored-value system, or a token-based software-only setup?

6. Is the smart card simply a digital signature enabler (for credit or debit), or does it have real cash value stored?

7. Do you want a system that has a preregistration requirement for either the seller or the buyer?

8. Do you want a system that charges the buyer, seller, or transaction processor?

9. Are you comfortable enough with financial EDI transactions that you can evolve to Internet financial EDI?

Options to consider when looking at payment instruments include:

| | |
|---|---|
| NetChex | Europay |
| NetBill | VeriFone |
| NetCash | Millicent |
| CheckFree | PayWord |
| CyberCash | MicroMint |
| DigiCash | KLELine |
| First Virtual Holdings | GlobeID |
| Mondex | eTILL |
| BlueMoney | |

Today, most payment mechanisms require a prior arrangement to be set up with the issuing entity and could be limited to the participating bank or financial institution. In the near future, we will see more interoperability, such as CheckFree incorporating CyberCash in its CheckFree Wallet, or Visa and MasterCard's SET joint standard. But this is only the beginning, since a specific storefront should not be limited to a particular cash or encryption solution that will serve only a segment of potential customers. Nor should the merchant be limited in the choice of a financial institution partner. A standard is reached when a critical mass of users is already on-line and using a specific mechanism. For back-end transactions, it is very likely that emerging practices will rely on extensions of the existing financial networks.

Finally, here is a note on the SET protocol that helps to clarify its purpose:

> SET is a payment protocol designed to protect consumers' bank card information when they choose to use bank cards to pay for goods and services on the Internet and other open networks. SET does not go beyond that scope or explore areas that are being addressed by the computer industry; specifically, it does not define the shopping or ordering process; it does not define payment method selection such as credit card, check, or mail device or operating system.*

* Visa/MasterCard press release, July 1996.

# INTERNATIONAL ELECTRONIC COMMERCE ORGANIZATIONS

## JAPAN

### Electronic COMmerce Promotion Council of Japan (ECOM)

ECOM is established with a view of linking distributors, manufacturers, and service providers who will use electronic commerce with computer vendors and information processing services that will build its infrastructure. ECOM's objective is to become the open forum for the development of common platforms.

Some of the working groups' areas of interest include standardization of product information, content integration (agent functions), business protocols between malls and content providers, common security technologies, shopping mall construction technologies, authentication, IC cards, and authentication centers.

*Contact:*
Secretariat
Time24 Bldg. 10F
2-45, Aomi, Kohtu-ku
Tokyo 135-73, Japan
Tel: + 81 3 5531 0061
Fax: + 81 3 5531 0068
e-mail: info@ecom.or.jp
Web: www.ecom.or.jp

## Cyberbusiness Association of Japan

Established in 1995, the Cyberbusiness Association of Japan has 94 member companies. Its current projects aim to evaluate the security and related operational technology over information networks. Major projects include the Telecom Service Association Trial, the JEMA EC Trial, and the Electronic Money Trial.

*Contact:*
Dr. Masayuki Nomura
Senior Manager, Planning Department
Nippon Telegraph and Telephone Corporation
Nittochi Uchisaiwai-cho Building
2-1 Uchisaiwai-cho
1-Chome Chiyoda-ku
Tokyo 100-19, Japan
Tel: + 81 3 3509 3676
Fax: + 81 3 3595 0286
e-mail: nomura@sphere.ad.jp

# EUROPE

## IBCC-Net: The Consortium of the International Bureau of Chambers of Commerce (IBCC) Network for Global Commerce

IBCC-Net is a system for the exchange of information among chambers of commerce and industry aimed at strengthening cooperation among chambers throughout the world.

The first specific objective is to contribute to the development of a global electronic environment for the open and nondiscriminatory exchange of information (e.g., data on technologies, products, and human resources), using international information networks to overcome obstacles of distance, time, and country borders for the benefit of SMEs. The second specific objective is to expand global electronic commerce in order to enable enterprises to carry out their business operations and management more effectively and more profitably.

*Contact:*
  Georges Fischer
  Deputy Director
  Paris Chamber of Commerce & Industry
  27 avenue de Friedland
  75382 Paris Cedex 08, France
  Tel: + 33 1 42 89 72 18
  Fax: + 33 1 42 89 72 08
  e-mail: fisxherg@ccip.fr
  Web: www.icc-ibcc.org/ibccnet.html

## French Association for Electronic Commerce and Exchange (AFCEE)

### Association Française pour le Commerce et les Echanges Electroniques

The AFCEE's objectives are to put in place a real Internet electronic market and to promote the emergence of electronic commerce in Europe. It hopes to influence and initiate Internet usage in education, culture, health care, and public service. The association sees itself as an intersection for information exchange, testing, research, and even financing relating to these initiatives.

*Contact:*
Julien Dufour
2 rue de Viarmes
75001 Paris, France
Tel: + 01 40 26 63 36
Fax: + 01 40 26 70 92
e-mail: Julien.Dufour@Utopia.EUnet.fr
Web: www2.atelier.fr/afcee

### Secure Electronic Marketplace for Europe (SEMPER)

SEMPER is a European R&D project in the area of secure electronic commerce over open networks, especially the Internet. It is executed by an interdisciplinary consortium, combining experts from social sciences, finance, retail, publishing, IT, and telecommunications, and it has established liaisons with several related efforts. SEMPER is part of the European Commission's ACTS (Advanced Communications Technologies and Services) Programme. SEMPER aims at providing an open and comprehensive approach to secure electronic commerce over the Internet and other public information networks.

The current phase of SEMPER addresses a coherent security model and a generic, open security architecture for the electronic marketplace. This architecture is independent of specific hardware, software, or network architectures. The most fundamental electronic commerce services, such as secure offering, order, payment, and information delivery, are also integrated in this first phase.

*Contact:*
Gerard Lacoste
IBM La Gaude
Centre d'Etudes et Recherches
Le Plan du Bois
F-06610 La Gaude, France
Tel: + 33 92 11 48 07
Fax : + 33 93 24 45 45
e-mail: lacoste@vnet.ibm.com
Web: www.semper.org

## Electronic Commerce Association (ECA)

ECA aims to encourage improvements in industrial, commercial, and governmental efficiency by offering guidance and practical solutions to enable organizations to make the most effective use of electronic commerce. The association will provide its members in the public and private sectors with information, support, and facilitation services to enable the general adoption of best business practices in the implementation of electronic commerce.

The ECA was formed by the business community in 1987, initially as the EDI Association (EDIA). Embracing the changing market, the ECA broadened its sphere of interest beyond the initial focus on EDI to incorporate the wider aspects of electronic commerce.

*Contact:*
Dr. Roger Till
Chief Executive
Ramillies House
1-9 Hills Place
London W1R 1AG, United Kingdom
Tel: + 0171 432 2502
Fax: + 0171 432 2501
e-mail: roger.till@eca.org.uk
Web: www.eca.org.uk

## European Commission—Electronic Commerce for SMEs

The European Commission supports the European Parliament and the Council of Ministers in policy making in the European Union. Directorate-General III is responsible for industrial policy and is also in charge of the information technology R&D program. "A Global Marketplace for SMEs" is an initiative of this directorate, and focuses on electronic commerce for the small to medium-size enterprises in Europe.

*Contact:*
Paul Timmers
Head of Sector
Electronic Commerce for SMEs
European Commission
Wetsraat 200, B-1049 Brussels, Belgium
Tel: + 32 2 299 02 45
Fax: + 32 2 296 83 87
e-mail: paul.timmers@dg3.cec.be

## Electronic Commerce Europe (ECE)

Founded in March 1997, ECE seeks to promote, coordinate, and assist in the development of electronic commerce in Europe. The association intends to carry out investigation and research in these areas and promote contacts among members by supporting and establishing courses, conferences, and practical work. It will contribute to a focused development of electronic commerce by exchanging information and cooperating with similar initiatives whether national or international and by influencing public opinion at all levels. The association will contribute to the establishment of good practices in the sector and will foster new initiatives aimed at accelerating penetration and acceptance of electronic commerce worldwide.

*Contact:*
Bill Bedford
High Street, Inkberrow
Worcester WR7 4DT, United Kingdom
Tel: + 44 1386 793 028
Fax: + 44 1386 793 268
e-mail: billbedford@attmail.com
Web: www.ec-europe.de

# CANADA

### EC World Institute

The Electronic Commerce World Institute is an independent, international organization that addresses the strategic business issues relating to electronic data interchange and electronic commerce around the world.

Created in 1992 by EDI associations from 11 countries, the nonprofit institute works to accelerate the development and adoption of EDI and electronic commerce in business and government. It provides a worldwide forum for information exchange and knowledge sharing, develops and markets awareness and training tools, facilitates understanding and implementation through consultative services, and engages in solutions-oriented R&D with industry and government. It is the coordinating office for the Internet Law and Policy Forum (ILPF).

*Contact:*
André Vallerand
President
World Trade Centre
380 rue Saint-Antoine Ouest, Bureau 3280
Montréal, Québec H2Y 3X7, Canada
Tel: 1 514 288 3555

Fax: 1 514 288 6355
e-mail: valleranda@ecworld.org
Web: www.ecworld.org

# COMMERCENET AND ITS GLOBAL PARTNERS

**Australia:**
Bruce McCleay
8 Greenhill Road
Wayville 5034
Adelaide, South Australia
Tel: + 61 8 8372 7823
Fax: + 61 8 8372 7800
e-mail: bmcleay@adelaide.on.net

**Brazil:**
Nilton B. Guarnieri, Jr.
Director
Open Concept
Alameda Campinas, 463 cj. 9 c
Sao Paolo SP, Brazil 01404-000
Tel & Fax: + 55 11 253 9921
e-mail:
  open.concept@originet.com.br

**Canada:**
  Walid Mougayar
  President & CEO
  CYBERManagement Inc.
  151 Bloor Street. Suite 470
  Toronto, Ontario M5S 1S4
    Canada
  Tel: 1 416 929 1011
  Fax: 1 416 929 1552
  e-mail: walid@cyberm.com

**Chile:**
Adolfo Casari
Gerente
ACTI—Associacion Chilena de
  Empresas de Technologias de
  Informacion, AG
Avenida Santa Maria, Piso 4
0508 Santiago, Chile
Tel: + 56 (2) 735 5755
Fax: + 56 (2) 735 5754
e-mail: acasari@rdc.cl

**Finland:**
Seppo Auvinen
Managing Director
EDI Management
P.O. Box 416 (Innopoli,
  Tekniikantie 12)
FIN-02151 Espoo, Finland
Tel: + 358 0 4354 3770
e-mail: Seppo.Auvinen@innopoli.fi

**France:**
Jean-Claude Pelissolo
Chief Operating Officer
LaSer
66 Rue des Archives
75150 Paris, Cedex 03, France
Tel: + 33 (1) 44 54 41 06
Fax: + 33 (1) 44 54 41 08
e-mail: jcpelissolo@Atelier.fr

**Germany:**
Dr. Heiko Schinzer
Lehrstuhl fuer
  Betriebswirtschaftslehre und
  Wirtschaftsinformatik
Unversitaet Wuerzburg
Neubaustrasse 66
97070 Wuerzburg, Germany
Tel: + 49 (931) 31 24 47
Fax: + 49 (931) 31 29 55
e-mail: schinzer@wiinf.uni-
  wuerzburg.de

**India:**
Ashok Nadkarni
commercenetindia.com
Sumangal G-8, Cross Road A,
  Marol MIDC
Andheri (East), Mumbai 400 093,
  India
Tel: + 91 22 820 4627/820 4631
e-mail:
  ashok@commercenetindia.com

**Italy:**
Dr. Paola Monti
MATE, s.r.l.
C.so Colombo, 10
20144 Milano, Italy
Tel: + 39 (2) 839 4414
Fax: + 39 (2) 835 8747
e-mail: pmonti@mate.it

**Japan:**
Chika Watanabe
Mitsubishi Corporation
3-1, Marunouchi 2-Chome
Chiyoda-Ku
Tokyo 100-86, Japan
Tel: + 81 3 3210 3573
Fax: + 81 3 3210 7107
e-mail: chika@tk.mitsubishi.co.jp

**Korea:**
Dr. Kapsu Kim
CN Korea Secretariat
140-013 SUNGJI Bldg.
40-712, 3-Ga, Hangang-Ro
Yongsan-Ku, Seoul, Korea
Tel: + 82 2 220 7118
Fax: + 82 2 220 0732
e-mail:
  kskim@decs20.dacom.co.kr

**Malaysia:**
George Gan
Hitechniaga
Enterprise 3 (Ru 1A)
Technology Park Malaysia
Bukit Jalil
57000 Kuala Lumpur, Malaysia
Tel: + 603 966 0966
Fax: + 603 966 0082
e-mail: georgeg@hitech.com.my

**Netherlands:**
Dr. Ellen Houwen
Giliadal 5
2317 HS Leiden,
  The Netherlands
Tel & Fax: + 0031 71 522 5367
e-mail: ehouwen@bart.nl

**Norway:**
Siri A.M. Jensen
Norsk Regnesentral—Norwegian
  Computing Center
Gaustadalleen 23
P.O. Box 114 Blindern
N-0314 Oslo, Norway
Tel: + 47 22 85 26 11
Fax: + 47 22 69 76 60
e-mail: Siri.Jensen@nr.no

**Russia:**
Petrov Serge
Chief Economist, Currency
  Department
Maritime Bank
Novoslobodskaya str.14/19 bldg.7
Moscow 103030, Russia
Tel: + 7 095 978 09 14
Fax: + 7 095 978 27 30
e-mail:
  petrov@maritime.comstar.ru


**South Africa:**
Wayne Friedman
Managing Director
Digital Mall
P.O. Box 891157
Lyndhurst 2106, South Africa
Tel: + 27 11 650 5044
Fax: + 27 11 882 6908
e-mail:
  wayne@commercenet.org.za


**Spain:**
Sonia Fernandez
ECTF
Santa Cruz de Marcenado 33
Madrid 28015, Spain
Tel: + 34 1 541 7264
Fax: + 34 1 559 9274
e-mail: soniaectf@tst.es


**Sweden:**
Magnus Harviden
Swebizz
Box 7195
103 88 Stockholm, Sweden
e-mail: swebizz@swebizz.se

**Taiwan:**
Dr. Han-Min Hsia
President NII Enterprise
  Promotion Association
Adviser to the President, Republic
  of China
8F, No. 81 Changan E. Road
  Sec. 2
Taipei, Taiwan
Tel: + 886 2 508 2353
Fax: + 886 2 508 0573
e-mail: nii@ohm.nkit.edu.tw


**United Kingdom:**
Jasper Judd
Managing Director
Rivus, Ltd.
10 Elvaston Place
London SW7 5QG,
  United Kingdom
Tel: + 44 (0)171 460 3458
Fax: + 44 (0)171 225 1136
e-mail:
  jasperj@resource.prestel.co.uk


**United States:**
Steve Terry (Secretary, GECB)
Director, International Business
  Development
CommerceNet, Inc.
4005 Miranda Avenue, Suite 175
Palo Alto, CA 94304 USA
Tel: 415 858 1930 x213
Fax: 415 858 1936
e-mail: swterry@commerce.net

**U.S. CommerceNet Southeast:**
Genelle Viars
CommerceNet Southeast
3340 Peachtree Road, N.E.
Tower Place, Suite 1800
Atlanta, GA 30326 USA
Tel: 404 812 5300
e-mail: gviars@commerce.net

**U.S. CommerceNet Great Plains:**
Douglas Perry
Multimedia Center Director
Applied Information Management
  Institute
1314 Douglas On-the-Mall
Omaha, NE 68102 USA
Tel: 402 422 5408
Fax: 402 422 3693
e-mail: dperry@omaha.org

**U.S. CommerceNet Northeast:**
Ron Parsons
Director, NE Regional Business
  Development
3209-A Corporate Court
Ellicott City, MD 21042 USA
Tel: 410 203 2707
Fax: 410 203 2709

# WEB INDEX OF COMPANIES CITED

| | |
|---|---|
| @Home | www.home.net |
| Actra Corp. | www.actracorp.com |
| Advantis | www.advantis.com |
| Agentics | www.agentics.com |
| AgentSoft | www.agentsoft.com |
| Amazon.com Books | www.amazon.com |
| American Greeting Cards | www.americangreeting.com |
| AmericaOnline | www.aol.com |
| AMP | www.amp.com |
| Andromedia | www.andromedia.com |
| Apple | www.apple.com |
| Ariba | www.ariba.com |
| Autonomy | www.agentware.com |
| BackWeb | www.backweb.com |
| BigYellow | www.bigyellow.com |
| BlueMoney | www.bluemoney.com |
| BroadVision | www.broadvision.com |
| c\|net | www.cnet.com |
| Camelot | www.camelot.com |
| Canada Post Corporation | www.mailposte.ca |
| CarPoint Network | www.carpoint.com |
| Cebra Inc. | www.cebra.com |
| Certco | www.certco.com |
| Certicom | www.certicom.com |
| CheckFree | www.checkfree.com |

| | |
|---|---|
| CIBC | www.cibc.com |
| Cisco | www.cisco.com |
| Citicorp/Citibank | www.citicorp.com |
| CommerceNet | www.commerce.net |
| CompareNet | www.comparenet.com |
| CompuServe | www.compuserve.com |
| ComputerESP | www.computeresp.com |
| Conductor Inc. | www.conductor.com |
| Connect, Inc. | www.connectinc.com |
| Consumers Edge | www.consumersedge.com |
| CouponNet | www.coupon.com |
| Cowles Media Company | www.cowles.com |
| Cross Route | www.crossroute.com |
| CUC International | www.cuc.com |
| CyberCash | www.cybercash.com |
| CYBERManagement Inc. | www.cyberm.com |
| CyberMedia | www.cybermedia.com |
| CyberSource Corporation | www.cybersource.com |
| DCT Online Trading | online.dct.net |
| DealerNet | www.dealernet.com |
| Diamond Shamrock | www.diasham.com |
| DigiCash | www.digicash.com |
| DimensionX | www.dimension.com |
| DirectIPO | www.directipo.com |
| e*Schwab | www.eschwab.com |
| E*Trade Securities, Inc. | www.etrade.com |
| EarthWeb | www.earthWeb.com |
| Elcom Systems | www.elcom.com |
| ENEN | www.enen.com |
| Epistemics | www.epistemics.com |
| E-Stamp | www.estamp.com |
| e-Travel | www.etravel.com |
| ETA | www.etauction.com |

| | |
|---|---|
| Europay | www.europay.com |
| eXpense | www.expense.com |
| Federal Express | www.fedex.com |
| Fidelity Investments | www.fidelity.com |
| Firefly Network | www.firefly.com |
| First Data Corp. | www.firstdata.com |
| First USA Paymentech | www.firstUSA.com |
| First Virtual Holdings | www.fv.com |
| Fruit of the Loom | www.fruit.com |
| Gamelan | www.gamelan.com |
| GCTech | www.gctec.com |
| GE | www.ge.com |
| Gemplus | www.gemplus.com |
| General Life Insurance | www.generalife.com |
| GlobeID | www.globeid.org |
| Hansa.net | www.hansa.net |
| Harbinger | www.harbinger |
| Hewlett-Packard Company | www.hp.com |
| IBM | www.ibm.com |
| iCat | www.icat.com |
| IDC | www.idc.com |
| IDT | www.idt.com |
| Informix | www.informix.com |
| Inquiry.com | www.inquiry.com |
| Intel Corporation | www.intel.com |
| Internet Liquidators | www.internetliquidators.com |
| Internet Secure | www.internetsecure.com |
| The Internet Shopping Network | www.isn.com |
| Interse | www.interse.com |
| InterWorld | www.interworld.com |
| Intuit | www.intuit.com |
| Inverse | www.inverse.com |
| IPOnet | www.iponet.com |

| | |
|---|---|
| Junglee | www.junglee.com |
| Keywitness | www.keywitness.com |
| KLELine | www.kleline.com |
| Manitoba Telecom Svcs | www.mts.mb.ca |
| Marshall Industries | www.marshall.com |
| MasterCard | www.mastercard.com |
| Mecklermedia | www.iworld.com |
| Microsoft | www.microsoft.com |
| Microsoft Network | www.msn.com |
| Milestone Systems | www.mstone.com |
| Millicent | www.millicent.com |
| Mondex | www.mondex.com |
| Net Logistics Inc. | www.netlogistics.com |
| NetBill | www.netbill.com |
| Netbot | www.netbot.com |
| NetBuyer | www.netbuyer.com |
| NetCash | www.netcash.com |
| NetChex | www.netchex.com |
| NetCount | www.netcount.com |
| NetDox | www.netdox.com |
| NetMarket | www.netMarket.com |
| Netscape | www.netscape.com |
| NetSeminars | www.netseminar.com |
| Netstakes | www.netstakes.com |
| NBTel | www.nbtel.nb.ca |
| onDisplay | www.ondisplay.com |
| OneWave | www.onewave.com |
| Online Mortgage Explorer | www.themortgage.com |
| ONSALE | www.onsale.com |
| Open Market | www.openmarket.com |
| Oracle | www.oracle.com |
| PackageNet | www.packagenet.com |
| PAWWS | www.pawws.com |

| | |
|---|---|
| PayLinx | www.paylinx.com |
| PCOrder | www.pcorder.com |
| PCQuote | www.pcquote.com |
| PhotoDisc | www.photodisc.com |
| PhotoNet | www.photonet.com |
| PointCast Inc. | www.pointcast.com |
| Premenos | www.premenos.com |
| Preview Travel | www.reservations.com |
| Quote.com | www.quote.com |
| RSA | www.rsa.com |
| SAQQARA Systems | www.saqqara.com |
| SBNet Solutions | www.sbnet.com |
| Security Dynamics | www.securid.com |
| Security First Network Bank | www.sfnb.com |
| Sharper Image Inc. | www.sharperimage.com |
| Sidewalk | www.sidewalk.com |
| Silicon Graphics Inc | www.sgi.com |
| Skyway | www.skyway.com |
| Software.net | www.software.net |
| Speedware | www.speedware.com |
| Sport Warehouse | www.sportwarehouse.com |
| Sterling Commerce | www.sterling.com |
| Tesserae | www.tesserae.com |
| Ticketmaster | www.ticketmaster |
| Time Warner | www.timewarner.com |
| TRADE'ex | www.tradeex.com |
| Travelocity | www.travelocity.com |
| Trilogy | www.trilogy.com |
| TRUSTe | www.truste.org |
| U.S. Robotics | www.usrobotics.com |
| Unibex | www.unibex.com |
| UPS | www.ups.com |
| Uvision | www.uvision.com |

| | |
|---|---|
| Vantive | www.vantive.com |
| VeriFone | www.verifone.com |
| VeriSign Inc. | www.verisign.com |
| VISA | www.visa.com |
| VocalTec | www.vocaltec.com |
| webMethods | www.webmethods.com |
| WitCapital Corporation | www.witcap.com |
| WOMEX | www.womex.com |
| WorldPoint | www.worldpoint.com |
| Worlds, Inc. | www.worlds.com |
| Sun Microsystems | www.sun.com |
| Ziff-Davis | www.ziffdavis.com |

# GLOSSARY OF ACRONYMS

| | |
|---|---|
| ABM | Automated Banking Machine (Canada) |
| API | application program interface |
| ATM | Automated Teller Machine (U.S.) |
| BIPS | Bank Internet Payment System |
| BOT | build, operate, transfer |
| CA | Certificate Authority |
| CGI | Common Gateway Interface |
| C-SET | Chip-Secured Electronic Transaction (Europe) |
| EDI | Electronic Data Interchange |
| FCC | Federal Communications Commission |
| FSTC | Financial Services Technology Corporation |
| HTML | Hypertext Markup Language |
| HTTP | Hypertext Transport Protocol |
| IETF | Internet Engineering Task Force |
| IPng | Internet Protocol next generation |
| IPv6 | Internet Protocol version 6 |
| ISP | Internet Service Provider |
| IT | information technology |
| JEPI | Joint Electronic Payments Initiative |
| OBI | Open Buying on the Internet |
| OECD | Organization for Economic Cooperation and Development |
| OFX | Open Financial eXchange |
| OPS | Open Profiling Standard |
| OTP | Open Trading Protocol |

| P8 | Political 8 (G7 countries, plus Russia) |
| PKI | public key infrastructure |
| SET | Secure Electronic Transaction |
| SVPN | Secure Virtual Private Network |
| TCP/IP | Transmission Control Protocol/Internet Protocol |
| VAN | Value-Added Network |
| VRML | Virtual Reality Markup Language |
| W3C | World Wide Web Consortium |
| WTO | World Trade Organization |
| XIWT | Cross-Industry Working Team |
| XML | eXtensible Markup Language |

# THE FUTURE OF DIGITAL MARKETS

To stay in touch with further developments relating to the concepts introduced in this book, you can choose from the following options.

## IN-HOUSE EDUCATION

The essence of this book with the methodology behind it can be delivered in a one-day seminar for your organization. There is also a learning workbook version which is a practical guide for following up effectively within your organization. Please contact CYBERManagement Inc. for further details. Walid Mougayar is the instructor.

## LIVE WEB SITE

The CYBERManagement Web site contains a continuously updated section on pertinent developments and a hyperlinked list to all companies and cases mentioned in the Web index. Web address: www.cyberm.com

## INTERACTIVE REMOTE LEARNING SITE

Through a partnership with Marshall Industries' Entertainment, News, and Education Network (ENEN), you can take a modular pay-per-view course based on the material in this book. Web address: www.enen.com/cyberm

# CYBER REVIEW, THE INTERNET STRATEGY EXECUTIVE NEWSLETTER

Written and published monthly by Walid Mougayar, this electronic newsletter will keep you informed of the latest original thinking and models for exploiting Internet commerce. Please send an e-mail to cyber@cyberm.com for a free 3-month subscription.

# EXECUTIVE PRESENTATIONS BY WALID MOUGAYAR

In these crisp, one-hour executive briefing sessions, Walid Mougayar enlightens with a dynamic style that leaves you learning and thinking. The presentations are focused on the business management and strategy aspects of how to exploit Internet commerce, and are always abreast of the most recent developments and best practices. Topics include:

- Success in the new electronic commerce agenda
- Creation of digital value and digital markets
- Future evolution of consumer-based commerce
- Electronic markets competitive strategy
- Different ways to participate in virtual markets and virtual value chains
- Segmentation and behavior of electronic markets
- Management actions and framework for deriving Internet business value

Walid Mougayar is available for speaking engagements worldwide exclusively through the W. Colston Leigh Bureau. Please contact Ronald J. Szymanski at 908-253-0640 or at rjs@leighbureau.com.

**CYBERManagement Inc.**
151 Bloor Street West, Suite 470
Toronto, Ontario M5S 1S4, Canada
Tel: 416 929 1014
Fax: 416 929 1552
e-mail: cyber@cyberm.com
Web: www.cyberm.com

# BIBLIOGRAPHY

## BOOKS

Allen, Catherine A. and Barr, William J. 1997. *Smart Cards: Seizing Strategic Business Opportunities*. Times Mirror Higher Education Group.

Bernard, Ryan. 1996. *The Corporate Intranet*. John Wiley & Sons, Inc.

Bogan, Christopher E. and English, Michael J. 1994. *Benchmarking for Best Practices*. McGraw-Hill.

Brandenburger, Adam M. and Nalebuff, Barry J. 1996. *Co-opetition*. Bantam Doubleday Dell Publishing Group, Inc.

Cronin, Mary J. 1996. *Global Advantage on the Internet*. Van Nostrand Reinhold.

Cronin, Mary J. 1996. *The Internet Strategy Handbook: Lessons from the New Frontier of Business*. Harvard Business Press.

Crumlish, Christian. 1995. *The Internet Dictionary*. SYBEX, Inc.

Dahl, Andrew and Lesnick, Leslie. 1996. *Internet Commerce*. New Riders Publishing.

Dertouzos, Michael. 1997. *What Will Be: How the New World of Information Will Change Our Lives*. HarperCollins Publishers, Inc.

Gascoyne, Richard J. and Ozcubukcu, Koray. 1997. *Corporate Internet Planning Guide: Aligning Internet Strategy with Business Goals*. International Thomson Publishing Company.

Godin, Seth. 1995. *Presenting Digital Cash*. Sams.net Publishing.

Goldman, Steven L., Nagel, Roger N., and Preiss, Kenneth. 1995. *Agile Competitors and Virtual Organizations: Strategies for Enriching the Customer*. Van Nostrand Reinhold.

Hagel, John III and Armstrong, Arthur G. 1997. *Net Gain: Expanding Markets through Virtual Communities*. McKinsey & Company, Inc.

Hammer, Michael and Champy, James. 1992. *Reengineering the Corporation*. Harper Business.

Kalakota, Ravi and Whinston, Andrew B. 1997. *Electronic Commerce: A Manager's Guide*. Addison Wesley Longman, Inc.

Kalakota, Ravi and Whinston, Andrew B. 1996. *Frontiers of Electronic Commerce*. Addison Wesley Longman, Inc.

Keen, Peter G. W., Mougayar, Walid, and Torregrossa, Tracy. 1998. *The Business Internet and Intranet: A Manager's Guide to Key Terms and Concepts*. Harvard Business School Press.

Kosiur, David. 1997. *Understanding Electronic Commerce: How Online Transactions Can Grow Your Business*. Microsoft Press.

Loshin, Pete. 1995. *Electronic Commerce: OnLine Ordering and Digital Money*. Charles River Media, Inc.

Lynch, Daniel C. and Lundquist, Leslie. 1996. *Digital Money: The New Era of Internet Commerce*. John Wiley & Sons, Inc.

Martin, Chuck. 1997. *The Digital Estate*. McGraw-Hill.

Mayer, Martin. 1997. *The Bankers: The Next Generation*. Penguin Group.

Miler, Steven. 1996. *Civilizing Cyberspace, Policy, Power, and the Information Super Highway*. Addison Wesley Longman, Inc.

Morgan Stanley. 1996. *The Internet Report*. Morgan Stanley, Inc.

Reeves, Byron and Nass, Clifford. 1996. *The Media Equation: How People Treat Computers, Television, and New Media Like Real People and Places*. Cambridge University Press.

Schneier, Bruce. 1995. *E-mail Security*. John Wiley & Sons, Inc.

Schwartz, Evan I. 1997. *Webonomics: Nine Essential Principles for Growing Your Business on the World Wide Web*. Broadway Books.

Schwartz, Peter. 1991. *The Long View*. Doubleday.

Stefik, Mark. 1996. *Internet Dreams: Archetypes, Myths, and Metaphors*. Massachusetts Institute of Technology.

Sterne, Jim. 1996. *Customer Service on the Internet: Building Relationships, Increasing Loyalty, and Staying Competitive*. John Wiley & Sons, Inc.

Sterne, Jim. 1995. *World Wide Web Marketing: Integrating the Internet into Your Marketing Strategy*. John Wiley & Sons, Inc.

Sun Microsystems. 1997. *Java Enterprise Computing: Enabling Breakaway Business Strategies*. Sun Microsystems, Inc.

Tapscott, Don. 1995. *The Digital Economy*. McGraw-Hill.

Vassos, Tom. 1996. *Strategic Internet Marketing*. Que Corporation.

## PUBLICATIONS

*Commercial Scenarios for the Web: Opportunities and Challenges*, Donna L. Hoffman, Thomas P. Novak, and Patrali Chatterjee. Owen Graduate School of Management, Vanderbilt University.

*CYBER Review* (vol. 1, nos. 1 and 2), Walid Mougayar, CYBERManagement Inc., 1996.

*Electronic Commerce and the Banking Industry: The Requirement and Opportunities for New Payment Systems Using the Internet.*

*Electronic Commerce: Effects on Electronic Markets,* Rolf T. Wigand and Robert I. Benjamin, School of Information Studies, Syracuse University, 1997.

*IBM and the Internet,* David H. Andrews, D. H. Andrews Group, 1996.

*Internet/Intranet: A Special Report,* International Business Machines Corporation, 1996.

"Manufacturing Systems Orders from Chaos," Tom Stein, *Information Week.* June 23, 1997, pp. 44–52.

*On the Road of Electronic Commerce: A Business Value Framework, Gaining Competitive Advantage and Some Research Issues,* Michael Bloch, Yves Pigneur, and Arie Segev, The Fisher Center for Information Technology & Management, Ecole des HEC, 1996.

*Technology Forecast: 1996,* Price Waterhouse Firm Services BV, Inc., 1995.

*The Future of Electronic Commerce,* David Bollier, The Aspen Institute, 1996.

*The Information Appliance, Special Report—Business Week,* McGraw-Hill, June 1996.

# WEB SITES

*A European Initiative in Electronic Commerce,*
   http://www.cordis.lu/esprit/src/ecomcom.html.

*Electronic Data Interchange (EDI) over the Internet,* Sue Gore, 1996,
   http://www.niit.org/insight/white/edi.html.

*Intermediaries and Cybermediaries: A Continuing Role for Mediating Players in the Electronic Marketplace,* Mitra Barun Sarkar, Department of Marketing, Michigan State University; Brian Butler, Department of Management, Carnegie Mellon University; Charles Steinfield, Department of Telecommunication, Michigan State University,
   http://www.usc.edu/dept/annenberg/vol1/issue3/sarkar.html.

*Internet-based SVPNs: The Cost of Ownership,*
   http://www.incog.com/execsumm.html.

*Living Apart Together in Electronic Commerce: The Use of Information and Communication Technology to Create Network Organizations,* John Nouwens and Harry Bouwman, Department of Communication, University of Amsterdam,
   http://www.usc.edu/dept/annenberg/vol1/issue3/nouwens.html.

*The Automation of Capital Markets,* Arnold Picot, Christine Bortenlanger, and Heiner Rohrl, Institute of Organization Ludwig-Maximilians-Universitat Munchen,
http://www.usc.edu/dept/annenberg/vol1/issue3/picot.html.

*The Emergence of a Networked World: Commerce, Society and the Future of the Internet,* Global Internet Project, http://www.gip.org/GIP2B.HTM.

*The Impact of Electronic Commerce on Buyer-Seller Relationships,* Charles Steinfield and Alice Plummer, Department of Telecommunication, Michigan State University,
http://www.usc.edu/dept/annenberg/vol1/issue3/steinfld.html.

*The Possibilities with Electronic Commerce,* ECRC.
http: //www.ecrc.ctc.com/poss.htm.

*The White House Framework for Electronic Commerce,*
http://www.whitehouse.gov/WH/New/Commerce

*Towards the Age of the Digital Economy,*
http://www.miti.go.jp/intro-e/a228101e.html.

*White Paper: The Java Electronic Commerce Framework (JECF),*
http://java.sun.com/products/commerce/doc.whitepaper.html.

# INDEX

ABMs, 94
Acronyms, 271, 272
Actions (*see* Strategy actions)
ActiveX, 208, 209
Actra Business Systems, 23
Add-a-Photo, 146
Advantage-driven users, 167, 168
AFCEE, 257
Agent Web model, 93, 94
AGENTics, 101, 103, 142
Agents, 88, 99–104, 172–174
Agentware, 103
Alternate delivery channel, 82
Amazon.com, 33, 60, 93, 121, 136, 142, 145, 170–172, 246
America Online (AOL) model, 93
American Greetings, 121, 146, 154
AMP, 76, 77
Apple, 125
Applets, 49, 155, 202, 203, 207
Ariba, 25
Australian Chamber of Manufacturers, 157
Authentication, 23, 61–64, 107, 128, 155, 158, 169, 201, 204, 250, 251
Automated banking machines (ABMs), 94
Avatars, 179
Awareness about availability of services, 74

Back-end process, 18, 231
Bandwidth costs, 64, 65

Bank Internet Payment System (BIPS), 56
Bank of America, 46, 251
BargainFinder, 173
Barker, Joel, 41
Bell Atlantic, 23
Benchmarking, 239–241
Benefits Management Network (BMN), 153–154
Bib Net, 25
Bibliography, 277–280
BigYellow, 96–99
Billboards, 223
BOT (build, operate, transfer), 196
Broadcasting, 85–87, 210
Browser war, 210
Build-a-Card, 154
Build-versus-buy, 192, 195
Business catalysts:
    competitive pressures, 34, 35
    consumer demands, 35, 36
    costs of business transactions, 32–33
    distribution costs/inefficiencies, 29–32
    globalization issues/location optimization, 36, 37
    government role, 37–39
    search for growth markets, 33, 34
Business process, 20, 25, 32, 48, 53, 75, 82, 86, 123, 200, 204, 212, 222
Business-to-business market, 17, 18, 27

Business-to-consumer market, 17, 18, 27
Business value of electronic commerce, 238–239
Bussbang, Jeffrey, 65, 139
BuyDirect, 167
Buyer/seller model, 85–87
Buying activities, 88

Cable TV networks, 95
CAFÉ, 184
Canada, 78
Canadian Imperial Bank of Commerce (CIBC), 94
Cannibalizing, 115
Canopy, 103, 174
CarPoint, 164
Case study (Marshall Industries), 217–231
  business drivers, 220, 221
  company background, 217, 218
  future activities, 227, 228
  ideas/concepts, 222, 223
  lessons learned, 228, 229
  NetSeminar, 226, 227
  questions to ask, 230, 231
  supply chain management, 225, 226
  virtual distribution, 221
  Web site features, 223–225
Cash cards, 250
Cassidy, Brian, 94
Casting technologies, 185–187
CatalogExpert, 103, 174
Cebra Inc., 150
CenterStage, 103
Certification authorities, 14, 64, 107, 129, 159
Certification process, 61–64, 73
Challenges and issues:
  behavioral/educational challenges, 70–75
  categorization, 52, 53

Challenges and issues (*Cont.*):
  channel conflict, 76, 77
  critical mass, 77, 78
  fulfillment process, 78, 79
  general observations, 51, 52
  legal/regulatory framework, 65–70
  organizational/business barriers, 75
  technological challenges, 54–65
Channel conflict, 76, 77
Chaos and complexity theory, 242
Chase Manhattan Bank, 156, 157, 252
CheckFree, 251
Cisco Systems, 45, 92, 115, 122, 126, 245
Click – Send, 160, 161
Client/server computing approach, 192
Clinton, Bill, 37
CNgroup, 109
Collaboration, 16, 84, 105, 107, 185, 210, 228
Commerce applications, 96–99
Commerce infrastructure, 95–97
CommerceNet, 56, 72, 102–111, 261–264
CommerceNet Southeast, 118, 119
Communications channel, 84
Community-of-interest networks (COINs), 110, 111
Companies cited, Web addresses, 265–270
Comparative buying, 59–60, 101, 173, 175
CompareNet, 59
Competitive analysis, 102
Competitive pressures, 34, 35
Competitors, 132
Component software, 49, 207
Computer ESP, 141, 142, 145, 163, 167
Conductor, 181

Connected Corporation, 153
Connectivity, 90, 91
Consumer attitudes, 70
Consumer demands, 35, 36
Consumer requirements (*see* Wired consumer requirements)
ConsumersEdge, 59, 145, 167, 187
Content liquidity, 45–48
Continuing education, 273–275
Convergence, 43–45
Cook, Scott, 70
Corporate anxiety, 236
Corporate communications, 84
Corporate planning, 34, 128
Cost of technology, 45, 47, 48
Critical mass, 52, 77–78, 150, 230
Cronin, Mary, 233
Cross Industry Working Team (XIWT), 56
CrossRoute, 25
Customer education, 118, 119
Customer expectations, 122, 123
Customer information intermediaries, 149, 159
Customer interface, 21, 237
Customer self-service, 170–171
Customer service, 8, 32, 33, 79, 120, 157, 179–181, 194, 195, 201, 238
Customs, 68
*Cyber Review*, 274
Cyberbusiness Association of Japan, 256
CyberCash, 55, 74, 183
CyberCoin, 183
CyberGold, Inc., 159
CYBERManagement Inc., 273–275
Cybermaturity, 116
CyberMedia, 153
CyberSource, 64
Cyberspace, 10, 65, 70, 113, 114, 131, 139, 179

Data reporting and analysis, 201
Database application approach, 192
DCT-On-Line Trading System, 154
DEC, 46
Delayering distribution channel, 30–32
Dell Computers, 92, 245
Deutsche Telekom, 46
Diamond Shamrock, 23, 156, 157, 252
DigiCash, 55, 249
Digital branding, 134
Digital cash, 55, 94, 182, 249, 250
Digital certificates, 61, 64, 71, 159, 182, 183, 204
Digital content, 9, 46, 200, 241
Digital economy, 39, 237
Digital ID, 58, 73, 129, 159, 228
Digital marketing, 133
Digital markets, 4, 14–15, 90, 132, 139, 141, 244–246
Digital rights intermediaries, 149, 158, 159
Digital signature, 22, 182, 183, 204, 251
Digital value creation, 12, 13, 226–227
Digital value token products, 126, 127, 201
Digital values, 243, 244
Digital wallets, 182, 183
Digital wealth, 96
Dills, Jim, 110
Diner's Club syndrome, 181
Dionne, Joseph L., 72
Direct Web model, 92
Directed content, 222
DirectIPO, 154
Disintermediation, 15, 30, 160
Distribution channels, 29–32, 91–94, 119–122
Domestic information appliances, 178
Drucker, Peter, 242

E*Trade, 154
E-Broker, 154
E-co system, 107–109
E-money laundering, 74, 75
e-Travel, 146
e-XPENSE, 146
e.Schwab, 154
Early and curious adopters, 167, 168
EC World Institute, 260
EchoSearch, 173
Edelman, Robert, 217, 222, 228, 234
Electronic data interchange (EDI), 8–10, 15, 18, 21–24, 46, 48, 78, 97, 100, 105, 107, 131, 148, 156–157, 197, 202, 204, 214, 215, 218, 220, 235, 251–253
Education, 116–119
Educational follow-up, 273–275
Electronic auctions, 147, 152, 189
Electronic back office, 200
Electronic business, 24, 230
    (See also Electronic commerce)
Electronic cash, 249
    (See also Digital cash)
Electronic catalog, 77
Electronic channels, 91–94
Electronic checks, 251
Electronic commerce, 7–27
    business-to-business vs. business-to-consumer market, 17, 18
    business value/measures, 238, 239
    buying/selling, 11, 12
    definitions, 9, 10
    digital value creation, 12, 13
    EDI, 21–24
    excuse for not doing, 235
    international organizations, 255–264
    Internet, 15, 16

Electronic commerce (Cont.):
    intranets, 24–26
    market size assessment, 27
    new intermediaries, 13, 14
    traditional vs. open, 18–21
    virtual marketplaces, 14, 15
Electronic commerce architecture, 199–202
Electronic Commerce Association (ECA), 258, 259
Electronic Commerce Europe (ECE), 259, 260
Electronic COMmerce Promotion Council of Japan (ECOM), 255
Electronic communities, 123, 164
Electronic consumer, 35–36, 167–169
Electronic interactions, 15, 35, 82
Electronic marketplace, 3, 4, 10, 14, 33, 82, 91, 92, 121, 122, 124, 128, 132, 137, 138, 140, 201, 220, 236, 239, 242
Electronic marketplace segmentation, 91–94
Electronic money, 127, 252
    (See also Digital cash)
Electronic Payments Forum (EPF), 56, 57
Electronic publishing, 10
Electronic purse, 128, 250
Electronic sales and marketing approach, 192
Electronic shopping, 10
Electronic storefront, 163, 192, 252
Electronic transactions, 44, 45, 61, 169, 182
Electronic Travel Auction (ETA), 176, 177
Electronic wallet, 44, 55, 127, 165
    (See also Digital wallets)
Employease Network, 153
Encrypted credit cards, 251

Encrypted end-user license agreements (EULAs), 64
Encryption key, 250
End-to-end Internet commerce, 199
ENEN, 154, 227
Enhanced product realization (EPR), 216
Enterprisewide legacy data approach, 193
Ethical hacking, 204
Europe, 40, 256–260
European Commission - Electronic Commerce for SMEs, 259
Excuses for not doing Internet commerce, 235
Executive briefing sessions, 274
Executive education, 116–118, 193, 237
Expedia, 245
Extranet, 17, 123, 211, 219, 225
Eyes, 172, 173

FastParts Trading Exchange, 156
Federal Express, 79, 126, 162
Fidelity Investments, 123
Financial EDI, 23, 251, 253
Financial institutions, 46
Financial Services Technology Consortium (FSTC), 56
Financial transaction brokers, 147, 154
Firefly Network, 173, 174
Firewalls, 47, 202, 204
First Data Corp., 55
First-generation malls, 166
First USA Paymentech, 55
First Virtual Holdings, Inc., 55
*Framework for Global Electronic Commerce*, 37–39, 68
Fraud, 73
Fruit of the Loom, 34, 120
Fuchs, Michael, 35

Fulfillment and logistics support, 148, 160, 161
Fulfillment process, 78, 79
Future of EDI, 21

Gambling, 75, 126
Gamelan, 98, 147, 155
Gaming, 126
GE Capital, 55
Gemplus, 128, 183, 250
GeneraLife, 126
Germany, 35
Globalization, 36–41
Government role, 37, 42
Gross, Mark, 141
Guiding principles, 237

Hanes, 34
Hansa.net Global Commerce Inc., 36
Hard-goods products, 124, 125
Health claim processing, 213
Hewlett-Packard, 9, 46, 97, 125, 128, 129, 174, 183, 250
Home banking, 10
@Home Network, 65
Human resources department, 128–130
Hype, 73

IBCC-Net, 256, 257
IBM, 46, 97, 125, 128, 180
Identify, 100, 101, 103, 142
IDML tags, 101, 103
ImagineCard alliance, 128, 183, 250
iMarkets, 2, 106, 108, 110, 244–246
Implementation (*see* IT strategies)
Indirect Web model, 92, 93
Industrial catalog, 77

Infomaster, 103
Information appliances, 44, 46, 99, 177, 178, 169, 183
Information superhighway, 16
Informix, 70, 126, 128, 183, 185, 250
InfoTest International, 216
Integrated shipping information, 125
Intel, 97
Intelligent agents (*see* Agents)
Inter-Internet development, 212–214
Interactive marketing, 10, 133
Interactive multimedia, 48, 49
Interactive personalized catalogs, 174
Interactive services, 115, 126, 201
Interactivity, 19, 29, 39, 171, 202
Intercasting, 56, 185–187
Intermediaries (*see* New intermediaries)
International electronic commerce organizations:
  Canada, 260
  CommerceNet, 261–264
  Europe, 256–260
  Japan, 255, 256
International trade, 8
Internet, 15, 16, 83, 84
Internet access, 19, 47, 77, 78, 123, 136
Internet addresses, 265–270
Internet appliances, 168
  (*See also* Information appliances)
Internet commerce, 7, 17
  (*See also* Electronic commerce)
Internet commerce infrastructure, 95
Internet commerce value chain, 94, 95
Internet computing, 8, 192, 193, 205–207, 209
Internet EDI, 156, 157

Internet e-mail, 48
Internet enablement framework, 199
Internet financial EDI, 251, 252
Internet jobs, 130
Internet Law and Policy Forum (ILPF), 260
Internet Liquidators, 152
Internet PC, 47
  (*See also* Networked PC)
Internet Service Providers (ISPs), 46
Internet Shopping Network, 125
InterNetShip, 126
Internetworked enterprise, 48
Interoperability, 58
Intranet, 15, 17, 23, 24–26, 64, 74, 83, 88, 92, 102, 115, 122, 123, 126, 129, 158, 194, 199, 202, 205, 207, 210–214, 219, 225, 231, 237, 239
Intranet applications, 24, 210, 214, 225
Intra-organizational commerce, 17
IPng (IPv6), 60
Ironside Technologies, 99
iSTAR, 46
IT strategies, 191–216
  BOT (build, operate, transfer), 195, 196
  costs of implementation, 202–204
  functional approaches, 198–199
  Internet computing, 205–207
  intranets, 210–214
  plug-and-go software, 207–210
  procurement service applications, 215, 216
  required subsystems, 195
  security architecture, 204
  standards, 197–198
  starting points, 191–193

IT strategies (*Cont.*):
  systems architecture framework, 199–202
  TCP/IP platform, 194
  Web automation, 214, 215
  Web delivery architecture, 205
  Webmaster, 194

Janes, Mike, 79
Jango, 60, 101, 103, 145, 174
Japan, 41, 255, 256
Java, 84, 108, 130, 155, 168, 202, 207, 208, 209
Java Electronic Commerce Framework (JECF), 209
Jobs, 130
Join Electronic Payments Initiative (JEPI), 56–58
Jones, Terry, 35

Kalakota, Ravi, 12
Kiosks, 44
KLELine, 55

Lawrence Livermore National Laboratories, 251
Learning organization, 116
Lebanon, 81
Legacy, 193
Legal framework, 65–70
Leigh Bureau, 274
Letterman, David, 234
Levert, Eric, 162
License Clearing House Services, 64
Light EDI, 21, 22
Live Agent, 103, 174
Location-optimized commerce on the Internet (LOCI), 36
*Long View, The*, 241
Lynch, Daniel, 184

Magaziner, Ira, 38, 70
Management, 2, 3, 5, 10, 53, 54, 75, 113, 115–117, 194, 218, 229, 233–246
Management readiness, 116
Management strategy, 137, 138
Management style, 137
Manitoba Telecom Services (MTS), 181
Mark Twain Bank, 55
Market maker, 142
Market-maker functions, 142–144
Market organization, 140–142
Market shares, 132, 133
Market size assessment, 27
Market-to-market connection, 145, 146
Marketing, 8–10, 25, 32, 33, 44, 76, 130, 149, 192, 204, 211, 220, 222, 238
Marketing communications, 131
Marketing mix, 84
Marketing strategy, 133–134
Marketplace concentrators/directories, 147, 155
Marketspace, 32, 33, 84, 115, 132
Marshall Industries, 24, 78, 98, 122, 126, 131, 163, 180
  [*See also* Case study (Marshall Industries)]
MarshallNet, 225
McGraw-Hill Companies Customer Privacy Policy, 72
Medical records, 127
Merchant services, 200
Metasearch engine capability, 173
Michelin, 25
Micro Web server, 45
Micropayment, 183
  (*See also* Microtransactions)
Microsoft, 35, 46, 71, 93, 97, 126, 133, 163, 183, 197, 209, 245
Microsoft's superintermediary strategy, 163, 164

Microtransactions, 184, 185
Middleware services, 207
Milestone Systems, Inc., 160, 161
Ministerial Declaration on Trade in
    Information Technology
    Products (ITA), 68
Mondex, 55, 74, 250
Monorail, 162
Moore's Law, 45
Mougayar, Walid, 273, 274
Multicasting, 174
Multimedia, 16, 48–49, 64–65, 86,
    97, 100, 147, 154, 169, 200,
    202, 206, 228
Multimedia content delivery, 147,
    154

National Bank of Canada, 55
Negroponte, Nicholas, 113, 127
NetAngels, 173
NetBot, 59, 101, 103, 142
NetBuyer, 59, 167
Netcasting, 44, 185
NetDox, 159, 160
NetInterview, 224
NetMarket, 141, 167, 187
Nets Inc., 233–234
Netscape, 23, 46, 71, 104, 183,
    207, 210
Netscape's ONE model, 208, 209
NetSeminars, 154, 224, 226, 227
Netstation, 162
Nettop, 162
Network Computing Architecture,
    209
Network information broker (NIB)
    system, 156
Network security, 64, 205
New intermediaries, 13, 14,
    139–164
    checklist, 149, 150
    classification of intermediaries,
        146–149

New intermediaries (*Cont.*):
    customer information
        intermediaries, 159
    digital rights intermediaries,
        158–159
    disintermediation, 160
    electronic auctions, 152
    marketplace concentrators, 155
    "multibroker," 150–151
    multimedia content delivery, 154
    on-line software delivery,
        152–153
    on-line support/service, 153
    outsourced professional services,
        153–154
    products/service brokers,
        155–156
    theory/behavior of virtual
        marketplaces, 140–146
    VAN-less EDI, 156, 157
    virtual trading communities,
        157, 158
New Net connections, 90
NewsPage, 173
NIB system, 156
Nonrefutability, 62
Nonrepudiation, 62
NYNEX, 96–99

Object-oriented software, 49
On-line customer service, 179, 180
On-line direct trading capabilities,
    154
Online Mortgage Explorer (OME),
    150–151
On-line software delivery, 147,
    152–153
On-line support/service, 147, 153
On-line transaction history, 180,
    181
OnDisplay, 103
ONE model of computing, 208,
    209

ONSALE, 152, 245
Open buying on the Internet (OBI), 197, 198
Open EDI, 21
Open financial exchange (OFX), 197
Open Market Inc., 46, 97
Open profile standard (OPS), 71
Open trading protocol (OTP), 198
Operating Resource Management (ORM), 25
Oracle, 46, 97
Oracle's Network Computing Architecture, 161, 209
Order-of-magnitude factor, 145
Order-related queries, 170
Organizational framework, 83
Organized markets, 140–142
OSI seven-layer infrastructure, 95
Outsourced professional services, 147, 153–154
Outsourcing, 195, 196
Overview of book, 4, 5

P3 project, 71
PageAgent, 103
Parallel Pull, 102
Parametric search capabilities, 125, 171
PartsNet, 155, 156
Payment instruments, 55–58, 181–184, 249–254
Performance benchmarking, 241
Personal ATM, 184
Personal information appliances, 178
Personalized interactive catalogs, 174
PersonaLogic Inc., 187
Pervasive users, 168, 169

Pervasiveness, 19
Phoenicians, 81
PhotoDisc, 154
PhotoNet, 146, 154
PKI, 61–64, 73
Platform for Privacy Preferences, 71
Plug-and-go software, 207–210
Plugged-IN, 224
PLUS Lotto, 185, 246
Point casting, 185
Point-of-sale devices, 44
PointCast Network, 173
Power of Vision, The, 41
Principles of virtual marketplaces, 140–146
Privacy, 70–72
Process benchmarking, 241
Procurement services, 9, 18, 23, 100, 148, 211–213, 215
Product generation process, 9
Products and services, 123–128
Products and services brokers, 148, 155
Public key cryptography, 62
Public key infrastructure (PKI), 61–64, 73
Push casting, 186

Quality ratings, 133
Questions to ask, 114, 115

Rapid software development, 49
Real estate COIN prototypes, 110, 111
Reengineering, 34, 235, 237
Regulatory framework, 65–70
Reintermediation, 32
Relationship cards (see Smart cards)
Relationship management, 10
Release Software Corporation, 153

Requirement-driven users, 168, 169
Reynolds, Chris, 161
Rodin, Robert, 217, 219, 221, 230

Sales associates, 121
Sales representatives, 76, 77
SAQQARA, 77, 97, 104
Scenario planning, 240–242
Schneier, Bruce, 204
Schwartz, Peter, 241
Second-generation malls, 167
Secure electronic transaction (SET), 197, 251, 254
Secure virtual private networks (SVPNs), 47
Security, 54–55, 84, 97, 107, 128, 182, 202, 204, 212, 235
Security First Network Bank (SFNB), 136
Segmentation of electronic distribution channels, 91–94
Self-service, 33, 36, 123, 126, 170–171, 181, 193, 224
Selling activities, 86, 87
SEMPER, 257, 258
SET protocol, 197, 251, 254
Silicon Graphics, 92, 126
Smart cards, 127, 128, 182–184, 250, 251
Smart catalogs, 174
Smart Telephone Card, 127
Social computing, 49
Soft-good products, 125, 126
Software agents, 172–174
Software.net, 152–153
SonicNet, 154
Spar, Debora, 65, 139
Spontaneity, 19
Sport Warehouse, 162
Standards, 60, 61, 197, 198
Strategic benchmarking, 241
Strategy, 82, 83

Strategy actions, 113–138
competitors/market share, 132, 133
customer expectations, 122, 123
distribution channels/supply chains, 119–121
education/training, 116–119
extend current systems to outside, 131, 132
human resources department, 128–130
management style, 137, 138
marketing strategy, 133, 134
products/services, 123–128
virtual marketplaces/intermediaries, 134–137
Sun Microsystems, 46, 47, 125, 207
SunTrust Bank, 162
Supply chain, 9, 24, 34, 64, 78, 90, 119–121, 134, 216, 225–226
Sweden Post, 182
Systems architecture framework, 199–202
Systems integration, 192
Systems integration approach, 192
Szymanski, Ron, 274

Tariffs, 68
Tax haven locations, 36, 37
Taxation, 67, 68
Taxonomy of everything (TOE), 109
Technical integration, 64
Technological challenges:
bandwidth costs, 64, 65
comparative buying, 59, 60
content, 60
infrastructure, 60
interoperability, 58
payment instruments, 55–58
public key infrastructure, 61–64, 73

Technological challenges (*Cont.*):
  security, 54, 55
  standards, 60, 61
  technical integration, 64
Technology drivers:
  content liquidity, 45–48
  convergence of
    technologies/capabilities, 43,
    44
  convergence of vendors/industry
    service capabilities, 44, 45
  cost of technology, 45, 47, 48
  human dimension to technology,
    48, 49
  proliferation of networks, 48
  rapidity of software development,
    49
Technology implementation (*see*
  IT strategies)
Telephone, 75, 124
Telephone companies, 46
Television, 44, 45, 77, 95, 127,
  147, 168, 177, 185
Templar software, 157
Tenenbaum, Jay M., 9, 105–118
Tesserae Information Systems
  (TIE), 101, 104
Thalheimer, Richard, 29
3-D, 179
Three-dimensional communities,
  174
Ticketless travel, 127
*Towards the Age of the Digital
  Economy: For Rapid Progress in
  the Japanese Economy and
  World Economic Growth in the
  21st Century*, 41
TRADE'ex, 157
Trading partners, 19
Trading Process Network Post
  (TPNPost), 157
Training, 116–119
Transaction engine approach,
  192

Transaction integrity, 62
Travelocity, 35
Trust, 70–72
TRUSTe, 71, 72
TuneUp.com, 153


Uncertainty of transaction journey,
  144
Unibex, 158
UNIClass, 103
Unifind, 104, 174
United States, 39
U.S. Treasury Secretary, 252
Universal digital wallet, 181–184
Universal payment switch/gateway
  approach, 192
User-centric model, 175–177
UUNET, 46


Value chain, 10, 12, 15, 29–32, 75,
  87–90, 94, 95, 110, 115,
  120–121, 132, 136, 140, 144,
  151, 160, 174, 221, 229
VAN-less EDI, 148, 156, 157
VANs (Value-Added Networks),
  21–23, 46, 148, 214, 251
VeriFone, 97, 183, 184, 253
VeriSign, Inc., 64
*Vibe* service, 65
Virtual distribution, 221
Virtual interactive services, 126
Virtual locker room, 187
Virtual marketplaces, 89, 90,
  140–146
Virtual Order, 79
Virtual private network, 47
Virtual Reality Modeling Language
  (VRML), 49, 178, 179
Virtual search engine, 225
Virtual shopping store, 187–189
Virtual trading communities, 148,
  157, 158

VRML, 49, 178, 179
vWallet, 183


W3C Consortium, 56
Wallet PC, 182
Waterhouse, 154
Web automation, 104, 214, 215
Web casting, 44, 185
Web-centric model, 175
Web delivery architecture, 205
Web-enabled applications, 199
Web index of companies cited,
    265–270
Web multicasting, 185
Web phone, 44
Web server, 45, 47, 192
Web server appliance, 45
Web to legacy, 198
Web TV, 44
WebCard, 181
webMethods, Inc., 104, 214, 215
Whiting, Randall, 9
Wired consumer requirements,
    165–189
  casting technologies, 185–187

Wired consumer requirements
    (*Cont.*):
  customer self-service, 170, 171
  efficient information access,
      171–175
  evolution, 167–169
  information appliances, 177, 178
  microtransactions, 184, 185
  on-line customer service, 179,
      180
  on-line transaction history, 180,
      181
  universal payment instruments,
      181–184
  user-centric queries, 175–177
  virtual reality experience, 178,
      179
  virtual retail store, 187–189
WiseWire, 173
Wismo calls, 170
WitCapital Corporation, 154, 155
WOMEX, 158
WorldPoint, 37


XML, 22, 109, 131

# ABOUT THE AUTHOR

Walid Mougayar is president of CYBERManagement Inc., a management education and consulting firm, which he founded in 1995. His clients include large organizations such as CIBC/INTRIA, Cowles Media Company, The Government of Canada (Revenue Canada), Hewlett-Packard Co., IBM, Oracle Corporation, Motorola Inc., Southam Inc., Sun Life of Canada, and TD-Bank. He is an internationally recognized consultant, writer, and speaker on electronic business, strategic Internet planning, and Internet commerce competitive strategy development. Mougayar is the founding chairman of CommerceNet Canada. A veteran of 14 years at Hewlett-Packard, he successfully led HP's Internet and Information Highway initiatives in Canada. He is coauthor of *The Business Internet and Intranets: A Manager's Guide to Key Terms and Concepts* (Harvard Business School Press, 1998). Mougayar also publishes the widely read electronic newsletter entitled *CYBER Review*. It covers leading developments in Internet strategy management and Internet commerce business models.